SOCIOLOGY OF SANITATION

Dedicated to

Dr Bindeshwar Pathak

Founder, Sulabh Sanitation and Social Reform Movement,
Sulabh International Social Service Organisation,
New Delhi

SOCIOLOGY OF SANITATION

B.K. Nagla

KALPAZ

ISBN: 978-93-5128-141-2
Price: ₹ 1090/-

First Published 2015

Published by

Kalpaz Publications
C-30, Satyawati Nagar,
Delhi - 110052
E-mail: kalpaz@hotmail.com Ph.: 9212142040

Laser Typesetting : Rajender Vashist, Delhi
Printed at : G. Print Process, Delhi

Cataloging in Publication Data--DK

Courtesy: D.K. Agencies (P) Ltd. <docinfo@dkagencies.com>

Nagla, B. K. (Bhupendra Kumar), author.
Sociology of sanitation / B.K. Nagla.
pages cm
Includes bibliographical references and index.
ISBN 978935128

1. Sanitation–Social aspects–India. I. Title.

DDC 363.720954 23

Contents

Dedicated to

Dr. Bindeshwar Pathak, Sociologist,Social Reformer and Founder, Sulabh Sanitation Movement, who gave the theory of "Sociology of Sanitation" to be included in the universal domain of Sociology, for teaching and research in the Universities of India, and across the globe. It will not only enlarge the scope of sociology, but will also be helpful in solving the problems of society in relation to sanitation, social deprivation, water, public health, hygiene, poverty, gender equality, welfare of children and empowering knowledge for sustainable development. This will strengthen sociological quest for knowledge on sanitation.

Dr. Pathak has given his entire life to the cause of sanitation, and in emancipation of scavengers with dignity and mainstreaming them. He has invented "Sulabh Shauchalya" as a tool of social change, which has revolutionised the field of sanitation.

Dr. Pathak has propounded the theory of Sociology of Sanitation, which is as follows:

"Sociology of Sanitation is a scientific study to solve the problems of society in relation to sanitation, social deprivation, water, public health, hygiene, ecology, environment, poverty, gender equality, welfare of children and empowering people for sustainable development and attainment of philosophical and spiritual knowledge."

Truly, he is founder and father of Sociology of Sanitation.

Foreword

Kudos to Professor B.K. Nagla for writing up a text on the sociology of sanitation, which besides being eminently readable, will also help in delineating the university course in this sub-specialization of sociology. A product of hard labour, innovative mind, diligent work, and learner-friendly approach, for which Professor Nagla is reputed all over in the academic fraternity, this book brings together at one place almost all the writings – sociological and the others – in English language on the issue of sanitation.

Although sometimes understood narrowly as dealing with the cleaning and upkeep of lavatories and toilets, the term sanitation indeed envelopes a large area. Soiled water jutting out of the kitchen sluice or the bathroom is as much a matter of sanitation as is the piling up of garbage and eco-wastes in public spaces. Against this backdrop, for any academic discipline that deals with sanitation, it is important that its contour – its scope – is demarcated clearly, in the sense of what would be included in it and what would be left out. To be kept in mind is that the sociology of sanitation is not just a study of the beliefs of purity and pollution, or the toilet technology, or caste inequality, or the condition and predicaments of the communities of scavengers, but rather deals with all of them in an integrated way.

For me, a sociology of sanitation is a critical study of the constellation of thoughts, technology, and practices that communities of people have historically devised, and are advised and instructed to follow, to restore to cleanliness their unclean states and environments, both inside and outside their houses. The cultural relativists say that the standards of cleanliness (and also of uncleanliness) vary from one society to another, and they have to, keeping in mind the resilience of culture and its ability to withstand the forces of change, however impetuously they might act.

This variability in yardsticks of cleanliness and uncleanliness is itself a subject of thorough investigation – for instance, why some communities encourage 'communal bathing', whereas the others proscribe it; why some clean them with leaves after defecation, while the others use water (in fact, a lot of it) for this purpose; why the pubic cloth used during menstruation is washed and reused in some communities, whereas the others inter it in a pit, for it could be used effectively for casting black magic; why some make pits, as in the preceding example, to deposit their phlegm and sputum, whereas the others litter these around; why some direct the used kitchen water to escape to the garden; and so on.

An empirically carried out sociological inquiry will make an authoritative contribution to the understanding of the binary opposition of 'dirt' and 'cleanliness'. Is dirt always 'out of place'? Is 'dirt' always 'dirty'? Perhaps not. Take this example. A woman plucks a pinch of dust from under the carpets spread in Gurudwaras for the visitors to walk on, and applies it to her forehead and also that of her child. For bio-medical specialists, dust harbours germs, causes ailments, and thus must be avoided, with our attempts concertedly working towards creating a dust-free environ; but for her, this dhul (dust) is that of the 'feet of devotees'. For divine grace, this dust must caress one's forehead, for it is 'sacred', 'worthy of reverence'. It is common to hear the submission, to take another instance, that the holy river of the Ganges does not require any 'cleaning', since it is 'eternally clean', having a divine origin; it has the unparallelled power to 'purify' itself and 'heal' others. The evidence the believers offer is that the Ganges water does not smell foul or have the birth of germs even when it is kept in a bottle for years and years together. Well known is the idea that people's beliefs often may not withstand a scientific scrutiny, but it does not displace the veracity of their thoughts they hold assiduously and unshakably.

Sociology has great potentiality to teach as well as make a significant contribution to directed and planned changes, in this context to the objective of creating a sanitized and hygienic environment. For attaining these objectives, Professor Nagla's book takes sensitive care of the sociological approaches, using them deftly, comprehending the myriad aspects of sanitation, thus laying the foundation of a sub-discipline of sociology, known as the 'sociology of sanitation'.

Vinay Kumar Srivastava
Professor of Social Anthropology and Head,
Department of Anthropology,
University of Delhi. Former Principal,
Hindu College, University of Delhi.

Preface

In the national Conference on Sociology of sanitation organized by Sulabh International Centre for Action Sociology (SICAS) and Sulabh International Social Service Organization (SISSO) held at Delhi on January 28-29, 2013, academicians and scholars recommend that the 'Sociology of Sanitation' be included as a sub-subject in schools and colleges which is also advocated by social activists, political leaders and others for making sanitation a part of school and college syllabus.

Apart from Lok Sabha Speaker Meira Kumar and Rural Development Minister Jairam Ramesh, the conference saw participation of Yogendra Singh, eminent sociologist and Professor Emeritus at Jawaharlal Nehru University, Indian Sociological Society President Prof Ishwar Modi, Patna University's Professor in Sociology Dr HetukarJha, Dr Manish Thakur from IIM-Calcutta, and Prof M.N. Karna, Emeritus Professor, North Eastern Hill University, Shillong, Prof B.K. Nagla etc. who allacademicians recommend that the 'Sociology of Sanitation' be included as a sub-subject in schools and colleges to address the complexities of the issue (*The Hindu*: 2013: Feb.6).

When former manual scavenger Usha Choumar was "liberated" a decade ago, her only mission was to ensure that her little daughter does not get into this "dirty business". Today she is an important functionary in Sulabh International, working in the field of sanitation, while her daughter goes to a public school with dreams of doing "something big". Now Choumar, having walked the ramp in New York on the invitation of the

United Nations, is on another mission — to see sanitation be made part of school curriculum. She asserts, "Unless we make our children, particularly those living in rural areas, understand the importance of sanitation, we cannot have a nation without scavengers, which unfortunately is a curse even after so many years of Independence". As for Usha Choumar, she has undertaken the task of raising the issue of introducing 'Sociology of Sanitation' in school curriculum not only in India but abroad. "Now that leading sociologists feel the importance of the subject, it is time that policymakers in India and globally understand the urgency of making sanitation a subject," she adds.

"The inclusion of this subject as an academic discipline will not only enlarge the scope of sociology, but also be helpful in solving the problems of society in relation to sanitation, social deprivation, water, public health, hygiene, poverty, gender equality, welfare of children and sustainable development," says Bindeshwar Pathak, founder of Sulabh International, which organized the conference.

Lamenting that India cannot claim the status of economic superpower till a vast majority of its population does not have access to clean toilets, Dr Pathak, who has been behind the liberation of manual scavengers like Usha Choumar in States like Rajasthan, Madhya Pradesh, Bihar and Uttar Pradesh, says the government should make 'Sociology of Sanitation' a new sub-discipline of sociology which would help children engage with sanitation at the theoretical, empirical and action level.

At the conference, it was strongly argued that existing sub-disciplines of sociology do not adequately capture and address the varied aspects, nuances and social complexities related to sanitation. Hence, a resolution was passed to approach the University Grants Commission (UGC) with the plea to include 'Sociology of Sanitation' as a recommended course in Sociology at graduate, post-graduate and research levels in a graded manner.

Referring to the resolution, Dr Pathak says it has been recommended that appropriate curriculum, literature and plan of action should be developed to achieve the goal of introducing sanitation as a sub-subject in schools and colleges. The tentative syllabus should include the definition, nature, scope and subject matter of 'Sociology of Sanitation' and the relation of the topic with other sub-disciplines of other social sciences and humanities. Dimensions of sanitation; policies, planning and executing agencies; and advocacy for community interventions were among other suggestions. It is also recommended that the Indian Sociological Society should be requested to begin a new research committee on Sociology of Sanitation and must promote research and teaching on sanitation at every possible level.

Talking about the future course of action in this connection, Dr Pathak says all departments of sociology at universities, colleges and other educational institutions, including schools, would be informed about this declaration adopted at the conference, while scholars would be encouraged to write comprehensive text and reference books on 'Sociology of Sanitation'. Similarly, the Indian Council of Social Science Research (ICSSR) will be approached to give priority to sanitation studies while promoting research.

"This new subject can generate employment opportunities and hence it is compatible to the UGC norms of 'employment generation potentiality' for introducing a new discipline/ course...We have also decided to write to all examinations boards across the country to give priority to sanitation studies so that children understands its important from the very beginning of their lives," he adds.

Responding to the call of Sulabh sanitation movement's founder Bindeshwar Pathak, Wardha-based Mahatma Gandhi International Hindi University (MGIHU) is introducing 'Sociology and Sanitation' in their curriculum. "It will be taught to sociology students from the next academic year commencing in June," vice-chancellor VibhutiNarain Rai told TOI. He added that Pathak had recently given a presentation on this subject at their campus and MGIHU had felicitated him for his efforts. Similarly, other universities, colleges and schools would also introduce the course in their respective academic institutions on the availability of study materials for the course on sociology of sanitation.

Keeping in view of the need of the society, SICAS organized a workshop to prepare a syllabus on Sociology of sanitation on June 13-14, 2013 at Sulabh Gram, New Delhi. An outline of the syllabus was prepared with the consultation of academicians including Dr Bindeshwar Pathak and SICAS also asked different scholars to write text books, namely, Professors Nil Ratan,

Nanduram, B. K. Nagla, Richard Pais, Anil Vaghela, Sanjay Mishra, Jitendra Prasad, M.N. Kaarna, HetukarJha, Goverdhan Ram, Mohammad Akram, Shaukath Azim. I am also one of them who is associated to write a text book for teaching sociology of sanitation in the schools and colleges. The present book is an outcome of the envisaged venture. I am particularly thankful to Dr Bindeshwar Pathak, the Sulabh International Centre for Action Sociology for having given me this opportunity to write a book on sociology of sanitation which is exceedingly meaningful exercise. The book is dedicated to Dr Pathak who has been devoted throughout his life for social justice and empowerment of weaker sections of the society. I thank to the functionaries of SICAS who provided me related literature for the book. I am grateful to my wife Prof Madhu Nagla who helped me in several ways – all the time for completing the work.

I am also thankful to Rohit and Radhica who helped me while writing the book in U.S.A. finally, I thank to prof. Neel Rattan and Kalpaz Publication for there co-ordination in the process of publication of the book.

B.K. Nagla

Biographical Note on Dr Bindeshwar Pathak

Context

Dr Pathak is known around the world for his wide ranging work in the sanitation field to improve public health, advance social progress, and improve human rights in India and other countries. His accomplishments span the fields of sanitation technology, social enterprise, and healthcare education for millions of people in his native country, serving as a model for NGO agencies and public health initiatives around the world.

Over a span of four decades Bindeshwar Pathak has advanced his vision for a safe, just, and dignified India through the introduction of dramatically improved sanitation. His project, Sulabh International, is improving India's sanitation, weakening the caste system, and helping those in the "untouchable" caste move into safer, more dignified jobs. Bindeshwar's systems are supported by municipal and user fees.

Background

Bindheshwar Pathak is an Indian Sociologist. He is the founder of Sulabh International, an India-based social service organisation which works to promote human rights, environmental sanitation, non-conventional sources of energy, waste management and social reforms through education. His work is considered one of the pioneers in social reform especially in the field of sanitation and hygiene. He received various national and international awards for his work with this organisation.

He was born on April 2, 1943, to a Brahmin (high caste) family, at Rampur Baghel village in Vaishali district of Bihar of British India. He comes from prosperous and respected family. His grandfather was a famous astrologer who, believe it or not, predicted the death of his own sibling at a certain age that actually happened. He also predicted that the wealth that his son, Dr Pathak's father would be left with would one day all whether away and that too, happened (Fair: 2012). His father is an ayurvedic (a holistic healing science) doctor.

> Dr Pathak was the proverbial child with a silver spoon. He grew up in a sprawling house with a large compound. There were nine rooms including a prayer room and another where only Atta, flour used to make most South Asian flat breads such as chapatti, roti, naan and puri. Groundwater too was drawn from this room. This house still stands today and though it is in ruin, it all the same stands. Bansal made a tour of the house and saw the unique well split into two by a wall. Her host told her that it was built in such a way that one side was used by men while the other was used by women. The reason for the split was that men should not catch a glimpse of women when the latter were drawing water to bathe. Bihar was and still is a very conservative state. One very distinctive feature that there was no toilet in the compound.
>
> Dr Pathak then told Bansal every morning at 4.00 a.m., there was total chaos in the house as women had to get up early and complete their personal cleanliness before sunrise. Some woman picked up a bucket; another was drawing water, while some-one would push another to hurry up. In case a woman in the house fell sick, she would have to relieve herself in a straw basket or a pot lined with ash (Bansal : 2011 : 291).

Dr Pathak graduated with a Bachelor's in Sociology in 1964 and earned his Master's degree in Sociology, topping the list from Patna University in 1980. He earned his Ph.D. on "Liberation of Scavengers Through Low-Cost Sanitation" in 1985 and his Master's degree in English, topping the list from Patna University in 1986. He earned his D.Litt. on "Eradication of Scavenging and Environmental Sanitation in India — a Sociological Study" in 1994. A prolific writer and speaker, Pathak has authored several books, the most well-known of which is *The Road to Freedom*, and is a frequent participant in conferences on sanitation, health, and social progress around the world. Other major works are as follows:

1. Constitutional Safeguards for weaker sections
2. Rural Violence in Bihar
3. Agricultural Engineering in Development: Human Resource Development-training and Education proramme
4. Social justice and development of weaker sections
5. Gandhi : Sanitation and Untouchability

Bindeshwar Pathak is a *Padma Bhushan* recipient from the Government of India. In 2003, his name was added to the Global 500 Roll of Honour. Bindheshwar Pathak also received the Energy Global Award in 2007 from Brussels-based Energy Globe at the European parliament, the Dubai International Award for Best Practices, and the Indira Gandhi Priyadarshini Award for Environment. Bindeshwar Pathak was elected to the Ashoka Fellowship in 2008. Stockholm Water Prize was awarded to him in year 2009 from the Stockholm international Water Institute, Sweden. In June, 2013, he also received the Legend of Planet award from the French senate in Paris, ahead of World Environment Day. Antarrashtriya Bhojpuri Samman was awarded to him in the 4th world Bhojpuri Sammelan in Port Louis. Known for its debating culture, the Cambridge Union Society is the oldest student debating society in the world and Cambridge University's largest. In January, 2011, Dr Pathak was invited by the Cambridge Union Society to deliver a lecture at the University of Cambridge. The lecture was well received by the students where Dr Pathak urged the students to join voluntary work in the field of sanitation.

Life Extraordinaire-Dr Bindeshwar Pathak

Louie Giglio views about Life Extraordinaire as: "Nothing is ordinary. Life is an endless series of little miracles. The difference between living and existing is noticing." When unexpectedly your paths cross with extraordinary people who can alter the way you thought so far, increasing its magnificence manifold, everything is a miracle. Your eyes are opened to the possibilities, life is an endless stream of grace that you just can't take for granted the little daisies tossed in your path and the very many blessings you are showered with. Here, we would like to describe the life extraordinaire of Dr Bindeshwari Pathak.

We want to present the story of Pathak in Rashmi Bansal's book "I have a Dream". We are reminded of this story and felt like sharing it without any attempt to be coherent in approach or effective in writing. We do not attempt to enunciate the minute details of his journey. It was a story that moved me deeply for the sheer grandness, simplicity, missionary zeal and absolute sensitivity to human suffering that it encompassed (see, Bansal: 2011; Unbounded Dreamer: 2012).

Pathak's story is the journey of a Brahmin boy of the 1940s whose grandmother forced him to eat cow dung and drink *gomutra* as a young boy because he happened to touch a member of the scavenger family in his village and thus had become unfit to live with his own family members. The boy grew up to found Sulabh International that has transformed the life of the manual scavengers and brought about a revolution to restore human dignity besides providing education & financial assistance to these people who have been oppressed through centuries of injustice.

He wanted to become a lecturer in Criminology for just one reason- his family was in business and sold medicines and in those days the business people were not held in much esteem by society (once he was going with his friend to his office; his friend asked him to get down from the rickshaw a hundred metres away from his office. On reaching the office of the friend some time later, his friend asked him *"Aurkabpahuncheaap?"* Pathak was shocked by humiliation when on expressing his surprise the friend told him that *"You are a supplier of medicines and I can't afford to be seen with you"*!). He wanted to change this by teaching in this new field and secure a dignified position in life and, therefore, left for Madhya Pradesh for his studies but on the way he met his cousin who forced him to abandon his plans and made him join an organisation that was celebrating Gandhi's birth centenary. As work progressed, due to internal politics, he was later transferred to another department and assigned the work of looking after the interests of manual scavengers. He realised that if he was to be able to do anything for them, he would have to become one of them, and thus a Brahmin came to live in the basti of bhangis. There was a great uproar back at his home; his friends would call him 'bhangiji' on seeing him; his father-in-law was terribly upset over what a graduate from Patna University had done and what would become of their daughter, and Pathak had to face greatly humiliating taunts from every quarter! Then two events changed his life completely.

In one of the families of the lower caste community, there came a newly wedded bride to her in-laws home after marriage. The very first day on her arrival, her *saas-sasur* forced her to go and clean the toilet. She cried bitterly and resisted, but to no avail. She was crying and crying and those around her were watching; Dr Pathak wept too on seeing all this. The second incident occurred one day in the marketplace when a bull suddenly charged towards a boy. At first several people rushed to protect him, but then one of the persons said that the boy is from the scavenger colony. Suddenly the crowd disappeared. Pathak and his friend were passing by and threw bricks at the bull to ward it off but the boy was terribly wounded and died on the way to the hospital. These two events shook the very core of Pathak and he suddenly forgot all about the insults and made up his mind to work for the scavenger community. It is this very spirit that we find driving the mission of Dr Pathak in context to Sulabh.

The journey ahead to the success of Sulabh Sauchalay took many years to materialise into reality; there were many hurdles from the Government and a plethora of other events that hindered progress, but slowly and slowly things changed and Sulabh became what it is today.

However, the greatness does not lie in the large scale construction of latrines in houses and public places across India, but in the simple but grand vision of the man- *to restore the lost individuality and dignity of the scavengers; to make them REALISE that they too are human beings entitled to live a dignified life just like others*. (When Ambedkar, a Dalit, was a boy, an official came to his school and asked the children to tell him one thing which they could see but could not touch. Some said 'sun', 'moon', 'air', etc. Ambedkar said *"paanikaghada"* (the earthen water pot) and pointed to the earthen pot of water in a corner of the classroom from which they were given water to drink but which they could not touch because they were lower caste children). Pathak also sends the scavenger community children to school, assists financially in the marriages of girls, etc. Today the women who used to clean toilets in the houses of upper caste women who did not even give them water in a glass, are now running small businesses and go to the same houses where they cleaned toilets and sit on the sofa and talk to those upper caste women. They enter temples where they could not earlier go. Pathak often takes women who were scavengers to 5 star hotels in Delhi for dinner and spends 3 lakhs just to make them realise *"Ki vo log bhiyahanaasaktehain"! (That they too can come here).* He says you cannot put a price tag on the feeling when you do such a thing. A feeling that you too are *somebody* in this world.That you too are a *human being.*

Pathak also wants to empower women and he has made a woman, who was once a scavenger, the president of Sulabh, Usha Chaumar. Today she walks the ramp with some of India's top models, meets dignitaries, gives speeches and accepts awards on behalf of Sulabh! He also sends his employees to United Nations and other places around the world to attend conferences and deliberately makes them stay in 5 star hotels and takes loan from banks to pay for their expenses!

There is profit but there is no concept of profit maximisation at Sulabh. The money is invested in building infrastructure, in paying salaries, and in welfare activities like vocational course and running Sulabh Public Schools where 60 per cent children are of scavenger community and 40 per cent from other backgrounds. He even helps to organise marriages and give aid to needy people who are not associated with Sulabh. Recently, if you read in the newspapers, Sulabh was approached by

Government of India on Supreme Court's directive to help the widows of Vrindawan; Pathak went there, registered the women, gave each of them money, provided them with meals and also took up the cause of looking after them (Unbounded Dreamer:2012).

Pathak's personal experience toward social revolution

In 1967, 25 year old Bindeshwar Pathak had missed getting a First Class that would have landed him a lecturer's job in a college. He tried being a school-teacher, a pay-roll clerk and even a street by street salesman of his grandfather's bottles of proprietary home-cure mixture. Deciding to get himself a Master's degree at Sagar University, MP, he boarded a train. At Hajipur, an elderly family friend talked him out of his move and promised him a 'good job' instead, in the Gandhi Centenary Committee at 'Rs.600 per mensum'. He got off the train and was led to Patna. The promised job wasn't quite there nor did life settle down for him, but he believes that his lifelong commitment to scavenger liberation through maintenance-free toilets began that day. **Contrasting Grandpas:** Or had it? Maybe it in fact began when he was a child and growing up in Vaishali and Sitamarhi. Maternal grandfather Pandit Jaya Nandan Jha had been to jail in the cause of India's freedom, even before Gandhi did in India. He had in fact been Gandhi's pilot to Hajipur and Vaishali. Pt. Jha was an egalitarian. The paternal grandfather was the opposite, though. "Time spent at the Pathak household were mystifying," says Bindeshwar. "Of the many 'rules', the one about not touching certain people intrigued me. Grandmother would sprinkle water on the paths such people had walked. And mutter some, as she did." One day, young Bindeshwar decided -as children are wont to- 'touch' a classified woman, just to see what happened- and hell certainly broke loose. He was given a ritual bath and administered a nugget of cow-dung and cow-urine, chased down by water from the Ganga.

As a child, Bindeshwar realised the injustices of the caste system. He once accidentally touched an untouchable woman; as punishment his grandmother made him swallow cow dung. That was the first of many experiences he had with the untouchable, scavenging community. After college, Bindeshwar joined the Bhangi-Mukti (scavengers' liberation) cell, a group dedicated to celebrating the birthday of Mahatma Gandhi and promoting a more just and integrated society. Through his work with Bhangi-Mukti, Bindeshwar lived and worked in an untouchable colony for three months. During his time in the colony he saw a newly married woman forced by her in-laws to clean toilets in Bihar. He also observed the way scavengers were dehumanised by mainstream society, and sought to declare them as a special class united in their disenfranchisement.

Even though Bindeshwar wrote his doctoral dissertation on scavenging, he realised that academia could not solve social problems. In his commitment to human rights and human dignity, he built up Sulabh as a systematic response to deal with the problem of manual scavenging. An inventor by nature, Bindeshwar ultimately focused on building an alternative to bucket toilets that was affordable and culturally acceptable. When building his organisation, Bindeshwar said, "The turning point was realising that the success of an organisation depends on its own resources. Self-reliance is important." To bolster his vision of a more just society, he combined theory with practice, and launched Sulabh International. Bindeshwar has transformed societal approaches to sanitation, built an enduring infrastructure for public sanitation and attracted new skilled talent to the sanitation sector.

He first came to understand the plight of scavengers in 1968 when he joined the Bhangi-Mukti (scavengers' liberation) Cell of the Bihar Gandhi Centenary Celebrations Committee. During that time, he traveled throughout India, living with scavenger families as part of his Ph.D. research. Drawing on that experience, he resolved to take action, not only out of sympathy for the scavengers but also in the belief that scavenging is a dehumanising practice that would ultimately have a destructive impact on modern Indian society.

He established the Sulabh International Social Service Organisation in 1970, combining technical innovation with humanitarian principles. The organisation works to promote human rights, environmental sanitation, non-conventional sources of energy, waste management and social reforms through education. The organisation counts 50,000 volunteers. He has made innovative use of biogas creation by linking Sulabh toilets to fermentation plants, he had designed over three decades ago and which are now becoming a byword for sanitation in developing countries all over the world. One of the distinctive features of Pathak's project lies in the fact that besides producing odour-free bio-gas, it also releases clean water rich in phosphorus and other ingredients which are important constituents of organic manure. His sanitation movement ensures cleanliness and prevents greenhouse gas emission.

Dr Pathak's story in his own words:

> In the welcome address of the National conference on Sociology of Sanitation on January 28, 2013, Dr Bindeshwar Pathak began telling his own story as to how he started his journey in the field of sociology and sanitation. Dr Pathak said: "I took up sociology as a subject in B.A. Part-I in Patna University and later as a subject in the Honours Class. I wanted to be a lecturer in the subject; however, after passing my Secondary School Examination, I became a school teacher. In the year 1968, by sheer coincidence, I joined the Bihar Gandhi Centenary Celebration Committee as a social worker. The General Secretary of the Committee asked me to engage myself fully to fulfil the dreams of Mahatma Gandhi – his unfinished agenda to restore the human rights and dignity of 'Untouchable' scavengers. This, he said, would be the best tribute from the committee to the Mahatma. I told him my story when, as a boy, I, out of curiosity, touched an 'Untouchable' Dom lady who used to come to deliver utensils made of bamboo at my house and after whose departure, my grandmother used to sprinkle water to purify the place. My grandmother seeing me having touched the lady forced me to take cow-dung and cow urine with Ganga water to purify me. I added, I belong to Brahmin caste, and further, I am not an engineer to find out an alternative to the toilets needing manual cleaning. The General Secretary looked at me seriously and said, 'I don't know your caste or whether you are an engineer or not, I see light in you having seen your dedication and commitment' ".

Pathak further said: "My background of Sociology prodded me to build a rapport with the community for which I had to work. I went to Bettiah, Champaran in Bihar, to live with the scavengers, the place, where incidentally, Mahatma Gandhi started his Satyagraha movement. My father and father-in- law had turned hostile seeing me going to work for scavengers. One afternoon, while going with some friends to the town, I saw a boy in a red shirt being attacked by a bull. People rushed to help him, in the meanwhile someone shouted from the back of the crowd that the boy belonged to the 'Untouchable' colony. On this everybody left him in an injured state. We took him to the local hospital but he died on the way. That day I took the solemn vow, forgetting my family, my caste, to work to fulfil Mahatma Gandhi's dream to rescue the 'Untouchables' from the shackles of slavery that are 5000 years old.

Once again, the background of Sociology came to my help indicating the need for some tools to test the hypothesis one is going to work upon. The tool, here, would be a technology that could find an alternative to bucket or dry toilet which needed manual scavenging. One such technology available was the sewerage system, which was costly to construct and maintain and hence existed in very few towns. I went through literature on the subject including the book, Excreta Disposal for Rural Areas and Small Communities by Edmund A. Wagner and J.N. Lanoix. Thereafter I innovated, invented and developed two-pit pour-flush Sulabh toilet, where one pit is used at a time; when it is filled up the flow is diverted to the other pit. After two years the residue in the first pit gets converted into bio-fertiliser which can be taken out by the householder himself. Sulabh alone has converted 1.3 million bucket toilets into Sulabh Shauchalayas and lakhs of scavengers have been freed from their inhuman profession of manually cleaning and carrying human excreta".

The Sulabh Founder said, "To rehabilitate the scavengers, I took help of one of the tools of Mahatma Gandhi – the tool of nonviolence. I didn't tear or burn the books of Vedas or Manusmriti. I persuaded the upper caste people and Pandits of temples to accept the scavengers as members of the society. I took them to Jagannath temple where after initial resistance the Pandits were convinced after discussion to let the erstwhile scavenger ladies perform Pooja in the temple. After the

Nathdwara visit the scavengers were given audience by the Hon'ble President of India, Mr. R. Venkataraman and the Hon'ble Prime Minister late Mr. Rajiv Gandhi. They were taken to Jagannathtemple.The head priest Pandit Devendra Kumar Sharma is here today amongst us. He will be awarded a cheque of 5 lakh by Sulabh in this function. There after they were taken to Varanasi where they worshipped Lord Shiva. The Pandits from Varanasi are also present here among us. They will take oath at this function today to eliminate untouchability from our society. The erstwhile scavengers have attended the UN General Assembly session and visited the Statue of Liberty in New York. They visited France to attend the Summit at Le Havre and Marseilles as well as Phoenix Ashram of Mahatma Gandhi in South Africa. The tool for this transformation has been education and training in vocations like making eatables, beauty care, stitching and embroidery in a Sulabh institute called Nai Disha in Rajasthan. They are sitting here among us in blue saries. Similarly, rehabilitated scavenger ladies from Arrah (Bihar) as well as New Delhi will be given blue saries at lunch today. Their children get free education, school dress and books and stationery in the Sulabh Public School in New Delhi".

This profile of Bindeshwar Pathak was prepared when he was elected to the Ashoka Fellowship in 2008. The highlight three things of Pathak as follows:

1. The New Idea
2. The Problem
3. The Strategy

The New Idea

An estimated 650 million of India's poorest citizens lack access to basic hygienic toilets; open defecation toilets are still common. When Bindeshwar started his work 40 years ago, he saw that sanitation offered a leverage point in matters both obvious and profound: Health, livelihoods, environment, social cohesion, and rights—particularly as pertains to the millions of India's "untouchable" caste.

Sulabh International advances transformative change in diverse communities. His solution brings together design, financing, public will, municipal resources and technologies that are basic and low cost. The pour-flush compost toilet (Sulabh-Shauchalayas) is outfitted with biogas converters to generate energy and reduce toxins and environmentally damaging practices such as dumping waste into rivers. By introducing a scalable, self-financing solution for sanitation, Pathak eliminates scavenging—the practice of removing human waste with manual tools—a job that falls to India's untouchables. Thus, the system he has introduced has created new roles for India's poorest citizens and charted a new, safe and dignified way for them to earn money.

The infrastructure Pathak has built is successfully used in twenty-five states and four territories. Many of his approaches have been adopted in other countries, and Sulabh International is actively involved in extending its work to Bhutan and Afghanistan. Additionally, he is building a University of Sanitation that will be a central resource center for everyone who needs to know about sanitation—users, technologists, municipal leaders, renewable energy experts and rights workers—to learn, share ideas, expand and deepen the work, and develop new ideas.

2. The Problem

In India, more than 65 per cent of the population lack basic sanitation facilities. That results in diseases such as cholera, diarrhea, dysentery, typhoid, infectious hepatitis, and hookworm. Studies show that more than 50 types of infections can be transmitted from human excrement, which causes or contributes to approximately 80 per cent of disease in developing countries. Disposal of human excrement causes significant environmental degradation as well. Sewage waste material is often dumped in rivers; areas without sewage facilities collect the waste on land. One of the U.N. Millennium Development Goals is to provide two billion people with toilets by 2015, but the goal is unlikely to be met because of the approaches currently used in many parts of the world. Rural populations have little access to proper toilet facilities, and urban slums are growing faster than toilets are being built. With few wastewater management facilities, both environmental damage and health hazards spread. Because of ignorance about sanitation and expensive sanitation technologies, many people— mostly those in the lower economic strata—live in unhygienic environments and constantly are threatened by preventable diseases. Furthermore, talking about excrement is a cultural taboo. Sanitation, therefore, is regarded as a matter of individual initiative—not a collective obligation of the community.

In 1878, an act was passed under British rule to implement public toilet systems. Even though the system was tried in some places around India, the toilets were too expensive to maintain and fell to disrepair. In the face of that failure, the subject of public sanitation was put aside, and defecation in public places continued. Due to the "dirty" undertones of the sanitation sector, people in "respectable" fields, such as engineering, business, and science, traditionally did not wish to work in the sector.

The job fell to "scavengers." Scavengers manually clean bucket toilets using rudimentary tools such as shovels and other buckets. Scavengers are relegated to the caste of untouchables and suffer discrimination. The caste has very little access to education, social services, or job mobility. With low literacy levels and few marketable skills, the scavengers' lives perpetuate a cycle of poverty.

3. The Strategy

Pathak's goal is to transform the sanitation sector and provide more opportunities for everyone. By making the sanitation sector more suitable for investment, he is increasing the rewards of working in the sector. Further, his programs are rehabilitating the scavengers and integrating them into society in a more respectful manner.

He developed the pour-flush compost toilet to promote better sanitation. The flush compost toilet requires one-tenth of the water required by traditional toilet systems and can be used for up to two years without waste removal. The system has helped eliminate open bucket toilets and is creating more opportunities for sanitary defecation. It also is recycling human waste and using it as agricultural fertiliser rather than allowing it to be dumped into local water supplies.

To give the affordable system greater exposure in India, Pathak came up with the idea of "pay and use." He receives initial financing from local governing bodies to build public toilet complexes, and Sulabh takes the maintenance guarantee. Although people in Bihar initially were skeptical of the pilot program in their state, more than 500 came to use the public toilets on the first day. Since Sulabh receives revenue through its public toilet system, it does not depend on external agencies for financing. Toilet complexes in slums and rural areas are subsidised with revenue from complexes in urban and more developed locations, which allowed the public toilet system to expand to over 1,400 cities in India, providing safe sanitation for all economic classes.

Under Sulabh International Academy of Environmental Sanitation, Pathak has been able to spread sanitation knowledge to citizen organisations, nurses, doctors, and officers from central, state, and local governments. He has held training workshops to enhance knowledge and skills in project planning and implementation of sanitation technologies through on-site construction, technical visits, and maintenance. He has also educated interested parties on various sanitation systems being implemented in the developing world, including biogas, bio-fertiliser, water treatment, duckweed technologies, solid waste management, and environmental protection. By institutionalising sanitation education, he brings people from all sectors together and removes taboos. Toilets are now becoming a source of economic gains, and he is able to engage top business professionals, engineers, and academics in the sanitation sector.

Even though his organisation is sanitation-oriented, it holds true to its fundamental mission to liberate scavengers and remove social discrimination and untouchability. Toilet technology has become a tool for social transformation. Along with sanitation programs, Pathak is providing technology and vocational training to help empower and generate alternative employment opportunities for scavengers. His approach to restore human dignity to the scavengers has five stages: (1) Liberation, (2) Rehabilitation, (3) Vocational training, (4) Social elevation, and (5) Proper education for future generations. Since scavengers traditionally have been trapped in a cycle of poverty and societal disenfranchisement, he is breaking that cycle through training and restoring dignity to the population. Through a combination of technological innovation and educational programming, he is using Sulabh to create a social revolution. Adopting flush toilets would end scavenging, enabling scavengers to pursue alternative forms of employment.

References

Ashoka Innovators for the Public (2008) *Profile of Bindeshwar Pathak*

Bansal, Rashmi (2011). *I have a Dream*, Chennai: Westland Ltd.

Dr Bindeshwar Pathak: *Wikipedia*, the free encyclopedia.

Fair, W.A.S.H (2012). "Fortnight of blissful life lessons with a 'philanthropist'." search from Sulabh International Social Service Organisation.

Life Extraordinaire- Shri Bindeshwar Pathak, *Unbounded Dreamer* on October 8, 2012

Life Foundation: Safeguarding Humanity, Dr Bindeshwar Pathak, Member of Advisory Board.

Sarkar, Sudeshna (2013). 'Flush of genius – Bindeshwar Pathak', *China daily Asia*, Friday, July 19.

Srivastava, Amitabh (2013). 'Pathak beats poverty and caste barrier to emerge as Bihar's unusual entrepreneur', *India Today*, Patna, March 23, 2013

Sulabh International Museum of Toilets: The profile of national Crusedar: Dr Bindeshwar Pathak.

1

Introduction

Most Indians still do not have access to modern sanitation. India has a population of almost 1.2 billion people, 55% of the population (nearly 600 million people) has no access to toilet. Most of these numbers are made up by people who have in urban slums and areas.

The absence of required sanitation in India has caused a loss of 6.5 per cent of the GDP per annum by the 20 per cent of the slum dwellers in India. Overall sanitation coverage in rural India is a dismal 34.8 per cent (where as according to NSSO : 2012, it is 32 per cent); for Scheduled castes and Scheduled tribes it is 23.7 per cent and 25 per cent respectively. The situation of sanitation is even worse in the tribal society of India. The situation in urban areas in terms of scale is not as serious as in rural areas This is an indication of alarming situation regarding Public Health, Social Deprivation, and Environmental Sanitation and so on in India. In this context, the present chapters deals with three things, namely,

I. Sociology of Sanitation: Concept and Genesis
II. Sanitation and its Relationship with other Disciplines and associated Dimensions:
   - Environmental,
   - Public Health,
   - Women and

- Sustainable development

III. Sanitation and its relationship with other social institutions

I
Sociology of Sanitation

Sociology emerged as a subject much later after history, philosophy and political science. Social awareness, individuals' relationship with one another and their participation as a community – all these are vital factors in sociological studies. Sanitation, hygiene, education are the sociological inter-locking factors. It is a well-known truism that sociology is practically non-existent in dictatorial regimes. It has been a remarkable step taken by the sociologist and social reformer Dr Bindeshwar Pathak to organise the National Conference on Sociology of Sanitation on January, 28-29, 2013 where various aspects of sociology like sanitation, public health, gender equality, social discrimination are explored. He has been working in the sphere of sanitation for the past four decades. It is the firm belief that a multifaceted approach is required to deal with the plethora of the issues embodying sanitation. Thus, he has propounded his theory of sociology of sanitation:

"Sociology of sanitation is a scientific study to solve the problems of society in relation to sanitation, social deprivation, water, public health, hygiene, ecology, environment, poverty, gender equality, welfare of children and empowering people for sustainable development and attainment of philosophical and spiritual knowledge to lead a happy life and to make a difference in the lives of others" (Wikipedia, the free encyclopaedia).

Sanitation refers to the safe disposal of human excreta (Mara, Lane and Scott and Trouba: 2010 WHO: int). This entails the hygienic disposal and treatment of human waste to avoid affecting the health of people. Sanitation is an essential part of the Millennium Development Goals. The most affected countries are in the developing world (Zawahri, Sowers, and Weinthal, 2011: 1153). Population increase in the developing world has posed challenges in the improvement of sanitation (Konteh, 2009: 69). According to Zawari, Sowers, and Weinthal (2011: 1154), lack of provisions of basic sanitation is estimated to have contributed to the deaths of approximately 3.5 million people annually from water borne diseases.

Mullegger, Lanergraber and Lechner (2011) of Eco San Club have discussed the issue of sanitation at length. This chapter has used their views for understanding various issues. There are 2.6 billion people who are living without adequate sanitation; the vast majority of population are in India, China, and Africa. Progress in provision of sanitation services is struggling to keep it with population growth, and Africa is lagging behind the most. Within 20 years, it is expected that an additional two billion will live in towns and cities demanding sanitation. The challenge is dubious, already today sanitation-related diseases and poor hygienic conditions cause 2.2 million deaths annually (mostly children under the age of five). Other consequences are the massive pollution of water and soil, the loss of innumerable school—(mainly girls) and working days, losses in tourism income, prevention of economic growth etc. In this context, there is an urgent need to understand the problem of Sanitation.

Sanitation in India

India may be 'on track" in achieving the 'The United Nations Millennium Development Goals (MDGs)' sanitation-target. MDG simply represent achievable levels. This is especially true for India's sanitation situation. Despite recent progress, access to improved sanitation remains far lower in India compared to many other countries. An estimated 55 per cent of all Indians, or close to 600 million people, still do not have access to any kind of toilet. Among them, Indians who live in urban slums and rural environment are affected the most.

In rural areas, the scale of the problem is particularly daunting as 74 per cent of the rural population still defecates in the open. The idea of building a facility for defecation in rural areas may not seem natural as the cash income is very low. Where such facilities exist, they are also often inadequate. In fact, this is not the issue of income but it should be the responsibility of the Gram Panchayats to provide such facilities in the villages. The sanitation landscape in India is still littered with 13 million unsanitary bucket latrines which require scavengers to conduct house-to-house collection. Over 700, 000 Indian still make their living this way.

The situation in urban areas is not as critical in terms of scale but the sanitation problems in crowded slum environments are equally serious. In these areas, the main challenge is to ensure safe environmental sanitation. Even in areas where household have toilets, the contents of bucket-latrines and pits, even of sewers are often emptied in context to environmental and health considerations. Sewerage systems, if they are even available, commonly suffer from poor maintenance which leads to overflow of raw sewage. Today, more than 20 Indian cities having population of more than 1 million people, including Indian megacities, such as Kolkata, Mumbai, New Delhi etc. antiquated sewerage systems simply cannot handle the increased load.

History of Sanitation

The earliest evidence of urban sanitation was seen in Harappa, Mohenjo-Daro and the recently discovered Rakhigarhi of Indus Valley civilisation. This urban plan included the world's first urban sanitation systems. Within the city, individual homes or groups of homes obtained water from wells. From a room that appears to have been set aside for bathing, waste water was directed to covered drains, which lined the major streets.

Roman cities and Roman villas had elements of sanitation systems, delivering water in the streets of towns such as Pompeii, and building stone and wooden drains to collect and remove waste water from populated areas - see for instance the Cloaca Maxima into the River Tiber in Rome. But there is little record of other sanitation in most of Europe until the High Middle Ages. Unsanitary conditions and overcrowding were widespread throughout Europe and Asia during the Middle Ages, resulting periodically in cataclysmic pandemics such as the Plague of Justinian (541-42) and the Black Death (1347–1351), which killed tens of millions of people and radically altered societies (Cipolla: 1980).

Medieval towns did have people to clear away the rubbish. However, the vast majority of people did not live in towns, they lived in the country where rubbish could just been buried or burnt or turned into compost or eaten by pigs etc. It wouldn't have seen such a problem. Bathing was less common than it is now, as few people had indoor plumbing. When you have to fetch water by hand, fill a tub, and empty it afterwards, bathing is less attractive. But some wealthy people did have bathrooms in their castles or palaces, and of course the rich had servants to fill and empty the baths, heat up the water etc. King Henry III of England, for example, had a spectacular bath, the Westminster Chronicle of 1225 writes that he took delivery that year of a French-made bath carved in stone in the shape of a peacock 'covered all over with eyes like a real peacock, made of precious stones called pearls, silver, and sapphires'. Squires would be expected to help the lords they served battle, among their other duties. Also largely dependent upon where you were. Places such as the Latin East and Spain where such things as public baths, with associated barbers/surgeons were maintained or rebuilt continued to be sued by the people of the area, of varying social levels of hygiene by location.

For the common people, bathing at home would mean a wooden tub or barrel, which would have to be filled with water by hand. The common people in towns enjoyed going to the public baths, Queen Matilda, wife of King Henry I of England, built the first public baths and public lavatories in London, for instance, Monasteries often had piped water, and had bath-house and lavers- stone troughs used for washing before and after meals.

Cassen (1978) argues that Indian levels of personal hygiene were probably well above those of medieval Europe. Slightly more information is available for being more unsanitary in urban areas than rural areas and for having worse housing and diet. Morality rates were probably higher in urban areas, despite their having a population concentrated in the "productive" age groups and relatively few males (Davis: 1951). But differences between the urban and rural areas are nearly as high as those of urban slums, and rural slums can be as unsanitary as urban ones (Jeffery: 1988:40).

We would like to give here some of the important development of the sanitation and hygiene in the different periods of time as follows:

- 2000 BC Ancient Indo-Aryan water purification. In this period water was purified by boiling and filtering.
- 460-377 BC: The Birth of Hygiene: During the time of Greek physician Hippocrates, "hygiene" became known as the branch of medicine dedicated to the "art of health", (as distinct from the therapeutics, the treatment of disease).

- 300 BC- AD 4000: The system of aqueducts built in Ancient Rome provided inhabitants with fresh running water, which was piped directly to homes of the wealthy, and to public fountains and baths. This greatly improved domestic sanitation and adequate disposal of sewage.
- 1600s-1700s: Human contact with waste was minimised in Japanese cities because it was collected for use as crop fertiliser. Sewage was not discharged to rivers so pollution of waterways was minimised.
- 1800s: England's population increased rapidly but its numbers of toilets did not. Most human waste made its way into rivers, polluting the water and giving rise to foul odours. In 1842 public health reformer Sir Edwin Chadwick published in his sanitary Health Report: "only two or three public privies... for the great bulk of inhabitants" "the whole area of the cellars of both houses were full of night soil (human excrement)" "a square court... occupied entirely as a dung receptacle of the most disgusting kind" "a dunghill in one street... is never removed... the malarious oozes through the wall, and runs over the pavement".
- As a result of his report, the 1848 Public Health Act was instituted, followed by the 1866 sanitary Act, making local authorities responsible for Sanitary regulation including sewage disposal, water supply and housing density and occupancy, and introducing penalties for persons suffering from dangerous infectious diseases who endangered others in public places.
- 1854: Dr John Snow showed that cholera was spread by water.
- 1860: The first septic tank was invented by Louis Moureas and used by communities to remove solids from waste before the liquid was discharged into a body of water. This design was improved by use of trickling sand filtration from 1893.
- 1865: In New York domestic garbage and filth of every kind is thrown into the streets. In winter, the filth and garbage etc. accumulate in the streets to the depth sometimes of two or three feet.

- 1800s- 1900s: Sewer Systems were constructed in many European and US Cities, initially discharging untreated sewage to water-waves. When discharge of untreated sewerage became increasingly unacceptable, experimentation towards improved treatment methods resulted in sewage farming, chemical precipitation, filtration, sedimentation, chemical treatment, and activated sludge treatment using aerobic microorganisms.
- 1900: The plague was brought to the Rocks area of Sydney by rats from ships. This led to one of the first major clean-ups of Sydney: slums were demolished, streets lime-washed, 1423 dead animals removed from Sydney harbor, 44,548 rats destroyed, more than 28,455 tons of garbage taken out to sea and another 25,430 tons of garbage burned.
- 1960s: Garbage compactors. The first patents for residential garbage compactors were filed in the USA.
- 2004: The National Health and Medical Research Council published Australian Drinking Water Guidelines, providing guidance on what constitutes good quality drinking water. Australia's drinking water is currently sourced from dams, rainwater, bore water and desalination plants, whilst increasingly treated grey water is being reused for irrigation and for selected household use.

As a matter of fact, the situation of sanitation has not been so bad in India if analysed from a historical perspective. The archeological excavations in India have revealed the Harappan Model of urban sanitation. We also know the views of the father of the nation, Mahatma Gandhi on sanitation. In the modern period, the world witnessed another economical and most effective Sulabh International Model of Sanitation introduced by Dr Bindeshwar Pathak. But even then the coverage of sanitation is far less than what is required on the developmental scale. Till now, access to proper sanitation has remained the privilege of only a small section of the society in India.

Concept of Sanitation

The word 'sanitation' is derived from the Latin word *Sanitas*, which means aim to protect and promote human health by providing a clean environment and breaking the cycle of disease.

It refers to the principles and practices relating to the collection, treatment, refuse as they impact upon people and environment (Mullegger, Lanergraber and Lechner: 2011).

The word hygiene comes from *Hygeia,* the Greek goddess of health, who as the daughter of Aesxulapius, the god of medicine. Since the advent of the Industrial revolution (c. 1750-1850) and the discovery of germ theory of disease in the second half of the nineteenth century, hygiene and sanitation have been at the forefront of the struggle against illness and disease (William:1981).

Sanitation is the hygienic means of promoting health through prevention of human contact with the hazards of wastes. Hazards can be physical, microbiological, biological or chemical agents of disease. Wastes that can cause health problems include human and animal faeces, solid wastes, domestic wastewater (sewage, sullage, and grey water), industrial wastes and agricultural wastes. Hygienic means of prevention can be by using engineering solutions (e.g. sewerage and wastewater treatment), simple technologies (e.g. latrines, septic tanks), or even by personal hygiene practices (e.g. simple hand washing with soap).

The World Health Organisation (WHO) states that: "Sanitation generally refers to the provision of facilities and services for the safe disposal of human urine and faeces. Inadequate sanitation is a major cause of disease world-wide and improving sanitation is known to have a significant beneficial impact on health both in households and across communities. The word 'sanitation' also refers to the maintenance of hygienic conditions, through services such as garbage collection and wastewater disposal (http://www.who.int.topics/sanitation/en). (WHO: int)

The term "sanitation" can be applied to a specific aspect, concept, location or strategy, such as:

(i) Improved Sanitation - refers to the management of human faeces at the household level. This terminology is the indicator used to describe the target of the Millennium Development Goal on sanitation, by the WHO/UNICEF Joint Monitoring Programme for Water Supply and Sanitation.

(ii) On-site Sanitation - the collection and treatment of waste is done where it is deposited. Examples are the use of pit latrines, septic tanks, and Imhoff tanks.

(iii) Food Sanitation - refers to the hygienic measures for ensuring food safety.

(iv) Environmental Sanitation – It helps the control of environmental factors that form links in disease transmission. Subsets of this category are solid waste management, water and wastewater treatment, industrial waste treatment and noise and pollution control.

(v) Ecological Sanitation – It is an approach that tries to emulate nature through the recycling of nutrients and water from human and animal wastes in a hygienically safe manner (see, for details, en.wikipedia.org/wiki/sanitation).

The United Nations Millennium Development Goals (MDGs) include a target to reduce by half the proportion of people without access to basic sanitation by 2015. In December 2006, the United Nations General Assembly declared 2008 'The International Year of Sanitation', in recognition of the slow progress being made towards the MDGs sanitation target. ["Peri-urban Water and Sanitation Services".Springer. 2010]. the year aims to develop awareness and action to meet the target. Particular concerns are:

The Joint Monitoring Programme (JMP) for Water Supply and Sanitation of WHO and UNICEF has defined improved sanitation as follows for global access to improved sanitation [WHO and UNICEF: 2012]:

1. Flush toilet
2. Connection to a piped sewer system
3. Connection to a septic system
4. Flush / pour-flush to a pit latrine
5. Ventilated improved pit (VIP) latrine
6. Pit latrine with slab
7. Composting toilet
8. Some special cases

The JMP publishes a report of updated estimates every two years on the use of various types of drinking-water sources and sanitation facilities at the national, regional and global levels. In

March 2012, the JMP released its latest updates. (WHO and UNICEF: 2012 a). According to the definition above, 1.8 billion more people used improved sanitation in 2010 than in 1990, bringing the percentage of people using improved sanitation to 63 per cent globally. However, the world remains off track for the sanitation target of the Millennium Development Goals. 2.5 billion lack improved sanitation (WHO and UNICEF: 2012: 2). According to the JMP, if current trends continue, in 2015 2.4 billion people will lack access to improved sanitation facilities. 15 per cent of the population still practise open defecation, defined as defecation in fields, forests, bushes, bodies of water or other open spaces. This represents 1.1 billion people. Though the proportion of people practising open defecation is decreasing, the absolute number has remained at over one billion for several years, due to population growth (WHO and UNICEF: 2012 a:5).

This outcome presents substantial public health risks as the waste could contaminate drinking water and cause life threatening forms of diarrhoea to infants. Most cities can neither afford a sewage drainage system, nor a sewage treatment system, as SunitaNarain spelled out in the magazine D+C Development and Cooperation. Improved sanitation, including hand washing and water purification, could save the lives of 1.5 million children who die from diarrheal diseases each year (WHO and UNICEF: 2012 b).

The standard sanitation technology in urban areas is the collection of wastewater in sewers, its treatment in wastewater treatment plants for reuse or disposal in rivers, lakes or the sea. Sewers are either combined with storm drains or separated from them as sanitary sewers. Combined sewers are usually found in the central, older parts or urban areas. Heavy rainfall and inadequate maintenance can lead to combined sewer overflows or sanitary sewer overflows, i.e. more or less diluted raw sewage being discharged into the environment. Industries often discharge wastewater into municipal sewers, which can complicate wastewater treatment unless industries pre-treat their discharges (Ujang: 2003).

The high investment cost of conventional wastewater collection systems are difficult to afford for many developing countries. Some countries have, therefore, promoted alternative wastewater collection systems such as condominial sewerage, which uses smaller diameter pipes at lower depth with different network layouts from conventional sewerage.

Sewage Treatment Plant in Australia

In developed countries treatment of municipal wastewater is now widespread (Typical U.S. water treatment standards), but not yet universal (for an overview of technologies see wastewater treatment). In developing countries most wastewater is still discharged untreated into the environment. For example, in Latin America only about 15 per cent of collected sewerage is being treated (see water and sanitation in Latin America)

II

Sanitation and its relationship with other disciplines and associated dimensions as follows:

- Ecological including environmental,
- Public Health,
- Women and
- Sustainable development

Ecological Sanitation

Ecological sanitation is sometimes presented as a radical alternative to conventional sanitation systems. Ecological sanitation is based on composting or vermicomposting toilets where an extra separation of urine and faeces at the source for sanitisation and recycling has been done. It thus eliminates the creation of *black water* and eliminates faecal pathogens. If ecological sanitation is practiced municipal wastewater consists only of grey water, which can be recycled for gardening. However, in most cases *grey water* continues to be discharged to sewers.

Sanitation and Public Health

The importance of the isolation of waste lies in an effort to prevent diseases which can be transmitted through human waste, which afflict both developed countries as well as developing countries to differing degrees. It is estimated that up to 5 million people die each year from preventable water-borne diseases as a result of inadequate sanitation and hygiene practices. The effects of sanitation have impacted the society of people throughout history (Ehlers: 1943). Sanitation is a necessity for a healthy life (George, Rose: 2008). The results of studies published in *Griffins Public Sanitation* show that better sanitation produces an enhanced feeling of wellbeing.

Relevant diseases include:

- Water-borne diseases, which can contaminate drinking water
- Diseases transmitted by the faecal-oral route
- Hookworm, where eggs can survive in the soil

There continues to be many countries that are struggling with diseases due to unhealthy living conditions and unfiltered water all in the name of bad sanitation (Heller and Castro:2009 ; Stewart and Gray : 2009; eBook Collection: 2012 and www.victorianweb.org/history/chadwick2.html).

Sanitation: A Woman's Issue

No issue touches the lives of women – particularly poor urban women – as intimately as that of access to sanitation. In low income settlements where there are no individual toilets, women have to queue for long periods to gain access to public toilets; some have to bear the indignity of having to defecate in the open, which exposes them to the possibility of sexual harassment or assault.

Although men also suffer from the burden of poor sanitation, they are more likely to resort to other means to relieve themselves. In many slums, men urinate and defecate along railway tracks and in open spaces. But women – whose anatomy, modesty and susceptibility to attack does not allow them to discreetly relieve themselves in public – have no choice but to wait until dark, usually early in the morning when there is less risk of being accosted. "Going to the toilet" for these women often means squatting in a private spot or waking up before dawn to queue at public toilets.

One woman interviewed in a Mumbai slum explained what it means to have no toilet: "We use the toilet outside our settlement, five minutes away. We have to stand in a queue for half an hour. That is why the men all go under the bridge and only the women use the toilets. Children also go out in the open."

A disproportionate share of the labour and health burden of inadequate sanitation falls on women. For women living in slums, a long wait at the public toilet can mean that children are left unattended, or that a household chore is delayed. Unhygienic public toilets and latrines threaten the health of women, who are prone to reproductive tract infections caused by poor sanitation. For women who are menstruating, the need for adequate sanitation becomes even more acute. Moreover, because it is generally women who are responsible for the disposal of human waste when provision of sanitation is inadequate, they are more susceptible to diseases associated with contact with human excreta.

Despite all this, the sanitation crisis affecting women has not been given a high priority on the agendas of human rights and women's organisations. United Nations and other international bodies tend to confine women's issues to reproductive health and education. Few, if any, governments focus on the impact of in-adequate sanitation on women. This could also be partially explained by the fact that improving access to sanitation was only recently recognised as a pressing internationally agreed target – in 2002 at the World Summit on Sustainable Development – so the issue has not been on the public agenda for long. Although women's lack of access to water in both rural and urban areas and its health implications – including severe back pain caused by carrying heavy vessels of water over long distances – has been the subject of several studies, women's lack of access to sanitation has not received the same attention. Preliminary UN-HABITAT analyses indicate the need for further study of the issue, as they show that lack of sanitation in slums increases health risks among all slum residents, women and children in particular.

Because rural women – no matter how poor – do not have to face the same dilemma as their urban counterparts when it comes to sanitation, poverty reduction efforts, which are currently focused on rural areas, particularly in sub-Saharan Africa and Asia, do not factor in women's access to sanitation in urban areas. Most rural households have access to at least one toilet – even if it is a crude pit latrine – which means that women in rural areas rarely queue to go to the toilet and are less likely to share toilets with dozens of other people. They are also more likely to keep the toilets clean, as their family's health often depends on it. [Sources: RasnaWarah 2005a; UN-HABITAT 2003a; Hardoy, et al. 2001; Mukherjee 2001)

Sanitation and Sustainable Development

In order to be sustainable, a sanitation system has to not only economically viable, socially acceptable, technically and institutionally appropriate, but it should also protect the environment and the natural resources. Thus sustainability in the sanitation sector refers to five integrated dimensions: technical, financial, institutional, social and environmental. The Sustainable Sanitation Alliance (SSA) links these sustainability criteria to the following aspects:

1. *Health and hygiene* includes the risk of exposure to human pathogens and hazardous substances; hygiene, nutrition and improvement of livelihood; effects on the health of downstream population.
2. *Environmental and natural resources* the required energy, water, and other natural resources; the potential emissions to the environment resulting from their use, the degree of recycling practiced, and their effects.
3. *Technology and operation* incorporates the functionality and the ease of construction, operation, maintenance and monitoring; suitability to achieve an efficient substance flow management; robustness as well as flexibility and adaptability of the system.
4. *Financial and economic issues* relates to the capacity of households and communities to pay for sanitation, economic benefits from the production of the recyclables, employment creation, increased productivity through improved health and the reduction of environmental and public health costs.
5. *Socio-cultural and institutional aspects* includes the socio-cultural acceptance and appropriateness of the system, convenience, gender issues, and impacts on human dignity, the contribution to subsistence economic and food security, and legal and institutional aspects.

Thus, *Sustainable Development* refers to the policy of promoting growth consistent with protection of environment, e.g., via shift to renewable resources and local community participation in development projects. For incineration options, the release of air pollutants, including certain toxic components is an attendant adverse outcome. Recycling and biofuel conversion are the sustainable options that generally have superior life cycle costs, particularly when total ecological consequences are considered (William: 1986), Composting value will ultimately be limited by the market demand for compost product.

In the above context, one of the major challenges before India is to provide sustainable sanitation and hygiene to its vast diverse and growing population. The Government of India has declared its commitment towards achieving MDG goals and universal sanitation coverage in the country by the year 2022, but with the current rural sanitation coverage of 32.7 per cent, this is a challenging task.

III

Sociology of Sanitation and its relationship with other Social Institutions

A social institution is an organised complex pattern of behaviour in which a number of persons participate in order to further group interest. Village, religion, Caste, family, kinship, the school, church, the hospital, political parties, professional associations and the panchayats are all social institutions. In each institution the roles by different are performed according to the rules or normative pattern of the society (Park and Park: 1977: 72). We are presenting below some of the institutions which are directly related with sanitation and its behavioural aspects communities and cultural practices of various ethnic groups whose nature is determined by social structure of particular society.

The introduction of on-site sanitation systems is much more than the application of simple engineering techniques - it is an intervention that entails considerable social change. If sanitation improvements in rural and urban areas are to be widely accepted, the relevant social and cultural factors have to be taken into consideration during planning and implementation. It is therefore necessary to understand how a society functions, including the communities and households within it, and what factors promote change.

As regards sanitation behaviour, defecation is often a private matter which people are unwilling to discuss openly, while the burying of faeces is widely practiced to ward off evil spirits. Contact with faecal matter is unacceptable to certain individuals in societies where it is the responsibility of low-income or low-caste groups, while taboos may dictate that separate facilities should be provided for particular social groups.

A particular cultural practice to be considered, which has direct technical consequences, is the method of anal cleansing used by the community. Whether water, stones, corncobs or thick pieces of paper are used will affect the design of the sanitation system. Culture also influences how people interpret and evaluate the environment in which they live. Investments in sanitation seek to improve health by providing a clean physical environment for households. There is a logical series of technical questions that need to be asked in order that acceptable technical solutions can be found. It may be confusing, therefore, when sanitation behaviour is found to vary widely between communities within the same physical environment. Predetermined rules cannot be applied. However, the sanitation behaviour of individuals usually has a rational basis, and people are often aware of the environmental causes of ill-health. Many societies have a detailed knowledge of the physical environment as a provider of resources for curative and preventive medicine and as a cause of illness. More than this, they have an understanding of the environment, not only in its physical sense, but also in relation to social and spiritual factors. This holistic view of the environment permeates many of the cultural beliefs and customs that impinge on both water use patterns and sanitation behaviour. (Franceys, R., J. Pickford & R. Reed: WHO: 1992:245). Some illustrations of these beliefs are given while discussing the concept of hygiene, beliefs about sanitation and disease, forces for change and response to change in the chapter on social structure and sanitation.

Improving Access

Removing the stigma around sanitation is very important so that the importance of sanitation can be more easily and publicly discussed. Health and other benefits flow from better hygiene, household sanitation arrangements and wastewater treatment. Research from the Overseas Development Institute suggests that sanitation and hygiene promotion needs to be better 'mainstreamed' in development, if the MDG on sanitation is to be met. At present, promotion of sanitation and hygiene is mainly carried out through water institutions. The research argues that there are, in fact, many institutions that should carry out activities to develop better sanitation and hygiene in developing countries. For example, educational institutions can teach on hygiene, and health institutions can dedicate resources to preventative works (to avoid, for example, outbreaks of cholera (ODI: 2006). There are also civil society organisations providing the necessary infrastructure where national governments cannot do that on their own. In Ghana, there is an umbrella organisation for those programmes, called CONIWAS (Coalition of NGOs in Water and Sanitation) as reported in the magazine D+C Development and Cooperation.

The Institute of Development Studies (IDS) coordinated research programme on Community-led Total Sanitation (CLTS) is a radically different approach to rural sanitation in developing countries and has shown promising successes where traditional rural sanitation programmes have failed. CLTS is an unsubsidised approach to rural sanitation that facilitates communities to recognise the problem of open defecation and take collective action to clean up and become 'open defecation free'. It uses community-led methods such as participatory mapping and analysing pathways between faeces and mouth as a means of galvanising communities into action. An IDS 'In Focus' Policy Brief suggests that in many countries the Millennium development goal for sanitation is off track and asks how CLTS can be adopted and spread on a large scale in the many countries and regions where open defecation still prevails (IDS: 2009). In United States, sanitation is a legislative requirement of occupational safety and health, which is governed by 29 CFR Part 1910.141 (CFR: 2008).

References

Aiello, A.E. E.L. Larson, R. Sadlak (2007), "Against Disease: The Impact of Hygiene and Cleanliness on Health", The Soap and Detergent Association, p.3-

Bartram, Jamie (2010), How Health Professionals can Leverage Health Gains from Improved Water, Sanitation and Hygiene Practices, *Perspectives in Public Health.* pp. 215-221.

Beyond Subsidies - Triggering a Revolution in Rural Sanitation' *Institute of Development Studies* (IDS) In Focus Policy Brief 10 July 2009.

Cassen, R. (1978), *India: Population, Economy, Society*, London: Macmillan.

Cipolla, Carlo M. (1980), *Before the Industrial Revolution: European Society and Economy (1000-1700)*, London: W.W. Norton and Company.

Code of Federal Regulations (CFR). "1910.141 Sanitation" (PDF). Retrieved 1 March 2008.

Davis, K. (1951), *The Population of India and Pakistan*, Princeton N.J.: Princeton University Press.

Ehlers, Victor (1943). *Municipal and Rural Sanitation*. New York: McGraw-Hill book company, inc

Franceys, R., J. Pickford & R. Reed (1992) A guide to Development On-Site Sanitation, Geneva: World Health Organisation (WHO) p.245.

George Rose (2008), *The Big Necessity: The Unmentionable Worlds of Human Waste and why it Matters*. New York: Metropolitan Books/ Henrey Holt and Company.

George, Tchobanoglous and Frank Kreith (2002), *Handbook of Solid Waste Management*, McGraw Hill.

Heller, Léo, and José Esteban Castro (2009). Water and Sanitation Services: Public Policy and Management. n.p.: Earth scan, 2009, eBook Collection (EBSCOhost). Web. 14 Nov. 2012.

Hoyt, E.P. (1972), "Hygiene in Ancient China", *Chest*, Vol.61, No. 2, p.133.

Japan External Trade Organisation (JETO). "Food Sanitation Law in Japan" (PDF). Retrieved 1 March 2008.

Jeffery, Roger (1988), *The Politics of Health in India*, London: University of California Press, p. 40.

Konteh, Frederick Hassan (2009), Urban Sanitation and Health in the Develoiping World: Reminiscing the Nineteenth Century Industrial Nations, Health and Place, March, Vol. 15(1): 69-78.

Mara, D.; Lane, J; Scott, B; Trouba, D. (2010), Sanitation and Health. PLOS Medicine, 7(11).

Mullegger, E., Langergraber, G. and Lechner, M. (2011)."Sustainable sanitation Practice, Planning Tools: Sustainable Sanitation Practice", EcosanClub, Issue 7. Available at:http://www.seecon.ch/sites/default/files/projects/files/spp_sswm_toolbox.pdf

Needham, J. and L. Gwei-Djen (1959), "Hygiene and Preventive Medicine in Ancient China", *Health Educational Journal*, Vol.17, p.170-179.

Park, J.E. and K.Park (1977), Text book on *Social and Preventive and Social Medicine*, Jabalpur: BanarsidasBhanot Publishers. P.71 (old book)

RasnaWarah 2005a; UN-HABITAT 2003a; Hardoy, et al. 2001; Mukherjee 2001. *habitat.press@unhabitat.org, website: www.unhabitat.org*

"Sanitation and Hygiene: knocking on new doors" (PDF). *Overseas Development Institute* (ODI). 2006. Retrieved 2007.

Stewart, Amy, and Tim Gray (2009). Governance of Water and Sanitation in Africa: Achieving Sustainable Development through Partnerships. n.p.: I.B. Tauris, 2009. eBook Collection (EBSCOhost). Web. 14 Nov. 2012.

Ujang , Z. (ed.) (2003). *Environmental Biotechnology: Advancement in Water and Wastewater Application*, IWA Proceedings, Malaysia.

US Fed News Service, Including US State News (2008), "Poor Sanitation Threatens Public Health".

WHO and UNICEF (2012) types of improved drinking-water source on the JMP website, WHO, Geneva and UNICEF, New York, accessed on June 10, 2012

WHO and UNICEF (2012 a), *Progress on Drinking-water and Sanitation*: 2012 Update, WHO, Geneva and UNICEF, New York

WHO and UNICEF (2012 b), *Progress on Drinking-water and Sanitation: Special Focus on Sanitation. 2012* Update, WHO, Geneva and UNICEF, New York

Williams, G. (1981), *The Age of Miracles- medicine and Surgery in the Nineteenth Century*, Chicago, IL: Academy Chicago Publishers.

William D. Robinson (1986), *The Solid Waste Handbook: A Practical Guide*, John Wiley and sons.

www.victorianweb.org/history/chadwick2.html.

Zawahri, N., Sowers, J. and Weinthal, E. (2011), The Politics of Assessment: Water and Sanitation MDGs in the Middle East. *Development and Change*, 42: 1153-1178.

2

Perspectives and Orientations

Sociological Perspectives

From Mooney, Knox, and Schacht, 2007. *Understanding Social Problems*, theories in sociology provide us with different perspectives with which to view our social world. A perspective is simply a way of looking at the world. Sociologists analyse social phenomena at different levels and from different perspectives. From concrete interpretations to sweeping generalisations of society and social behaviour, sociologists study everything from specific events (the micro level of analysis of small social patterns) to the "big picture" (the macro level of analysis of large social patterns).

The pioneering European sociologists, however, also offered a broad conceptualisation of the fundamentals of society and its workings. Their views form the basis for today's theoretical perspectives, or paradigms, which provide sociologists with an orienting framework—a philosophical position—for asking certain kinds of questions about society and its people. In this context, the present chapter deals with the following things:

(1) Perspectives and Orientations

(2) Approaches to Public Health

(3) Social Perspective on the sanitation challenges

[To explain the different perspectives and orientations, examples are given from the Report on South Asian people's perspective on sanitation Synthesis review Bangladesh, India, Nepal, Pakistan and Sri Lanka. This report is cited as Water Aid, FANSA and WSSCC (2011) *South Asian people's perspective on sanitation: Synthesis review* (see note 1)].

Sociological Theory

Sociological theory has occupied a prominent position within the discipline from its very foundation. However, as a major subfield it has been hampered by at least two major problems: (1) theory, particularly within the context of a paradigmatic culture, has often viewed as separate from and irrelevant to research and empirical reality while (2) theory texts have tended to be descriptive, historical and philosophical compendiums of large number of theorists rather than analyses of evolution, structure, and forms of sociological theory.

In reaction to such problems, Kinloch (1977) attempts to analyse the emergence, context (i.e., social, intellectual, and biographical conditions), and evolution of the major types of theory in sociology. Such an approach views sociological theory as a dynamic, situational, and changing process—a systematic reaction to particular social situations by intellectual thinking in particular philosophical conditions of social reality; the organic-structure-functional, conflict-radical, and social-behaviourist-social psychological paradigms. The result is an assessment of the basis, development and structure of sociological theory and its possible alternatives.

The Three Main Sociological Perspectives

A theory is a set of interrelated propositions or principles designed to answer a question or explain a particular phenomenon; it provides us with a perspective. Sociological theories help us to explain and predict the social world in which we live. Sociologists today employ three primary theoretical perspectives: the functionalist perspective, the conflict perspective, and the symbolic interactionist perspective (sometimes called the interactionist perspective or simply the micro view). Each perspective offers a variety of explanations about the social world and human behaviour. These perspectives offer sociologists theoretical paradigms for explaining how society influences people, and vice versa. Each perspective uniquely conceptualises society, social forces, and human behaviour (see Table 1).

Table 1: Sociological Perspectives

Sociological perspectives	*Level of Analysis*	*Focus*
1. Functionalism	Macro	Relationship between parts of society; How aspects of society are functional (Adaptive).
2. Conflict Theory	Macro	Competition of scarce resources: How the elite control the poor and weak.
3. Symbolic Interactionism	Micro	Use of symbols; Face - to - Face interactions

1. Functionalist Perspective

According to the functionalist perspective, also called functionalism, each aspect of society is interdependent and contributes to society's functioning as a whole. The government, or state, provides education for the children of the family, which in turn pays taxes on which the state depends to keep itself running. That is, the family is dependent upon the school to help children grow up to have good jobs so that they can raise and support their own families. In the process, the children become law abiding, tax paying citizens, who in turn support the state. If all goes well, the parts of society produce order, stability, and productivity. If all does not go well, the parts of society then must adapt to recapture a new order, stability, and productivity. For example, during a financial recession with its high rates of unemployment and inflation, social programs are trimmed or cut. Schools offer fewer programs. Families tighten their budgets. And a new social order, stability, and productivity occur.

The functionalist perspective is based largely on the works of Herbert Spencer, Emile Durkheim, Talcott Parsons, and Robert Merton. According to functionalism, society is a system of interconnected parts that work together in harmony to maintain a state of balance and social equilibrium for the whole. For example, each of the social institutions contributes important functions for society: Family provides a context for reproducing, nurturing, and socialising children; education offers a way to transmit a society's skills, knowledge, and culture to its youth; politics provides a means of governing members of society; economics provides for the production, distribution, and consumption of goods and services; and religion provides moral guidance and an outlet for worship of a higher power. The functionalist perspective emphasises the interconnectedness of society by focusing on how each part influences and is influenced by other parts. For example, the increase in single parent and dual-earner families has contributed to the number of children who are failing in school because parents have become less available to supervise their children's homework. As a result of changes in technology, colleges are offering more technical programs, and many adults are returning to school to learn new skills that are required in the workplace. The increasing number of women in the workforce has contributed to the formulation of policies against sexual harassment and job discrimination. Functionalists use the terms *functional* and *dysfunctional* to describe the effects of social elements on society. Elements of society are functional if they contribute to social stability and dysfunctional if they disrupt social stability. Some aspects of society can be both functional and dysfunctional. For example, crime is dysfunctional in that it is associated with physical violence, loss of property, and fear. But according to Durkheim and other functionalists, crime is also functional for society because it leads to heightened awareness of shared moral bonds and increased social cohesion.

Functionalists believe that society is held together by social consensus, or cohesion, in which members of the society agree upon, and work together to achieve, what is best for society as a whole. Emile Durkheim suggested that social consensus takes one of two forms: Mechanical solidarity is a form of social cohesion that arises when people in a society maintain similar values and beliefs and engage in similar types of work. Mechanical solidarity most commonly occurs in traditional, simple societies such as those in which everyone herds cattle or farms. Amish society exemplifies mechanical solidarity.

In contrast, organic solidarity is a form of social cohesion that arises when the people in a society are interdependent, but hold to varying values and beliefs and engage in varying types of work. Organic solidarity most commonly occurs in industrialised, complex societies such those in large American cities like New York in the 2000s.

Sociologists have identified two types of functions: manifest and latent (Merton: 1957). Manifest functions are consequences that are intended and commonly recognised. Latent functions are consequences that are unintended and often hidden. For example, the manifest function of education is to transmit knowledge and skills to society's youth. But public elementary schools also serve as babysitters for employed parents, and colleges offer a place for young adults to meet potential mates. The baby-sitting and mate-selection functions are not the intended or commonly recognised functions of education; hence they are latent functions.

Thus, the functionalist perspective achieved its greatest popularity among American sociologists in the 1940s and 1950s. While European functionalists originally focused on explaining the inner workings of social order, American functionalists focused on discovering the functions of human behaviour. Among these American functionalist sociologists is Robert Merton (1910), who divides human functions into two types: manifest functions are intentional and obvious, while latent functions are unintentional and not obvious. The manifest function of attending a church or synagogue, for instance, is to worship as part of a religious community, but its latent function may be to help members learn to discern personal from institutional values. With common sense, manifest functions become easily apparent. Yet this is not necessarily the case for latent functions, which often demand a sociological approach to be revealed. A sociological approach in functionalism is the consideration of the relationship between the functions of smaller parts and the functions of the whole.

Functionalism has received criticism for neglecting the negative functions of an event such as divorce. Critics also claim that the perspective justifies the status quo and complacency on the part of society's members. Functionalism does not encourage people to take an active role in changing their social environment, even when such change may benefit them. Instead, functionalism sees active social change as undesirable because the various parts of society will compensate naturally for any problems that may arise.

Besides the criticism, the functional theory is very important in context to the maintenance of the society which is also applicable to the problem of sanitation as South Asian people's perspective on sanitation Synthesis review Bangladesh, India, Nepal, Pakistan and Sri Lanka mentions: *"Sanitation is essential for life. It is an important part of our religion too.' Cleanliness helps a person get a better education and higher "position in society. Hand-washing with soap after defecation is very important for maintaining hygiene. Food hygiene prevents diseases and keeps children healthy."* (Water Aid: 2011). This depends upon the people's understanding and awareness of sanitation. Water Aid review first focused on people's understanding of the concept of sanitation and hygiene. *"Sanitation is all about cleanliness, no open defecation, proper solid "waste disposal, using safe water in all domestic activities, washing "hands in right manner and keeping the environment clean."*

The safety of men, women and children was often found to be compromised by poor sanitation. Open fields – especially in the night or during the rainy season – or railway tracks were described as unsafe and instances of people losing their limbs, or even their lives, and of women being molested were frequently reported, Impact on health, education and poverty Many people across all the countries believed that keeping one's body and environment clean, leading a healthy life and protecting oneself from disease constitute sanitation and hygiene. Those who had a clear understanding of hygiene perceived that living in an unhygienic environment led to all kinds of diseases. They said that following simple hygiene practices, like washing hands before meals or cooking food, keeping the drinking water covered and so on, would eliminate many of the diseases. They were clear that it would therefore also contribute towards reducing poverty. Section 2 of water Aid indicates: *"Everyone in the village goes to the nearby fields for defecation. It is dirty, troublesome, time consuming and dangerous as well, especially for women and physically challenged people. It is very common for pigs to attack us from behind when we are squatting in the field. We are forced to take someone along when going out to the fields."* Veerkala, 50, Kota Dewara, Uttar Pradesh, India *"We waste so much time in going to the doctor and then waste so much money on medicines. By just paying a little bit of attention to sanitation we can save all that time and money and thereby enhance our economic condition."* Ram Avtar, a prominent member of the community, Bhora village, Jalaun district, Uttar Pradesh, India views: For others, especially the very poor, 'rights' did not matter, as feeding their children and having clean drinking water were priorities. In some situation people do not agree to each other and therefore they create conflict instead of cooperating.

2. Conflict Perspective

The functionalist perspective views society as composed of different parts working together. In contrast, the conflict perspective views society as composed of different groups and interest competing for power and resources. The conflict perspective explains various aspects of our social world by looking at which groups have power and benefit from a particular social arrangement. For example, feminist theory argues that we live in a patriarchal society—a hierarchical system of organisation controlled by men. Although there are many varieties of feminist theory, most would hold that feminism "demands that existing economic, political, and social structures be changed" (Weir and Faulkner 2004, p.xii).

The origins of the conflict perspective can be traced to the classic works of Karl Marx. Marx suggested that all societies go through stages of economic development. As societies evolve from agricultural to industrial, concern over meeting survival needs is replaced by concern over making a profit, the hallmark of a capitalist system. Industrialisation leads to the development of two classes of people: the bourgeoisie, or the owners of the means of production (e.g., factories, farms, businesses); and the proletariat, or the workers who earn wages. The division of society into two broad classes of people—the "haves" and the "have-nots"— are beneficial to the owners of the means of production. The workers, who may earn only subsistence wages, are denied access to the many resources available to the wealthy owners. According to Marx, the bourgeoisie use their power to control the institutions of society to their advantage. For example,

Marx suggested that religion serves as an "opiate of the masses" in that it soothes the distress and suffering associated with the working-class lifestyle and focuses the workers' attention on spirituality, God, and the afterlife rather than on such worldly concerns as living conditions. In essence, religion diverts the workers so that they concentrate on being rewarded in heaven for living a moral life rather than on questioning their exploitation.

Thus, the conflict perspective, which originated primarily out of Karl Marx's writings on class struggles, presents society in a different light than do the functionalist and symbolic interactionist perspectives. While these latter perspectives focus on the positive aspects of society that contribute to its stability, the conflict perspective focuses on the negative, conflicted, and everchanging nature of society. Unlike functionalists who defend the status quo, avoid social change, and believe people cooperate to effect social order, conflict theorists challenge the status quo, encourage social change (even when this means social revolution), and believe rich and powerful people force social order on the poor and the weak. Conflict theorists, for example, may interpret an "elite" board of regents raising tuition to pay for esoteric new programs that raise the prestige of a local college as selfserving rather than as beneficial for students.

Whereas American sociologists in the 1940s and 1950s generally ignored the conflict perspective in favour of the functionalist, the tumultuous 1960s saw American sociologists gain considerable interest in conflict theory. They also expanded Marx's idea that the key conflict in society was strictly economic. Today, conflict theorists find social conflict between any groups in which the potential for inequality exists: racial, gender, religious, political, economic, and so on. Conflict theorists note that unequal groups usually have conflicting values and agendas, causing them to compete against one another. This constant competition between groups forms the basis for the everchanging nature of society.

Critics of the conflict perspective point to its overly negative view of society. The theory ultimately attributes humanitarian efforts, altruism, democracy, civil rights, and other positive aspects of society to capitalistic designs to control the masses, not to inherent interests in preserving society and social order. We may cite here the example of *Water resources and conflicts.*

Water is the source of life, but as such it can also be a source of competing demand, leading to conflict. During the 20th Century, world population tripled, while world demand for water increased six- fold. At the international level, trans boundary water issues have always caused heated debate, and in fact a number of prominent people have said that the wars of the 21st Century will be fought over water. Upstream and downstream users have argued over their share of water since time immemorial (*Water Conflict Chronology*: 2004). Water resources have rarely, if ever, been the sole source of violent conflict or war. But with the high numbers of international water courses which are shared between countries, water and its use may be a cause of tension and may strain relations between countries. Water remains therefore a security concern for many countries. Although water may give rise to armed conflict, freshwater can be, due to its essential nature, a powerful incentive for co-operation. Water as a potential cause of conflict and water as an agent of co-operation can be seen as two sides of the same coin (See UNESCO's and Green Cross: 2004). Research has shown much more historical evidence of water as a catalyst for cooperation, rather than conflict. A number of examples of workable treaties on water can be cited, even between states such as India and Pakistan, and Israel and Jordan, which may be in conflict over other matters. Rivers provide us the basis for concrete ideas on sharing and cooperation over a resource that no person can live without. As water is essential to every aspect of life – health, human rights, environment, economy, welfare, politics and culture – it is well beyond the scope of any individual country or sector to deal with it unilaterally. The link between conflict prevention, peace building and natural resources management therefore deserves closer attention. Women, who know best about the vital nature of clean water and safe sanitation, play a crucial role in peace building actions through water resources management and cooperation. Due to its fundamental importance, water is often an issue during armed conflicts and can become a target during wars. Flood-control dikes may be destroyed in order to flood areas threatened by an adversary and water supplies and wells may be deliberately contaminated to harm the opponent. In addition, water scarcity and insufficient sanitation frequently accelerate in armed conflicts. The civilian population – above all women and children – is the first to suffer from the disruption of water supply, and often thirst has proved to be more deadly than guns. People affected by natural and man- made disasters are more likely to become ill and die from diseases related to inadequate sanitation and water supplies than from any other single cause. Minimum standards are urgently needed for post-disaster and emergency sanitation services (WHO: 1997).

When water is scarce, women and girls pay dearly. They may have to travel longer distances to obtain water, and conditions are more dangerous. Conflicts that exacerbate water scarcity hence lead to a double hardship for women: the negative impacts of lack of water are compounded by the well-documented abuses against women's fundamental human rights that occur during wartime. Women are disproportionately affected by natural disasters, such as floods and earthquakes, as a result of gender inequalities regarding political and economic status, human rights, education and health. Women have high death rates in disasters, as they often do not receive warnings or other information about hazards and risks. Their mobility in disasters may be restricted or affected due to cultural and social constraints. Gender inequality can complicate and extend the time for women's recovery, for example, if women do not receive timely care for trauma experienced in disasters. During the floods in *Mozambique* in 2000, with clean water in short supply, many women were forced to resort to using floodwater for cooking, thereby increasing the risk of disease outbreak.

3. Symbolic Interactionist Perspective

Both the functionalist and the conflict perspectives are concerned with how broad aspects of society, such as institutions and large social groups, influence the social world. This level of sociological analysis is called macro sociology: It looks at the big picture of society and suggests how social problems are affected at the institutional level.

Micro sociology, another level of sociological analysis, is concerned with the social psychological dynamics of individuals interacting in small groups. This is called symbolic interactionist perspective, also known as symbolic interactionism, directs sociologists to consider the symbols and details of everyday life, what these symbols mean, and how people interact with each other. Although symbolic interactionism traces its origins to Max Weber's assertion that individuals act according to their interpretation of the meaning of their world, the American philosopher George H. Mead (1863–1931) introduced this perspective to American sociology in the 1920s.

Symbolic interactionism reflects the micro-sociological perspective, and was largely influenced by the work of early sociologists and philosophers, such as George Simmel, Charles Cooley, George Herbert Mead, and Erving Goffman. Symbolic interactionism emphasises that human behaviour is influenced by definitions and meanings that are created and maintained through symbolic interaction with others. Sociologist W.I. Thomas (1966) emphasised the importance of definitions and meanings in social behaviour and its consequences. He suggested that humans respond to their definition of a situation rather than to the objective situation itself. Hence Thomas noted that situations that we define as real become real in their consequences. Symbolic interactionism also suggests that our identity or sense of self is shaped by social interaction. We develop our self-concept by observing how others interact with us a label us. By observing how others view us, we see a reflection ourselves that Cooley calls the "looking glass self."

According to the symbolic interactionist perspective, people attach meanings to symbols, and then they act according to their subjective interpretation of these symbols. Verbal conversations, in which spoken words serve as the predominant symbols, make this subjective interpretation especially evident. The words have a certain meaning for the "sender," and, during effective communication, they hopefully have the same meaning for the "receiver." In other terms, words are not static "things"; they require intention and interpretation. Conversation is an interaction of symbols between individuals who constantly interpret the world around them. Of course, anything can serve as a symbol as long as it refers to something beyond itself. Written music serves as an example. The black dots and lines become more than mere marks on the page; they refer to notes organised in such a way as to make musical sense. Thus, symbolic interactionists give serious thought to how people act, and then seek to determine what meanings individuals assign to their own actions and symbols, as well as to those of others.

Consider applying symbolic interactionism to the American institution of marriage. Symbols may include wedding bands, vows of lifelong commitment, a white bridal dress, a wedding cake, a Church ceremony, and flowers and music. American society attaches general meanings to these symbols, but individuals also maintain their own perceptions of what these and other symbols mean. For example, one of the spouses may see their circular wedding rings as symbolising "never ending love," while the other may see them as a mere financial expense. Much faulty communication can result from differences in the perception of the same events and symbols.

Critics claim that symbolic interactionism neglects the macro level of social interpretation—the "big picture." In other words, symbolic interactionist may miss the larger issues of society by focusing too closely on the "trees" (for example, the size of the diamond in the wedding ring) rather than the "forest" (for example, the quality of the marriage). The perspective also receives criticism for slighting the influence of social forces and institutions on individual interactions.

Symbolic interactionism means feeling and realisation of the people as MdAbul Hossain of the BaroGozia community living in Ghorodhap Union of JamalpurSadarUpazilla of Jamalpur district, Bangladesh views: "*We used to feel embarrassed when guests coming to the village "would make faces and cover their nose and mouth.*" Group of men and women, Kali Talai-Goras, Sheopur district, MP, India The level of understanding of sanitation and hygiene, and its articulation, was influenced to an extent by both the educational attainment of respondents and interventions in the area. Interventions made communities more educated and aware, and in turn people in these communities described sanitation as 'hygienic toilets', 'closed drainage' and 'rubbish-free settlements'. For such communities, it also meant regular maintenance of the facilities and sustained availability of services. Similarly, it was observed, especially in India and Sri Lanka, that the higher the educational status of community leaders and respondents, the better knowledge they possessed and the better they could articulate their understanding of sanitation. However, at the same time even the illiterate respondents had a basic understanding of sanitation and hygiene. For instance, Mina Begum of AadibasiSundarpara of Shyamnagar, Satkhira, Bangladesh, is illiterate and belongs to a minority group. To her, sanitation means a hygienic latrine, safe drinking water, washing hands with soap, and disposing of children's faeces in the latrine. (Water Aid: 2011).

Furthermore, Water Aid (2011) reveals that almost all women and most male respondents reported feeling acutely embarrassed in front of neighbours as well as outsiders in the absence of a private toilet. Privacy and dignity are especially important to women, Dignity, apart from practical aspects of convenience. For instance, JeevanPaudel from Ilam and Dhan Prasad Subedi from Dhading, Nepal, are differently-abled people whose lives have been dignified by sanitation interventions in their settlements. They said that sanitation is an essential component of life that affects the healthy environment of any community. Availability of safe water was seen as essential to sustain sanitation services. Section 2 6 South Asian people's perspective on sanitation Synthesis review Bangladesh, India, Nepal, Pakistan and Sri Lanka *"There is a need for separate toilets for each house because people without toilets are cornered by others and face difficulties entertaining guests."* GayaniMendis, resident of semi-urban area of Galle, Sri Lanka *"We find it shameful that we do not have toilets and that our men do not listen to us."* Group of women, Balerpada in Burla Notified Area, Sambalpur, Orissa, India *"In the absence of sanitation facilities, people feel degraded, especially when guests arrive. Many people have migrated from "this place just because of poor sanitation."* SughranBibi, a housewife of Jungle Barali, district Vehari, Punjab, Pakistan *"Sanitation is the basis for happiness and satisfaction. It urges me to get up early and remains as the first thought for the day to keep my home and surrounding clean. As the day starts with cleaning, the whole day then becomes very active and happy."* All such views reflect people's perspective from phenomenological understanding.

Besides the above, we may mention here broadly two major type of theories: (1) Scientific Theories (positivistic theory) and (2) Humanistic Theories (symbolic interactionism). These are discussed by the sociologists to refer the particular behaviour, for instance, deviant behaviour. However, these theories reflect the particular of the individual in society. The scientific theories

(e. g. anomie theory of R.K. Merton and differential association theory of Edwin H. Sutherland etc.) focus on the causes of deviant behaviour as scientific explanation. While the other humanistic theories (labelling theory, Phenomenological and conflict theory) deal with the meanings of the particular behaviour and with the impact of these meanings on people's behaviour.

Control Theory

Control theory differs from the other major theories discussed above. First both anomie and differential association theories approach the problem of explaining the behaviour hand-on and ask: what causes the particular behaviour? But control theorists approach the problem in a roundabout way and ask: what causes conformity to the particular behaviour. They figure that if they can find out what causes conformity, they will automatically find out what causes the particular behaviour. The particular behaviour may be normal or abnormal. For what causes the particular behaviour is simply the *absence* of what causes conformity. Second both anomie and differential association theorists reject the Freudian idea of that the particular behaviour (e.g. may be normal or deviant) can naturally or by itself burst forth from our inborn animal impulses. They instead theorise that deviant behaviour is produced by an anomic social condition or has to be learned by the individual. But most control theorist seems to accept the Freudian idea to one degree or another. So they argue that the particular behaviour need not to be learned and that the inborn animal impulses, if not properly controlled, will naturally turn into deviant behaviour.

Generally, in the eyes of control theorists, what causes conformity is social control over the individual and therefore the absence of social control causes deviance as for the more specific nature of social control, various control theorists tell the story a little differently. There are two groups of control theorists, one telling the story with original research data to back it up and the other telling the same story but the without the data. Let us discuss only the first group. It consists of three sociologists—Walter Reckless, Ivan Nye, and Travis Hirschi.

Reckless Containment: In his version of control theory, which he calls *containment theory,* Reckless assumes that there are powerful forces pushing the individual to a deviant course of action.

Nye: Social Control: Like Reckless, the second control theorist Ivan Nye assumes that there are powerful forces pushing all of us towards deviance. Unlike reckless, Nye simply relies on Freudian psychology and singles out our animal instincts as the motivating force of deviance. Since all of us are born with the same animal instincts, we all have the same natural tendency to behave like an animal by breaking social norms. Yet most of us do not actually break the norms, while some of us do. In order to explain this difference between conforming and deviant behaviour, Nye, like reckless, uses the concept of control. According to Nye's version of control theory, society uses social control to help us check our animal instinct or deviant tendencies so that we will become law-abiding citizens. Social control, then, is seen as preventing us from deviation or ensuring our conformity, and the lack of social control is seen as creating the opposite result.

Hirschi: Bond of Society: Like Nye the third control theorist, Travis Hirschi assumes that we are all animals endowed with the ability to commit deviant acts. Most of us do not take advantage this ability—as Hirsci's control theory suggests—because of our strong *bond* to society. Our strong bond to society, then, ensures our conformity; conversely, if our bond to society is weak or broken, we will commit deviant acts. You may have perceived that Nye looks at our relation to society from the sociological standpoint of how society controls us as individuals. In contrast, Hirschi looks at the same relations from the psychological point of how we as individuals tie or *bond* ourselves to society. According to Hirschi, there are four ways that individuals bond themselves to society.

The first is by *attachment to others*. Individuals attach themselves to conventional people and institutions. In the context, they may show this attachment by loving and respecting their parents, making friends with conventional peers, liking schools, and working hard to develop intellectual skills. A commitment to conformity is the second way. Individuals invest their time and energy in conventional types of action, such as getting an education, holding a job, developing an occupational skill, improving a professional status, building up a business, or acquiring a reputation for virtue. At the same time, people show a commitment to achievement through these activities. The third way is *involvement in conventional activities*. People simply keep themselves so busy doing conventional things that they do not have time for wrong things. *A belief in the moral validity of social rules* is the fourth way that people bond themselves to society. Individuals have a strong moral belief that they should obey the rules of conventional society. A young person may show such moral belief through a respect for the police or through a positive attitude toward the law.

If these four elements of the individual's bond to conventional society are strong, the individual is likely to get stuck in conformity. If these four elements of the bond are weak, the individual is likely to slide into deviance. In summary, all the control theorists suggest that containment, social control, or bond to society prevents individuals from committing deviant acts, and the lack of it prompts them into committing wrong things.

We cite here to control the situation in which people have differences. In the case Section 2 Water Aid (2011) cites the views of the people as: *"We should not shy away from acknowledging the differences amongst us. If two people stress on something and the other two stand against them, how can anything happen in such a situation?"* Women of Kota Dewara, Uttar Pradesh, India *"There are some proud and prejudiced people in our community. They do not cooperate with the majority of poor and disadvantaged groups. For example, one such person did not allow the passage of a drain through his land. This resulted in a series of meetings and dialogues, and protests. But the drain remains incomplete while the locals wait for legal action against the individual."*

The two critical outcomes of this approach were the emergence of vested interests and the creation of a dependency syndrome where community participation and involvement was at a minimum. The latter was more observed in places prone to natural disasters and relief interventions like the Tsunami regions of Sri Lanka or the flood-affected plains of North Bihar in India. Included or excluded? Infrastructure-led, patronage-based sanitation is also a social and environmental disaster and does little for an inclusive approach. Consider the following voices from Orissa, Galle, and Vehari, Sound and appropriate technology Inappropriate design, poor quality of construction and a lack of follow up and maintenance arrangements were critical issues present in all countries without exception. These were often not only the perceived reasons for failure, but also a deterrent to participation in subsequent projects. Several countries in the region are prone to natural disasters like cyclones and floods, yet the toilets here are not often designed to withstand or survive such calamities; as a result, communities that had begun to use toilets are often forced to revert back to open defecation. Poor design and poor quality of construction are often a result of a lack of supervision during the construction and implementation phase.

"Sanitation programmes are successful when NGOs and communities, particularly the youth, jointly discuss the good and bad effects of sanitation, everyone participates in all phases of development, female family members are actively involved, hygienic latrines are low cost and affordable, and Union Parishad and NGO staffs work jointly."

II
Approaches to Public Health

Park and Park (177:688) discuss approaches to public health:

1. Regulatory Approach: The regulatory approach or legal approach seeks to protect the health of the public through the enforcement of laws and regulations, e.g. Epidemic Diseases Act, Food Adulteration Act etc. The best laws are there but implementation is very poor. They remain on paper if they are not used in later and spirit. They are only used in emergency situation or in limited situation e.g., fairs, festivals or epidemics. In areas involving personal choice (e.g., giving up smoking, family planning) laws have no place in a democratic society. The legal approach also has the disadvantage that it requires vast administrative machinery to enforce laws and also involves considerable expenditure.

2. Service Approach: The service or administrative approach aims at providing all the health facilities needed by the community in the hope that people would use them to improve their own health. The service approach proved a failure when it was not based on the felt needs of the people. For example, when water seal latrines were provided free of cost, in some villages in India under the Community Development Programme, people did not use them. This serves to illustrate that we may provide free service to the people, but there is no guarantee that the service will be used by them.

3. Educational Approach: The educational approach is major means today for achieving change in health practices and the recognition of health needs. It involves motivation, communication and decision-making. The result, although slow, are permanent and enduring. Sufficient time should be allowed to have the desired change brought about. There are certain problems which can be solved only through education, e.g., nutritional problems, infant and child care, personal hygiene, family planning. The educational approach is used widely today in solution of community health problems. It is consistent with democratic philosophy which does not order the individual.

The educational approaches may be classified as: (a) individual and family approach (b) small group approach, and (c) mass approach. Since individual vary so much in their socio-economic conditions, traditions, attitudes, beliefs and level of knowledge a single educational approach may not be suitable. Mixtures of approach must be evolved depending upon local circumstances.

III

Social Perspective on the sanitation challenges

In their collection on, 'Social Perspective on the sanitation challenges', Milet, Bas Van, Spaargaten, Gertet. al (2010) present a timely collection of social scientific papers from the perspectives of Science and Technology Studies, Environmental Sociology and Urban Studies dealing with innovative sanitation issues and concepts, perceptions and decision-making support. Together they comprises a valuable resource for political scientists, environmental engineers and urban planners involved in the study, design and implementation of sanitation projects worldwide and whose work relates to meeting the ambitious Millennium Development Goal on sanitation. If the goal is to half the number of people without sustainable access to safe drinking water and basic sanitation by 2015, we may not only need new technologies but rather innovative sanitation concepts, new tools for decision-making and an understanding of diverse stakeholder perspectives along the sanitation chain. In developed countries the sanitation challenge is to initiate a transition from strongly centralised, water-based infrastructure regimes towards more sustainable, source-separation oriented, sanitation regimes. This calls for social scientific research and demonstration on different levels and scales, including concept development, institutional learning and governance building.

In the developing world the sanitation challenge is to provide sanitation services to the poor and the very poor, without compromising on sustainability. In this realm, the book presents new configurations that employ the best practices of sanitation technology and management for rural and urban contexts.

The sanitation challenge in both worlds is to go beyond traditional dichotomies between 'small, appropriate' and 'modern/advanced' sanitation solutions in solving the global sanitation challenge and to develop rural and urban sanitation with a mix of scales, strategies, technologies, payment systems and decision-making structures, that better fit the physical and social systems (human systems) for which they are designed. Here we present some more studies regarding sanitation management as follows:

Social Perspectives on the Sanitation Challenge is unique in its presentation of social scientific research findings from urban planners, sociologists, economists, political scientists and environmental engineers who are involved in international sanitation research and implementation. Theoretically the volume includes insights from Science and Technology Studies, Environmental Sociology and Urban Studies. Its empirical scope, stretching from Western Europe to Sub-Saharan Africa, is deliberately wide to stress the global character of the sanitation challenge that we all face (Milet, Bas Van, Spaargaten, Gert *et. al:* 2010)

Misra, and Goldar (2008) undertaken a study to gain an understanding of the baseline water supply and sewerage services in Delhi, and assess consumer coping strategies and associated costs, their preferences for service improvements, willingness to pay and affordability for the preferred options. For this purpose, a representative sample survey of around 8,000 households and about 2,000 non-domestic consumers was carried out. The survey results bring out the deficiencies in services, and the significant coping costs the consumers are bearing. The survey data reveals that the consumers are willing to pay- and can afford-the extra cost that service improvement will entail. The analysis of survey data indicates that, for poor households in informal settlements, substantial improvements in water supply can be made by introducing/implementing paid group connections. Significant social gains, which could be as high as Rs. 5,500 to Rs. 8,000 million per annum, are expected from the efficiency improvements in the present system and other reforms that could be undertaken by the Delhi jal Board. The study on consumer coping costs, WTP and affordability clearly shows that domestic and non-domestic consumers in Delhi are bearing a huge cost to cope with the inadequacies of water supply and sewerage services currently being provided. Nearly one-fifth of households in authorised colonies are making use of additional water sources, such as their own borewells, housing society borewells or bottled water. Domestic consumers face considerable difficulties due to limited hours water supply, low pressure and water quality problems. These problems have compelled the consumers to invest in large storage, booster pumps, filters and acqua-guard.

The study demonstrates that significant social gains are expected by improving efficiency of the WSS delivery system. Taking into consideration possible energy efficiency improvements and least cost design of infrastructure, the reduction in operating expenditures are likely to be about 20 per cent and 33 per cent, respectively. Such an improvement of the public piped water and sewerage service could eliminate the need for customer coping strategies altogether and the amount of cash currently injected in the sector by customers could over 100 per cent of DJB operating expenditures and contribute 80 per cent towards DJB capital expenditures. Such an optimistic scenario also allows investment of about Rs. 4,250 million per year for seven years (equivalent to $700 million) to address some of DJB's systemic technical, commercial and financial problems, yielding an internal rate of return of 25 per cent and an overall saving of resources of Rs. 8.000 million per year. However, even assuming a more "realistic scenario" with slower efficiency improvements will allow an annual investment of a maximum of Rs. 2,900 million per year for seven ears (equivalent to $450 million) to fix DJB operations and at the same time, yield an internal rate of return of 25 per cent, with an overall saving of resources of about Rs. 5,500 million per year. Overall, a saving of Rs. 5,500 to Rs. 8,000 million per year is expected, depending on the efficiency improvements and other reforms that could be undertaken by the DJB.

Paper by Srinivasan (2006) explores equity, accountability and environmental concerns in solid waste management in Chennai city. Through the study of the urban local body, a private agency and a civil society organisation engaged in this activity, the paper highlights issues related to effectiveness and equity, role of the urban poor in this service, and the relevance of an effective policy framework. In the context of increasing private sector participation in public service provision, and global awareness related to the impact of urban footprints on the planet, the study rings out some interesting lessons on the nature of public-private partnership in SWM, and the role of the state in guaranteeing social and ecological equity and accountability. It also points to the urgent need for a change in the way the state itself approaches solid waste management, stressing policy mandates across the country. The study is based on qualitative research methodology, and involved in-depth interactions and discussions with residents, agency officials and conservancy workers, detailed examinations of secondary literature on SWM systems, and intensive field observation of SWM processes in the three agencies in Chennai.

Solid waste management, typically as straight forward public health service to be provided by local administration, is, in reality, a complex, multi-layered issue. At one level, efficiency and efficacy of service provision have significant implications for public health and sustainability of operations, and recent years have seen private sector participation being explored as a means of enhancing service provision. The aspects that have received far less attention, but are of equal or even greater importance, include ecological and worker safety and equity in service provision. This study is essentially an attempt at a holistic examination of SWM, analysing these crucial issues to derive lessons for policy and action.

The private sector participation in SWM, s in most other areas, is a difficult and contentious issue. This study reveals that there is a strong case for moving away from the traditional polarisation between champions of privatisation on the one side and those advocating complete state responsibility on the other, towards a more fruitful partnership. At the same time the overall context- liberalisation, privatisation, globalisation and the changing, in some cases diminishing, nature of state intervention- in which these partnerships are emerging, gives rise to concerns regarding the accountability of both the public and private sectors.

The study clearly shows that the public sector, on its own, has not been able to respond effectively to the SWM challenge. On the other hand, it also clearly shows that private and civil society participation also poses several challenges especially in terms of equity and accountability. Further, it also emerges that the nature and efficiency of civil society responses to SWM problems is shaped by a host of local conditions and variables, quality of volunteers and leadership, and most importantly the response of the ULB.

In addition, the study indicates that while ecological considerations are slowly gaining ascendance in SWM policy, certain sections of people continue to remain missing from the large SWM discourse- these are the conservancy workers, people who work on the dumpsites and on the streets, as well as the urban poor for whom SWM is a luxury that they cannot afford to spend time, effort or money on. The study points to the pressing need for an inclusive policy that addresses these concerns as well.

The key lesson that Chennai has to offer is that while crucial roles exists for the private sector- for profit ad not-for-profit the intervention of the state and public policy is imperative to safeguard ecological and equity interests, and enable greater accountability of both public and private actors. This lesson is of relevance not only to the SWM arena but also to a broader range of concerns surrounding initiatives such as he "Shanghasiation" of Mumbai, debates around which are becoming increasingly significant after the July 2005 floods.

As Dreze and Sen (1995), points out with respect to the liberalisation debate, it is not the question of more governance or less governance, or of more markets or less market, but of going beyond the market. This study of SWM in Chennai clearly establishes that it is not a question of expanding or restricting private sector participation but of going beyond it. It is important to focus on the ends, i.e. ecological safe and equitable solutions to the problem of SWM, rather than just on the question of more or less private sector participation.

A survey of households in six villages in Birbhum district of west Bengal provides evidence that decentralisation in delivery of water supply leads to better quality of services. The participation of local government in distribution of water supply, and household contribution to operation and maintenance appear to have a positive impact on quality.

Quality of piped water has been observed to be better in villages where the local government participates in operation and maintenance. Quality indicators are found to be better in Illambazar and Ruppur Gram panchayats where the local government participates in operation and maintenance. These indicators are worse in Pourandarpur gram panchayat where the public Health Engineering department shares some of the maintenance activity along with panchayat samiti. Division of responsibility according to the comparative advantage of local government and Public Health engineering department has yielded the best result. Household contribution for maintenance also has been found to have a positive impact on quality of water supply services. Overall the results of study suggest that decentralisation has a positive impact on quality of water supply.

Article by Mehrotra (2006) offers a menu of options for reform of Uttar Pradesh's public health system. Though some actions have been taken some actions have been taken after the introduction of the national Rural Health Mission in late 2005, a large number of very serious problems remain. Unless they are addressed, the monitorable targets of the Eleventh Five-year Plan in regard to health and nutrition in India will not be met, since UP has such a large weight in the unmet needs of public health in the country.

Focusing attention on the immediate issues arising out of the implementation of NRHM is clearly one priority of policy makers. However, the preventive/promotive public health measures and he population-wide health measures that underpin a medical, clinical care are delivery system, which is the sine qua non of serious improvements in both health outputs and health outcomes, so far do not seem to be forthcoming, except in the case of a slight increase in institutional deliveries.

Pathway to Success (Compendium of Best Practices in Rural Sanitation in India)

One of the major challenges before India is to provide sustainable sanitation and hygiene to its vast diverse and growing population. The Government of India has declared its commitment towards achieving MDG goals and universal sanitation coverage in the country by the year 2022, but with the current rural sanitation coverage of 32.7 per cent, this is a challenging task. The Ministry of Drinking Water and Sanitation has already risen to the occasion with renewed strategies and approaches. The existing Total Sanitation Campaign has been revamped and renamed as the **Nirmal Bharat Abhiyan (NBA)** in April 2012 by adopting community-led and people-centered strategies with a saturation approach backed by post-achievement incentives.

One of the major shifts in the approach under NBA has been to adopt a more holistic approach in addressing issues related to sanitation. Apart from addressing the issues of building individual household toilets, community toilets, and constructing toilets in anganwadis and schools, the Government has placed a lot of emphasis on providing the much-needed flexibility to households to choose the sanitation technology they prefer from a variety of options based on socio-cultural aspects, hydro geographical conditions, and economic status.

The Government has also streamlined steps to make available sanitation material and equipment within the reach of the common people by providing incentives for the setting up of Production Centers and Rural Sanitary Marts in rural areas. These Marts ensure that a variety of pans, soakages, compost pits, vermin-composting processes, and washing platforms are made available at nominal cost to the general public. Another area that has been accorded prime importance is the management of solid and liquid waste (SLWM), which is essential for promoting a hygienic and healthy environment. Under the SLWM component, the Government is promoting innovative and adaptable initiatives like compost pits, vermin composting, common and individual bio gas plants, and low cost drainage apart from collection, segregation, and disposal of household waste at the village level.

These initiatives will be unsuccessful if the general public is not educated about the benefits of incorporating safe sanitary practices and if they remain unaware of the various facilities and incentives being provided by the Government. A comprehensive *Sanitation and Hygiene Advocacy and Communication Strategy Framework (2012-2017)*has been launched by the Ministry with the objective of rolling out a number of communication activities in a phased manner to sensitise the general public about various aspects of sanitation. An intensive audio visual and radio campaign has been launched at the national level while the States and the Gram Panchayats have been urged to also include Interpersonal Communication and direct media activities. The need to broaden communication on rural sanitation and its various facets has been accepted and is being initiated with vigor

As a part of this information dissemination approach to be able to bring about much-needed behavioral change, it is essential that we share stories of successes that have emerged from various States and UTs over the last decade. One State and 28,002 Gram Panchayats across the length and breadth of the country have been awarded Nirmal Gram Puraskars so far, as an acknowledgment of the significant sanitation initiatives taken up in their areas. Many of these GPs are shining examples of how to overcome extraordinary odds to achieve this status.

The Ministry, with the assistance of Water and Sanitation Program (WSP), has put together a second volume of *Compendium of Best Practices on Rural Sanitation titled 'Pathway to Success'. This is in continuation with the first volume, titled 'From Dreams to Reality'*, released in 2010. The 16 success stories documented in the Compendium can be lessons of great inspiration and serve as models for various Gram Panchayats, Districts, and States across India in overcoming hurdles and obstacles in various fields as diverse as Community Participation, Sustainability, Resource Mobilisation, Solid and Liquid Waste Management, Program Implementation, IEC Practices, and Institutional Reforms.

The community members, grass root sanitation workers, Panchayati Raj Institutions, and government officials have been documented here for the wonderful work and sincere efforts they have put in to provide a clean and healthy environment and hope that they will continue to be role models for the NBA program. *Download Report(Source: Pankaj Jain, MDWS:*New Delhi, March 13, 2014*)*

Social Development Perspectives

The days of solving water supply and sanitation (WS & S) problems with concrete and pipes alone are over. Integrated approaches to WS&S now have people at the centre. A social development perspective, which supports this approach, means understanding and involving users and responding flexibly towards their concerns. Social development objectives in WS&S include ensuring that dialogue and interventions: are responsive to demand; reach poor or disadvantaged populations and socially excluded groups; promote empowerment, local voices, and ownership; and recognise the different needs and contributions of women and men. A social development perspective is supported by social analysis and by incorporating social issues and participatory approaches into development planning.

The response to WS&S which evolved during the 1980s was the basic services approach. It identified lack of access to basic services which are the basic rights such as water, healthcare, and education as both a cause and a symptom of poverty (Jarman: 1997). The World Summit for Social Development held in Copenhagen in 1995 persisted with the point that over one billion people in absolute poverty live lives characterised by deprivation of basic human needs, including those of safe drinking water and sanitation facilities. The Social Summit urged that in formulating strategies for eradicating absolute poverty, governments and the international community should implement the commitment to meet basic needs including providing 'on a sustainable basis, access to safe drinking water in sufficient quantities and proper sanitation for all' (UNICEF, 1995). The DFID White Paper supports this commitment, along with an emphasis on demand responsiveness and participatory approaches. In his introduction to social development issues in an urban context, Jarman (1997) examines the relationship between poverty and water supply and sanitation in the city, providing best practice examples of interventions.

Gender perspective on Water resources and Sanitation

It has been observed that a difference between women's perspective of sanitation and men's. For women it especially meant keeping themselves, their houses and their children clean. Women from some rural communities in states like Tamil Nadu said that a clean house gave them immense 'happiness' and 'pride', A matter of dignity Understanding of sanitation was closely related to open defecation and the need for toilets, especially in crowded urban settlements. In fact, an open defecation-free environment and use of toilets were repeatedly identified with sanitation across all countries (Water Aid: 2011).

Within the next 20 years freshwater will become the most important strategic resource, essential for sustaining life and achieving sustainable development. Its control will be a source of power and the key to economic development, and it will be one of the root causes of socio-political stress. The global commitments made in the areas of water and sanitation do not specifically address the equitable division of power, work, access to and control of resources between women and men. It will be critical to mainstream gender perspectives into the planning process to ensure that the specific needs and concerns of women and men from all social groups are taken into account in development, use and management of water resources and sanitation. In most cultures, women are primarily responsible for the use and management of water resources, sanitation and health at the household level. Over the years, women have accumulated an impressive store of environmental wisdom, being the ones to find water, to educate children in hygiene matters and to understand the impact of poor sanitation on health. At the same time, women and girls are often obliged to walk many hours every day fetching water, while men are rarely expected to perform such tasks. The importance of involving both women and men in the management of water and sanitation has been recognised at the global level, at least since the 1977 United Nations Water Conference at Mar del Plata and during the International Drinking Water Supply and Sanitation Decade, 1981-1990.

Note

1. Running head South Asian people's perspective on sanitation Synthesis review Bangladesh, India, Nepal, Pakistan and Sri Lanka. South Asia is a region of great contrast. On one hand there are promising GDP growth rates, but these are countered by poor human development, poverty and disease, with hundreds of

millions of men, women and children with no access to sanitation. There is political commitment to change, with new policies and investment for public services, but there are also significant barriers to enabling people to live safe and dignified daily lives. The biggest, and often overlooked, problems are exclusion and inequality. Millions of poor and marginalised people continue to be denied their basic rights, and as development initiatives concentrate on numbers, the excluded are marginalised still further. It is now time to move from talk to action; to ensure that economic growth translates into human development and wellbeing for the people of South Asia. This review is the result of a series of open-ended interviews and focus group discussions with a cross section of poor and marginalised social groups across Bangladesh, India, Nepal, Pakistan and Sri Lanka.

References

Cliffs Notes article on: *Three Major Perspectives in Sociology*

De, Indranil (2009), "Can decentralisation Improve Rural Water Supply Services?"*Economic and Political Weekly,* pp. 68-72.

Dreze, J. and S.Sen (1995), "India: Economic Development and Social Opportunity, Delhi: Oxford University Press.

Hirschi, Travis (1969). *Causes of Delinquency,* Berkeley and Los Angeles: University of California Press.

Jarman, J. (1997) 'Water supply and sanitation' in J. Beall (ed.), *A City for All: Valuing difference and working with diversity,* Zed Books, London.

Kinloch, Graham C. (1977). *Sociological Theory: Its development and Major Paradigms,* New York: McGraw Hill Book Company.

Kuhn, T.S. (1962), *The Structure of Scientific Revolution,* Chicago: University of Chicago Press.

Mehrotra, Santosh (2008), "Public Health System in UP: What can be Done?" *Economic and Political Weekly,* Vol. XLIII, No. 49, Dec. 6-12, pp. 46-53.

Merton, R.K. (1957). *Social Theory and Social Structure,* New York: Free press of Glencoe, pp. 131–194.

Milet, Bas Van, Spaargaten, Gert et. al. (2010) *Social Perspective on the Sanitation challenges,* Springer.

Misra, Smita and Bishwanath Goldar (2008), "Likely Impact of Reforming Water Supply and Sewerage Services in Delhi". *Economic and Political Weekly,* Vol. XLIII, No. 41. pp. 57-66.

Mooney, Linda A., David Knox, and Caroline Schacht, (2007). *Understanding Social Problems*, Thomson.

Nye, F. Ivan (1958). *Family Relationship and Delinquent Behaviour*, New York: John Wiley.

Park, J.E. and K .Park (1977), Text book on *Social and Preventive and Social Medicine*, Jablapur: BanarsidasBhanot Publishers. P.668 (old book).

Reckless, Walter C. (1973).*The Crime Problem*, New York: Appleton-Century-Crofts, pp. 55-57.

Report South Asian people's perspective on sanitation Synthesis review Bangladesh, India, Nepal, Pakistan and Sri Lanka. This report is cited as Water Aid, FANSA and WSSCC (2011) *South Asian people's perspective on sanitation: Synthesis review.*

Srinivasan, Krithika (2006), "Public, Private and Voluntary Agencies in Solid Waste Management: A Study in Chennai City", *Economic and Political Weekly*, Vol. XLI, No. 22, pp. 2259-2267.

Sutherland Edwin H. and Donald R. cressy (1974).*Criminology*, Philadelphia, Pa.: Lippincott, pp. 71-93.

The *Water Conflict Chronology* by the Pacific Institute for Studies in Development, Environment, and Security, http://www.worldwater.org/conflict.htm, 13 December 2004.

Thio, Alex (1978). *Deviant behaviour*, Boston: Houghton Mifflin Co.

UNESCO's and Green Cross International's joint programme *From Potential Conflict to Co-operation Potential: Water for Peace* (*PC>CP: Water for Peace*), http://www.unesco.org/water/wwap/pccp/index.shtml and http://www.gci.ch/GreenCrossPrograms/WATERRES/pdf/executif_summary.pdf, 13.12.2004.

Weir, Star and Constance Faulkner (2004). Voices of a new generation: a *Feminist anthology*, Pearson/ Allyn and Bacon, p. xii

World Health Organisation (WHO), 1997, Strengthening interventions to reduce helminth infections: an entry point for the development of health-promoting schools . Geneva: WHO.

3

Sanitation, Health and Society

Context

Indian sanitation is in crisis as reported by Live Mint and The Wall Street Journal on Jan. 1, 2014. The Indian state has done little to provide preventive public health services. New data released by the National Sample Survey Office (NSSO) have once again underlined the abysmal state of sanitation in the country, particularly in rural India where two-thirds of the country lives.

Only 32 per cent of rural households have their own toilets, according to the recently released results of a large-scale survey conducted by NSSO in 2012. An additional nine per cent have access to toilets although the access figure could be an over estimate. The results of the last census had also highlighted India's gaping sanitation deficit. Census results showed that less than half of Indian households had a toilet at home; there were more households with a mobile phone than with a toilet.

The woefully inadequate progress in sanitation makes India an outlier even among developing countries. Of the estimated billion people who defecate in the open, more than half reside in India. Poor sanitation impairs the health of Indians, leading to high rates of malnutrition and productivity losses. India's sanitation deficit leads to losses worth roughly six per cent of

India's gross domestic product (GDP), according to World Bank estimates, by raising the disease burden in the country. Children are affected more than adults. The rampant spread of diseases inhibits children's ability to absorb nutrients, stunting their growth.

It is well known that child malnutrition rates in India (and much of South Asia) exceed those of even sub-Saharan Africa. High levels of gender inequality in South Asia and poor health of women, which lead to a very high proportion of low birth weight babies, partly explains this phenomenon. Another key driver is India's sanitation deficit. As health economist Dean Spears argues on 4 July 2013 that in a large part of India's malnutrition burden is owing to the unhygienic environment in which children grow up. Poor sanitation and high population density act as a double whammy on Indian children, half of whom grow up stunted. It is not a coincidence that states with the poorest levels of sanitation and highest levels of population density such as Bihar, Jharkhand and Madhya Pradesh also have the highest levels of child malnutrition in the country.

The unhygienic environment in which children have to grow up owes to India's historic neglect of public health services. While the Indian state has been making interventions to ensure access to curative medical services, it has done precious little to provide preventive public health services to citizens even though such services are more cost-effective than medical services.

The absence of an effective public health network in a densely populated country like ours has resulted in an extraordinarily high disease burden. Water-borne diarrhoeal diseases alone result in annual deaths of about 200,000 children below four years of age in the country, according to a recent study published in the Lancet medical journal. While the poor pay the biggest price of an ineffective public health system in terms of increased health expenditure, reduced earnings and death, even the rich are not spared. Children of wealthy families suffer high levels of morbidity and although deaths are rare, stunting is common.

In a 2005, *Economic and Political Weekly* article, World Bank economist Monica Das Gupta traces the neglect of public health in India to the decisions of policy-makers in post-independent India, who focuses on disease-specific interventions rather than on an overarching public health network focused on prevention. India is one of the few Asian economies that did not invest in an integrated public health system involving food safety, water management, waste disposal, vector control, sanitation systems, health education and other health regulations. Partly as a result of that legacy, and partly because public health investments may be difficult to sell to an electorate that may value private goods (such as food grains) over public goods, India's public health systems are in a shambles.

The long-running debate on high child malnutrition in the country over the past few years, which culminated in the food security Bill, represents another lost opportunity to put the issue of public health on the forefront.

The only silver lining on the horizon is the growing political consensus on the importance of toilets. If political personalities as disparate as Jairam Ramesh and Narendra Modi have come to acknowledge the urgent need for providing toilets, that must be seen as a welcome development. Hopefully, the political consensus will add heft to a campaign for providing effective public health services. NSSO results show that centrally sponsored schemes such as the total sanitation campaign have only led to large leakages, without achieving much success in improving rural sanitation levels.

A society cannot progress unless its members progress and achieve refinement. The opportunity for progress and refinement should percolate down to the last member of society. Health plays a prominent role in achieving this goal. Thus, a vital component of a developed society is the health of its citizens. A healthy body harbours a healthy mind and there is an urgent need to create awareness regarding health and sanitation. Proper sanitation is needed to build a healthy society. Despite all progress and development today, the modern world especially India suffers from poor sanitation. This lack of proper sanitation leads to ill health of members of the society.

It seems that lack of sanitation has emerged as one of the prominent stumbling blocks in the process of development of society in the 21st century. Keeping this view as a serious challenge before us, the present chapter makes an attempt to raise issues related sanitation, health and society. These concerns have been raised by a number of social scientists time and again at different platforms.

Before, we move for the discussion on sanitation, health and society, we would like give conceptual clarification of the terms which we are going to use in this chapter. These are as follows:

1. Sanitation
2. Hygiene
3. Scavenging
4. Purity and pollution,
5. Environment
6. Wastage: public and private space

1. Sanitation

Sanitation generally refers to principles, practices, provisions, or services related to cleanliness and hygiene in personal and public life for the protection and promotion of human health and well-being and breaking the cycle of disease or illness. It is also related to the principles and practices relating to the collection, treatment, removal or disposal of human excreta, household waste water and other pollutants. The World Health Organisation states that: Sanitation generally refers to the provision of facilities and services for the safe disposal of human urine and feces. Inadequate sanitation is a major cause of disease world-wide and improving sanitation is known to have a significant beneficial impact on health both in households and across communities. The word 'sanitation' also refers to the maintenance of hygienic conditions, through services such as garbage collection and wastewater disposal. According to Mmom and Mmom (2011) environmental sanitation comprises disposal and treatment of human excreta, solid waste and waste water, control of disease vectors, and provision of washing facilities for personal and domestic hygiene. It aims at improving the quality of life of the individuals and contributing to social development.

2. Hygiene

Hygiene refers to the set of practices perceived by a community to be associated with the preservation of health and healthy living. While in modern medical sciences there is a set of standards of hygiene recommended for different situations, what is considered hygienic or not can vary between different cultures, genders and sectarian groups. Some regular hygienic practices may be considered good habits by a society while the neglect of hygiene can be considered disgusting, disrespectful or even threatening.

Concept of Hygiene: Hygiene is an old concept related to medicine, as well as to personal and professional care practices related to most aspects of living. In medicine and in home (domestic) and everyday life settings, hygiene practices are employed as preventative measures to reduce the incidence and spreading of disease. In the manufacture of food, pharmaceutical, cosmetic and other products, good hygiene is a key part of quality assurance i.e. ensuring that the product complies with microbial specifications appropriate to its use. The terms cleanliness (or cleaning) and hygiene are often used interchangeably, which can cause confusion. In general, hygiene mostly means practices that prevent spread of disease-causing organisms. Since cleaning processes (e.g., hand washing) remove infectious microbes as well as dirt and soil, they are often the means to achieve hygiene. Other uses of the term appear in phrases including: body hygiene, personal hygiene, sleep hygiene, mental hygiene, dental hygiene, and occupational hygiene, used in connection with public health. Hygiene is also the name of a branch of science that deals with the promotion and preservation of health, also called hygienics. Hygiene practices vary widely, and what is considered acceptable in one culture might not be acceptable in another.

3. Scavenging

Scavenging refers to the removal of human waste/excreta (night soil) from unsanitary, "dry" toilets, "dry toilets", i.e., toilets without the modern flush system. Manual scavenging involves the removal of human excreta using brooms and tin plates. The excreta are piled into baskets which scavengers carry on their heads to locations sometimes several kilometers from the latrines (NHRC: 2013). Manual scavenging is said to have started in 1214 in Europe when the first public toilets appeared(Pathak:1995). The water closet was invented by John Harrington in 1596. In 1870, S.S. Helior invented the flush type toilet, and it became common in the Western world.There is evidence of existence of wet toilets in the civilisations of Harappa and Mohenjo-Daro. These cities had toilets, which were connected to underground drainage system lined with burnt clay bricks (as given in the primary History Indus Valley: Home Life: 2013) and in later stage manual scavenging became a caste-based occupation and the vast majority of workers involved are women as reported in the National Conference of Elimination of Manual Scavenging.

4. Purity and Pollution

The notions of purity and pollution are critical for defining and understanding caste hierarchy. According to these concepts, Brahmins hold the highest rank and Shudras the lowest in the caste hierarchy. The Varna System represents a social stratification which includes four varnas namely- Brahmans, Kshatriyas, Vaisyas and Shudras. The Shudras were allocated the lowest rank of social ladder and their responsibilities included service of the three Varnas. The superior castes tried to maintain their ceremonial purity

Dumont holds the notion of purity and pollution interlinked with the caste system and untouchability. The hierarchy of caste is decided according to the degree of purity and pollution. It plays a very crucial role in maintaining the required distance between different castes. But the pollution distance varies from caste to caste and from place to place.

Dipankar Gupta observes that the notion of purity and pollution as Dumont observed is integrally linked with the institution of untouchability. But unlike untouchability the notion of purity and pollution is also a historical accretion. Over time this notion freed itself from its specific and original task of separating untouchables from the others and began to be operative at different planes of the caste system. Here, purity is related to the upper caste persons who are not involved in the occupation of scavenging and pollution is related to the lower caste persons who are involved in the occupation of scavenging which made them untouchables (Dalits) and unclean.

5. Environment

In general, an environment is any set of things, forces, or conditions in relation to which something exists or takes place.

Sociologists typically distinguish between natural environments and social environments. The later includes both material culture (such as buildings and computers) and the abstract cultural and structural characteristics of social systems that constraint and shape the terms on which social life is lived. Since sociology's major contribution to understanding human behaviour focuses on the influence of factors external to individuals, the existence of various kinds of environments is a fundamental assumption that underlies all sociological work. Here, we mean human behaviour which reflects environmental sanitation. Environmental sanitation means the control of all those factors in man's surroundings, which may or may not cause adverse effects on his health.

6. Waste Management

Trash has played a tremendous role in history. The bubonic plague, cholera and typhoid fever, to mention a few, were diseases that altered the populations of Europe and influenced monarchies. They were perpetuated by filth that harbored rats, and contaminated water supply. It was not uncommon for Europeans to throw their garbage and even human wastes out of window. They figured that stray dogs would eat whatever they threw out.

The study of garbage has given us much insight into civilisation of yesteryear (Crowell:2012).Human by their very nature careless with trash. It is not a trait of the 20th century. Garbologists have discovered that people let trash fall where it may. As the timeline of garbage suggests, there has been a problem of trash from man's earliest time. Four basic means of dealing with trash have been used over and over in history.

1. Dumping:
2. Burning
3. Recycling
4. Waste Minimisation

Some cultures are very wasteful, considering everything disposable. Many Mayan sites demonstrate such careless consumption. Consumption and waste of resources is probably related to supply available more than any other factor. When gasoline is plentiful and cheap, automobiles get larger (no body is thinking about future supplies). When it becomes scarce and expensive, automobiles get smaller.

How does the waste we toss today compare to the waste that was thrown away by other civilisation? It is hard to be specific. Until recently trash quantity was calculated by volume not weight. Weight is influenced by moisture content, which varies greatly depending upon climate and weather conditions. The various studies that have been conducted vary too greatly to get a clear picture of per capita refuse per day.

Studies fail to substantiate the notion that Americans are more wasteful than similar civilisations of the past. Note that the nature of waste varies greatly from one civilisation. There is an archaeological account of Native Americans in Colorado about 6500 BC who killed 200 buffalo in one day and butchered 150 of them, carrying away enough meat to feed 150 people of 23 days. They left the remains behind (some 18,380 pounds of bones, which had remained for 6500 years). Soft tissues had decomposed years ago). 150 modern day Americans would produce about 14,150 pounds in 23 days, most of which would have decomposed rapidly. Based on the weight of the bones that remained, the Native Americans in that clan produced about 5.3 pounds of waste a day as compared to 2.5 pounds a day, which is a moderate figure for middle class American consumption.

It is not the question of the nature and quantum of waste but it is much more important of waste management. For instance, the study by Khandewale (1996), reported that garbage is collected only sometimes. As many as 35 respondents mentioned that garbage is collected 'weekly' (14 per cent), and 40 respondents observed that garbage is collected 'occasionally'. Another 45 respondents gave entirely different version. Unless the garbage of the locality is cleaned daily, it would pose serious hazards to the health of its residents. But often, this aspect of sanitation is ignored. This is possible to understand through the relationship of sociology of sanitation and health in context to sanitation, health and society.

Relationship of Sociology of Sanitation with Sociology of Health

Sociology of Health

Sociology of Health is a specialisation within the field of sociology. Its main interest is in the study of health, health behaviour and health care institutions. In the first instance, sociology of health was regarded as medical sociology and proposed by Charles McIntire in 1894. It is defined as "professional endeavour devoted to social epidemiology, the study of cultural factors and social relations in connection with illness, and the social principles in medical organisation and treatment". Broadly speaking medical sociology is sociology of health which includes studies of health professional, relationship with other segments of society, social factors in the aetiology, prevalence, prevalence, incidence and interpretation of disease (Park and Park: 1977:71)

Health Impacts of Sanitation

For any social and economic development, adequate sanitation in conjunction with good hygiene and safe water are essential to good health (Mara, Lane and Scott and Trouba: 2010). Lack of proper sanitation causes diseases. Most of the diseases resulting from sanitation have a direct relation to poverty. The lack of clean water and poor sanitation has caused many diseases and the spread of diseases. Sanitation is very important in order to keep good health. One of the most significant diseases that arise from poor sanitation is diarrhoea. Deaths resulting from diarrhoea are estimated to be between 1.6 and 2.5 million deaths every year (Mara, Lane and Scott and Trouba:2010). Most of the affected are young children below the ages of five. Other diseases that are caused by poor sanitation include schistosomiasis, trachoma, and soil transmitted Helminthiases.

Poor sanitation accounts for almost 50 per cent of underweight child since it has a direct link to diarrhoea. Children suffering for diarrhoea are more vulnerable to become underweight. According to Mara, Lane, and Scott and Trouba, about 26 per cent acute respiratory infections occur in children who are malnourished, which has a direct link to diarrhoea. Sanitation is a serious issue that is affecting most parts of the world especially the developing countries. On a global scale, the most affected are children who in most cases lose their lives due to diseases caused by poor sanitation. Major initiatives need to be set up if the MDG goal on sanitation is to be achieved by 2015.

In many suburban and rural areas households are not connected to sewers. They discharge their wastewater into septic tanks or other types of on-site sanitation. On-site systems include drain fields, which require significant area of land. This makes septic systems unsuitable for most cities. The reuse of untreated wastewater in irrigated agriculture is common in developing countries. The reuse of treated wastewater in landscaping, especially on golf courses, irrigated agriculture and for industrial use is becoming increasingly widespread.

Madhu Nagla discusses, 'Social Construction of Hygiene and Sanitation in Haryana'. We are giving some of the excerpts which are inferred from her paper as follows:

1. Idea and Practice of Sanitation
2. Hygiene and Sanitation in Community Understanding
3. Disposal of Excreta and Habit of Defecation

1. Idea and Practice of Sanitation

Sanitation is an important index of socio-economic development. Low sanitation levels lead to a host of diseases, making sanitation a key public health issue ad concomitant of a clean water supply. Reddy and Snehlatha (2011) did field work in two urban slums of Hyderabad, Andhra Pradesh and concludes that sanitation implies much more than defecation issues and it converges on several important aspects of life, such as shame and dignity and personal hygiene. Women themselves defined what appropriate sanitation is. Cleaning tasks are primarily performed by women who receive little support from men. Reddy and Snehlatha (2011) argue for the need to give women a central role in decision-making, designing, planning and implementation of sanitation programmes. Women's definitions of the minimum standards of hygienic practices are clearly brought out by study. Idea and practice of sanitation revolves around women. In our study, the women are disposing the stool of children outside their houses. Majority of the houses are having flush latrines, therefore, they need not to go outside except very poor people.

2. Hygiene and Sanitation in Community Understanding

There are many hygiene behaviours, however, according to WHO they include: hand-washing, having and using latrines, safe disposal of excreta and storing drinking water supply. Community members across socio-economic group highlighted the hygiene and sanitation behaviour. The vignettes given below are only a few from the large numbers recalled during the FGDs.

(a) Hand washing: Having clean hands is important to prevent disease. For example, one common way to get a cold or serious disease such as hepatitis A or diarrhoea is by rubbing your nose, mouth or eyes after your hands have been contaminated with germs. Hand washing is a complex behaviour, for which several things are needed such as knowledge, skills and an enabling environment. Knowledge of hand washing times that is important for health reasons. These critical hand washing times are usually considered to be: before eating, after defecation, after handling excreta of infants. Rubbing both hands with soap or ash and using enough water is important. Dongre et al (2007) found that need based, focused, skill based child to child education is effective for behaviour change. Mukhopadhyay et al., (2012) found in their study that many food handlers disregard their illnesses like diarrhoea, sore throat and skin infections and continued to do work under such conditions. Disregarding these illnesses can contribute to the occurrence of frequent food borne diseases to their consumers in eateries.

Knowledge and practice of hand washing with soap is common in the study population. However, fifty per cent respondents wash their hands using soap and water and rubbing both hangs together. The entire households had soap for washing hands however; washing of hands with soap was only observed after defecation not after urinating. Washing hands, before eating is also not found common, however, after eating food is found among 80 per cent of the respondents.

3. Disposal of Excreta and Habit of Defecation

The condition of the disposal of the house dirt and waste need to be seen against the background of the local traditions, customs and practices which reflect the lack of understanding of the rule of sanitation and hygiene and in turn knowledge about the disease. People are used to the conditions as they are today in the nature of things, a characteristics feature of village life. They will hardly think about it or talk about it. This has created indifference in these people regarding the disposal of house filth or waste and general sanitary conditions of the village. It may be out of place to quote Karve's explanation of the indifference of the people to environmental sanitation. Karve says. "When people cannot afford to spend adequately even on food and clothing they do not just bother about environmental sanitation...experience strengthens the view that sanitation is inextricably woven with the economic and social life of people, and to the extent to which the latter improves, the sanitary consciousness of the people also correspondingly improves..."(Report on Environmental Sanitation in Rural India: 1957:62-63). Curtis and Cairncross (2003) found that inadequate hand washing after defecation and the cleaning was important source of transmission of enteric diseases in the countries like Bangladesh and India. On the other hand, Curtis, Cairncorss and Yonli (2000) evidenced that hand washing after defecation; especially by the children was significant factor in diarrhoea transmission.

Generally in the city houses are usually swept daily and the refuse is thrown out near some empty plot or some vacant place. Alternatively sweepers of the municipal corporation come and load in their carts and throw them outside the city. In the planned colonies the refuse is not thrown outside the house but house maids collect them in some polybags and dispose it off in the big bins collected in the corner of the colonies.

One of the respondent replied that "they also want to live like the other rich people live, but in the rich locality the municipality people regularly come and clean it. On the other hand they hardly both to clean it and they do not come regularly".

Another respondent said that "it is not the house waste or filth which bothers but it is the disposal part which worries us. There is no proper place to dispose them, Moreover, the refuse of polythene bags create many problems. When the wind blows therefore, it turns into heaps and ultimately it stinks and invites breeding of mosquitoes and flies."

Another respondent said "that heaps of the house refuse may be seen decaying and emitting foul smell. Here house flies and mosquitoes are found on large scale and thus result in the malaria and other diseases."

(a) Habits of Defecation: The proper disposal of human fecal material is important for the environmental sanitation of a community. Report on Environmental Sanitation in Rural India (1957:75) reports that a complete drainage systems laid out has been unearthed in Mohenjo-Daro and in all these places, there are latrines and bathrooms in each house, with drains. All their men and women among Hindus go to the fields for defecation with the exception of one family. Among the Muslim families, latrine was there, but only females were using that as they are supposed to observe *purdah* (Hasan: 1979:73). Furthermore, nearly 90 per cent did not want to have latrines in their houses as they feel it is unhygienic and uncomfortable. The foul smell inside the latrine makes them feel bad. Hasan also observed that inside the house feel failed to excrete and resulting in to constipation or their bowels did not move. Going outside in the morning has an additional advantage as one enjoys morning walk and breeze.

In the present situation of the village, people have latrines, except very few houses. However, the houses in which latrines were there, we asked them that where the children defecate? Except those houses where mothers and fathers were educated their children defecate in the latrine and in the toddler stage they defecate on the floor of the house or in plastic pot and then stool are thrown in the latrine and pot is washed. Children aged between 3-4 years to 6-7 years defecate outside the house where drainages are there. They reported that it is convenient for children as well as for parents to send them outside the home for defecation as for this age group of children as they have only one latrine and in the morning time all the members go for defecation, therefore there is rush for it. Therefore, for this age-group of children it is better to send them outside. Generally, latrines do not have tap water, only one container filled with water along with the mug is there to wash the latrine and flush it out with mug of water. They have given the argument that by fixing tap in the latrine for water, water will be spent in the liberal manner. There is already a shortage of water and it has to be collected during either from the supply of municipality water or from private sources. Private source of water is very popular in Haryana. Generally each household has private connection of water by paying Rs. 100-150 per month. The private water supply owners bring tanks and whosoever pays them they fill their tanks and charge the money. Thus, the role of parents' education, economic condition and role of water supply is the determining variables in the hygienic behaviour(MadhuNagla).

Sanitation and Public Health

The importance of the isolation of waste lies in an effort to prevent diseases which can be transmitted through human waste, which afflict both developed countries as well as developing countries to differing degrees. It is estimated that up to 5 million people die each year from preventable water-borne diseases (Pacific Institute), as a result of inadequate sanitation and hygiene practices. The effects of sanitation have impacted the society of people throughout history (Ehlers: 1943). Sanitation is a necessity for a healthy life (George: 2008). The results of studies published in Griffins Public Sanitation show that better sanitation produces an enhanced feeling of wellbeing.

Relevant diseases include:

1. Waterborne diseases, which can contaminate drinking water
2. Diseases transmitted by the fecal-oral route
3. Hookworm, where eggs can survive in the soil

There continues to be many countries that are struggling with diseases due to unhealthy living conditions and unfiltered water all in the name of bad sanitation [Castro and Leo (2009), Amy, and Gray (2012) and www.victorianweb.org].

Solid waste

The term solid waste is applied to unwanted or discarded waste material from houses, street sweepings, commercial, industrial and agricultural operations, arising from man's activities. In the cities it is called refuse; in the country side it is called litter; and in general, it is called solid wastes. It is a conglomeration of dust, ash, vegetable and putrescible matter, paper and packing of all kinds; rags and other fabrics, ploy bags, glass and many other combustible and incombustible debris.

Health issues are linked with man's total environment. The accumulation of solid wastes in man's environment constitutes a positive health hazard because of the following reasons which are given by Park and Park (1977:222).

- The organic portion of solid wastes ferments and favours fly breeding
- The garbage in the refuse attracts rats;
- The pathogens may be conveyed to man through flies and dust;
- There is possibility of water pollution if rain water passes through deposits of fermenting refuse;
- There is risk of air pollution, if there is accidental or spontaneous combustion of refuse;
- Piles of refuse are a nuisance from an aesthetic point of view.

Therefore, there should be an efficient collection, removal and disposal of refuse without the risk to health. It is fundamental environmental health service. In fact, the social development of a community is reflected in the collection and disposal of its refuse.

Composition, Quantity and Sources of Refuse

The composition and volume of refuse reflects the living conditions of the people. It also varies from season to season and from locality to locality. The affluent societies are producing more and more bulky refuse of all kinds, cardboard, plastics, empty tins, glass and metal. Strictly speaking, refuse should not contain night-soil. In India and similar other emerging countries, it not uncommon to find nights oil in collections of refuse. There are various types of the sources of refuse as follows:

1. Refuse that is collected by the street cleaning service or scavenging is called street refuse. It consists of leaves, straw, paper, animal droppings and litter of all kinds.
2. Refuse that is collected from markets is called market refuse. It contains a large proportion of putrescible vegetable and animal matter.
3. Refuse that is collected from stables is called stable litter. It contains mainly animal droppings and lift-over animal feeds.
4. Industrial refuse comprises a wide variety of wastes ranging from completely inert materials such as calcium carbonate to highly toxic and explosive compounds.

5. The domestic refuse consists of ash, rubbish and garbage. Ash is the residue from fire used for cooking and heating. Rubbish comprises paper, clothing, and bits of wood, metal, glass, dust and dirt. Garbage is waste matter arising from the preparation, cooking and consumption of food. It consists of waste food, vegetable peelings and other organic matter. Garbage needs quick removal and disposal because it ferments on storage.

Storage

The first consideration should be given to the proper storage of refuse, while awaiting collection. The galvanised steel dust bin with close fitting cover is a suitable for storing refuse.

Collection

The method of collection depends upon the funds available. House-to-house collection is by far the best method of collecting refuse. In India, there is no house-to-house collection system. People are expected to dump the refuse in the nearest public bin, which is usually not done. Refuse is dispersed all along the street, and some is thrown out in front and around the house. As a result, an army of sweepers is required for sweeping the streets in addition to the gang for collecting the refuse from public bins. The refuse is then transported in refuse collection vehicles to the place of ultimate disposal. Dead animals are directly transported to the place of disposal.

The collection methods normally practiced need drastic revision and improvement in the interest of better hygiene. The Environmental Hygiene Committee (1949) recommended that municipalities and other local bodies should arrange for collection of refuse not only from the public bins but also from individual houses. A house to house collection will result in a simultaneous reduction in the number of public bins. The open refuse cart should be abandoned and replace by enclosed cans. Mechanical transport should be used wherever possible as it is more practical than the 19th century methods. There is wide variety of refuse collection vehicles of all shapes and sizes.

Disposal of solid waste is most commonly conducted in landfills, but incineration, recycling; composting and conversion to biofuels are also avenues. In the case of landfills, advanced countries typically have rigid protocols for daily cover with topsoil, where underdeveloped countries customarily rely upon less stringent protocols (George and Kreith: 2002). The importance of daily cover lies in the reduction of vector contact and spreading of pathogens. Daily cover also minimises odor emissions and reduces windblown litter. Likewise, developed countries typically have requirements for perimeter sealing of the landfill with clay-type soils to minimise migration of leachate that could contaminate groundwater (and hence jeopardise some drinking water supplies) [Hiriya Landfill, Israel].

Methods of Disposal

There is no single method of refuse disposal which is equally suitable in all circumstances. The choice of a particular method is governed by local factors such as cost and availability of land and labour. The principal methods of refuse disposal are:

- Dumping
- Controlled tipping or Sanitary Land-fill
- Incineration
- Compositing
- Manure pits
- Burial

Dumping

Refuse is dumped in low lying areas partly as a method of reclamation of land but mainly as an easy method of disposal of dry refuse. As a result of bacterial action, effuse decreases considerably in volume and is converted gradually into humus. The drawbacks of open dumping are: (1) he refuse is exposed to flies and rodents, (2) it is a source of nuisance from the smell and unsightly appearance; (3) the loose refuse is dispersed by the action of wind and (4) drainage from dumps contributes to the pollution of surface and ground water. A WHO committee (1967) condemned dumping as a most insanitary method that creates public health hazard, a nuisance, and severe pollution of the environment. Dumping should be outlawed and replaced by sound procedures.

Controlled Tipping

Controlled tipping or sanitary landfill is the most satisfactory method of refuse disposal where suitable land is available. It differs from ordinary dumping in that the material is placed in a trench or other prepared area, adequately compacted, and covered with earth at the end of the working day. The term modified sanitary landfill has been applied to those operations where compaction and covering are accomplished once or twice a week.

Incineration

refuse can be disposed of hygienically by burning or incineration. It is the method of choice where suitable land is not available. Hospital refuse which is particularly dangerous is best disposed by incineration. Incineration is practiced in several of the industrialised countries, particularly in large cities due to lack of suitable land. Incineration is not a popular method in India because the refuse contains a fair proportion of fine ash which makes the burning difficult. A Preliminary separation of dust or ash is needed. All this involves heavy outlay and expenditure, beside manipulative difficulties in the incinerator. Further disposal of refuse burning is a loss to the community in terms of the much needed manure. Burning therefore has a limited application in refuse disposal in India.

Composting

Composting is a method of combined disposal of refuse and night soil or sludge. It is a process of nature whereby organic matter breaks down under bacterial action resulting in the formation of relatively stable humus like material, called the compost which has considerable manurial value for the soil. The principal by-products are carbon di-oxide, water and heat. The heat produced during composting – 60^0C or higher, over a period of several days- destroy eggs and larvae of flies, weeds seeds and pathogenic agents. The end product-compost- contains few or no disease producing organisms, and is a good soil builder containing small amounts of the major plant nutrients such as nitrates and phosphates.

Manure Pits

In rural areas in India, there is no system for collection and disposal of refuse. Refuse is thrown around the house indiscriminately resulting in gross pollution of the soil. The problem of refuse disposal in rural areas can be solved by digging manure pits by the individual householders. The garbage, cattle dung, straw and leaves should be dumped into the manure pits and covered with earth after each day's dumping. Two such pits will be needed, when one is closed, the other will be in use. In 5 to 6 months' time, the refuse is converted into manure which can be returned to the field. This method of refuse disposal is effective and relatively simple in rural communities.

Burial

This method is suitable for small camps. A trench wide 1.5 meter wide and 2 meter deep is excavated, and at the end of each day the refuse is covered with 20 to 30 cm of earth. When the level is in the trench is 40 cm from ground level, the trench is filled with earth and compacted, and a new trench is dug out. The content may be taken out after 4 to 6 months and used in the fields. If he trench is 1 meter in length for every 200 persons, it will be filled in about one week.

Food preparation

Sanitation within the food industry means the adequate treatment of food-contact surfaces by a process that is effective in destroying vegetative cells of microorganisms of public health significance, and in substantially reducing numbers of other undesirable microorganisms, but without adversely affecting the food or its safety for the consumer (U.S. Food and Drug Administration, Code of Federal Regulations, 21CFR110, USA). Sanitation Standard Operating Procedures are mandatory for food industries in United States, which are regulated by 9 CFR part 416 in conjunction with 21 CFR part 178.1010. Similarly, in Japan, food hygiene has to be achieved through compliance with food sanitation law (JETO:2008).

Additionally, in the food and biopharmaceutical industries, the term sanitary equipment means equipment that is fully cleanable using clean-in-place (CIP) and sterilisation-in-place (SIP) procedures: that is fully drainable from cleaning solutions and other liquids. The design should have a minimum amount of dead leg (Treatment of dead leg plumbing areas) or areas where the turbulence during cleaning is insufficient to remove product deposits. In general, to improve clean ability, this equipment is made from Stainless Steel 316L, (an alloy containing small amounts of molybdenum). The surface is usually electro-polished to an effective surface roughness of less than 0.5 micrometre to reduce the possibility of bacterial adhesion.

The Emergence of Public Health

The birth of the public health occurred in England around 1840. The evils of the industrial revolution on one hand, and the frequent visitations of cholera on the other, led to the rapid growth and development of public health in the western world. The industrial revolution of the 18th century brought in its wake new problems to society- creation of slums, accumulation of refuse and human excreta, overcrowding, women and child health and social problems, industrial and crowd diseases,. Cholera which if often called the "father of public health" hit the western world in the first quarter of the 19th century. Johanna Peter Frank (1745-1821), a liberal health philosopher of his time, conceived public health as good health laws enforced by the police, and enunciated the principle that State is responsible for the health of the people. The great Cholera epidemic of 1832 led Edwin Chadwick (1800-1890), a lawyer in England investigate the health of inhabitants of the large towns with a view to improving the conditions under which they lived. Chadwick's report on the "The Sanitary conditions of the Labouring Populations (1842) focused on the attention of people and government on the urgent need to improve public health. Filth was recognised as man's greatest enemy, and with this began an anti-filth crusade. This great movement, often described as the "great sanitary awakening" led to the Public Health Act of 1848 in England and acceptance of the principle that the State is responsible for the health of the people. Cholera continued to occur time and again in the western world during the 19th Century. In 1854, John Snow, by an epidemiological investigation of the Cholera epidemic in Broad Street, London established first time the method of transmission of Cholera. In 1856, William Budd, another pioneer produced similar evidence about typhoid fever. These two discoveries clinched the role of water in the transmission of Cholera and typhoid fever, long before their causative organisms were identified. Then came the demand from people of clean water. A comprehensive piece of legislation was brought into force in England, the Public Health Act of 1875 for the control of the physical environment and public health. The torch had already been lit by Chadwick, but the man who was responsible move than any other for sanitary reforms in England was Sir John Simon (1816-1904). He built up a system of public health which became the admiration of the rest of the world.

The development of the public health movement in America follows closely the English pattern. In 1865, Shattuck, a book seller and publisher, published his report on the health conditions in Massachusetts. Like Chadwick's report it stirred the conscience of the people to the improvement of public health. France, Spain, Austria, Germany, Italy, Belgium and the Scandinavian countries all developed their public health. By the beginning of the 20 the Century, the broad foundations of public health- clean water, clean surroundings, wholesome conditions of houses, control of offensive trades, etc. were laid in all the countries of the civilised world. After the First World War, there were three particular new comers to the public health scene- Yugoslavia, Turkey and Russia. These three countries in 1920 presented the typical picture of the underdeveloped world. Today, there are quite advanced public health.

Western public health made rapid strides in the western world, its progress was slow in the developing countries such as India where the main health problems continue to be those faced by the western world 100 years ago. The establishment of the World Health Organisation providing a Health Charter for all people provided a great fillip to the public health movement in these countries.

Concept of Public Health

Public health during the 19th Century was largely a matter of sanitary legislations aimed at the control of the physical environment e.g., water supplies, sewage system and housing. At the beginning of the 20th Century, a new concept began to take shape that the State has a direct responsibility for the health of the individual. It was initiated as mother and child health services. School health services were developed concurrently. Public health nursing was a direct outgrowth of this concept. Then came the industrial and mental health services within the purview of public health. Winslow in 1920 defined public health as "the science and art of preventing disease, prolonging life and promoting health and efficiency through organised community effort".

Public health made significant progress during the past 70 years. Many of the once major health problems have been brought under control. The health of the people has vastly improved consequent upon improvements in the standard of living, spread of literacy and control of the environment. The old problems were solved, new health problems began to emerge (viz. cardiovascular diseases, hypertension, cancer, mental illness, AIDS/HIV, alcoholism, drug addiction) especially I the affluent societies. These problems posed a challenge to public health which is now engaged in this broad field of effort.

Public health in its modern concept is quite different from public health of a generation ago. Although the term public health is still widely used, its original meaning has changed. A recent definition of public health is "the organised application of resources to achieve the greatest health for the greatest number. Public health by this definition would encompass not only government activity but also voluntary and other organised community action taking place all the way from local to international levels. It would include not only prevention but also treatment and rehabilitation. It would be concerned and not just with the communicable diseases and sanitation, but also with the chronic diseases and accidents, not only with the health of mothers and children, but also of fathers and grandparents. In view of the changed meaning and scope of public health, the term community health is preferred by some leaders in public health.

Thus the public health as understood till recently, was defined by C.E.A. Winslow, a former professor of public health at Yale University as follows:

"Public health is the science and art of (1) preventing disease, (2) prolonging life, and (3) promoting health and efficiency through organised community effort for :

- The sanitation of the environment
- The control of communicable diseases
- The education of the individual in personal hygiene
- The organisation of medical and nursing services for the early diagnosis and preventive treatment of disease, and
- The development of social machinery to insure everyone a standard of living adequate for the maintenance of health,

so organising these benefits as to enable every citizen to realise his birth-right of health and longevity.

Winnslow's definition of public health which was given in 1920 is considered too broad, and created an umbrella under which almost anything could be gathered and fails to meet the criteria of modern public health. The concept of public health is different today to what it was 70 years ago, from the control of physical environment and communicable diseases, public health has moved to the preventive, therapeutic and rehabilitative aspects of chronic diseases and behavioural disorders which are currently the major health problems in the developed countries. The current emphasis in the field of health is also on the application of modern management techniques for improving the efficiency of health care delivery systems. An operational definition of public health therefore must change with the times. A new definition of public health which meets the modern public health is as follows" Public health is the planning, carrying out and evaluation of health measures and system services that both maintain and improve the health of a population group and prevent and control diseases within that population group".

This definition gives increased emphasis to planning and evaluation of health activities, programmes and systems. In turn, this implies increased attention to the precise definition of health needs while retaining the epidemiological approach to the establishment of factors environmental and personal that contributes to these health problems. The definition illuminates that challenge that now confronts public health, as it is now termed community health (Park and Park: 1977:4).

References

Amy, Stewart, and Tim Gray (2012). Governance Of Water And Sanitation In Africa : Achieving Sustainable Development Through Partnerships. n.p.: I.B. Tauris, 2009. eBook Collection (EBSCOhost). Web. 14 Nov. 2012.

Barbalace, Robert Crowell (2011) The History of Waste, *Environmental Chemistry*. <http://environmentalchemistry.com/yogi/environmental/wastehistory.html>. Web. 07 July 2011.

Castro, Jose Esteban and Leo Heller (ed.) (2009), *Water and Sanitation Services*, Routledge, Taylor and Francis Group.

Curtis, Valerie and S.Cairncross (2003), "Effect of Washing Hands with Soap on Diarrhea Risk in the Community: A Systematic Review", *The Lancet Infectious Diseases*, 3: 275-281.

Curtis, Valerie, S.Cairncross and R.Yonli (2000), "Domestic Hygiene and Diarrhea, Pinpointing the Problem", *Tropical Medicine and International Health,* 5: 22-32.

Dongre, A.R. et al., (2007), "An Approach to Hygiene Education Among Rural Indian School Going Children", *Online Journal of Health and Allied Sciences,* Vol.6, 4, Oct-Dec.

Dumont, Louis (1980), *Homo Heirachicus: The Caste System and Its Implications,* Complete revised English edition, Chicago: University of Chicago press (First published in 1966).

Ehlers, Victor (1943). *Municipal and rural sanitation.* New York: McGraw-Hill book company, inc.

George Tchobanoglous and Frank Kreith (2002).Handbook of Solid Waste Management, McGraw Hill professional.

Gupta, Dipankar (ed.) (2004). Caste in Question: Identity or Hierarchy?, New Delhi: Sage Publication.

The Hiriya Landfill Project (1998). Tel Aviv, Israel.

Japan External Trade Organisation (JATO: 2008) "Food Sanitation Law in Japan", Quoted from Wikipedia.

Khandewale, Shreekant V. 1996), health Administration and the Weaker sections in an Indian Metropolis, ebook.

Mara D, Lane J; and Scott B, and Trouba D (2010) Sanitation and Health, PLOS Med 7 (11).

Mmom, P.C. and Mmom, C. F. (2011). 'Environmental sanitation and Public health challenges in a rapidly Growing City of the Third world: The case of Domestic waste and Diarrhoea Incidence in greater Port Harcourt Metropolis, Nigeria' *Asian Journal of Medical Sciences* 3 (3).

Mukhopadhyay, Prianka et al., (2012), "Indentifying Key Risk Behaivours Regarding Personal Hygiene and Food Supply Practices of Food Handlers Working in Eating Establishments Located within a Hospital campus in Kolkata", *Al Ameen Journal of Medical Science,* 5 (1): 21:28.

Nagla, Madhu, 'Social Construction of Hygiene and Sanitation in Haryana' in the process of publication in the *Journal of Sulabh International,* New Delhi.

National Human Rights Commission (NHRC) (2013). 'Human Rights and manual scavenging', Know Your Rights Series.

Park, J.E. and K. Park (1977), *Text book on Social and Preventive and Social Medicine,* Jabalpur: BanarsidasBhanot Publishers. pp. 94, 222, (old book)

Pathak, Bindeswar (1995). 'History of Toilets', *International Symposium on Public Toilets,* Hong Kong, May 25–27.

www.victorianweb.org].

4

Culture and Sanitation

Introduction

Culture is the accumulated store of symbols, ideas, and material products associated with a social system, whether it is an entire society or a family. India is a nation of ancient and firmly entrenched tradition and culture. For thousands of years, religion, geography and the necessities of a rural agrarian society have sculpted a complex caste system based on status, hierarchy, and, above all, a strict division of labour. As India is becoming increasingly urbanised, and her people are leaving their traditional rural communities and entering into an environment marked by fluidity, change and drastically different technological and physical conditions, traditional divisions of labour and living habits forged in rural settings are increasingly out of step with contemporary conditions. Yet, Indians continue to cling to traditional cultural mores, often causing great problems, especially for the poor.

Is India's lack of toilets a cultural problem?

Is anybody really surprised that nearly half of India's 1.2 billion people have no toilet at home? Not really. The India Human Development report has been saying this for a while.

The situation is worse in the villages, where two-thirds of the homes don't have toilets. Open defecation is rife, and remains a major impediment in achieving millennium development goals which include reducing by half the proportion of people without access to basic sanitation by 2015.

Is the lack of toilets and preference for open defecation a cultural issue in a society where the habit actually perpetuates social oppression, as proved by the reduced but continued existence of low caste human scavengers and sweepers? It would seem so.

Mahatma Gandhi, India's greatest leader, had, in the words of a biographer, a "Tolstoyian preoccupation with sanitation and cleaning of toilets". Once he inspected toilets in the city of Rajkot in Gujarat. He reported that they were "dark and stinking and reeking with filth and worms" in the homes of the wealthy and in a Hindu temple. The homes of the untouchables simply had no toilets. "Latrines are for you big people," an untouchable told Gandhi.

Many years later when Gandhi began encouraging his disciples to work as sanitation officers and scavengers in villages, his diligent secretary and diarist Madhav Desai noted the attitudes of villagers. "They don't have any feeling at all," he wrote. "It will not be surprising if within a few days they start believing that we are their scavengers."

India's enduring shame is clearly rooted in cultural attitudes. More than half a century after Independence, many Indians continue to relieve themselves in the open and litter unhesitatingly, but keep their homes spotlessly clean. Yes, the state has failed to extend sanitation facilities, but people must also take the blame.

In the upstart suburb of Gurgaon, where Soutik Biswas (Delhi Correspondent of BBC) lives, his educated, upwardly mobile, rich neighbours sent their pet dogs outside with their servants to defecate and refuse to clean up the mess. As long as their condominium is clean, it is all right. These are the same people who believe that the government is at the root of all evil [Biswas, Soutik (Delhi Correspondent of BBC News in India):2012].

The present chapter discusses social components in scavenging and cleanliness – culture and dirt, attitudes, beliefs and values associated with dirt, problems of scavenging, purity and impurity, development and sanitation.

Social Construction of Hygiene and Sanitation

Dirt and Hygiene

Idea about dirt and hygiene vary from culture to culture and has changed from century to century. What is dirty in one place is clean in another. What was seen as clean by our forebears is unacceptably dirty in the late twentieth century. The explanation offered by anthropology for dirt is that it is matter out of its proper place. As each society has rules that create order, violations of that order constitute a threat to society. As physical objects which are in the wrong place, or hard to classify are labelled as "dirty", so the label "dirty" is given to marginal behaviours and social categories which provide a threat to the social order (Douglas: 1966). Hence the lipstick has to stay in its proper place on the lips, and the dirty old man has to keep his behaviour within society's boundaries.

To combat the dangers of dirt there is hygiene, which serves to preserve order, to chase away dirt and to preserve health. As dirt is multiple in natures and ubiquitous, so is corollary to hygiene. Rules about hygiene are to be found throughout every society. Hygiene is not only the private practice of individuals, but it is requirement of each society. Hygiene provides not only a barrier to the transmission of disease, but it also provides a barrier to disorder, chaos and social collapse.

Simply providing public services, whether in water supply, sanitation, curative services or health education does not, in itself guarantee improvement in health status. Just because a service is there does not guarantee that it will be used, or that it will be used to the best possible health advantage. Some households contrive to preserve health even without these services. A framework that goes beyond the provision of services, beyond the standard public health perspective, is needed, if we are to find more effective way of working.

Berman et al. (1994) offer a solution and suggest that at household level external conditions and internal processes come together to produce health. They propose that households combine their own knowledge, resources and behavioural patterns with available technologies, services, information and support from outside the home, to produce desired outcomes, one of which is good health. Similarly, in a paper on the public and domestic domains of disease transmission, Cairncross (1996) points out that the endemic disease that is responsible for the vast majority of the toll of death and illness in developing countries is largely transmitted within households.

What is Hygiene?

What image comes to mind when one thinks of hygiene? A European might think of a spotless bathroom, or of a child learning to put her hand in front of her mouth when she coughs. An African might think first of a well-swept courtyard and a child leaning not to eat with her left hand, whilst someone from Asia might first imagine a veranda carefully smeared with dung and a child learning to brush her hair. Hygiene means different things to different people. Hygiene is a social phenomenon in the context of the social reality.

Boot and Cairncross (1993) provide a useful definition of hygiene: "the practice of keeping oneself and one's surrounding clean, especially in order to prevent illness or the spread of infection". The idea of hygiene thus comprises two concerns, the avoidance of dirt, and the prevention of disease. The ideas about hygiene are not absolute. They vary from culture to culture and have through history. If we are to understand hygiene it is necessary to explain both dirt and concept of disease causation. According to McLaughlin (1971) "dirt is the evidence of the imperfection in life". He suggests that there is no such thing as absolute dirt: soup on a plate before we eat it is food, the leftovers on the plate are dirty; lipstick on a girl's lips may make the boyfriend want to kiss them, lipstick on a cup will ensure that he does not drink from it. Secretions; pus, vomitus, urine and faces are inescapably dirty. The anthropologist, Mary Douglas was one of the first to realise that dirt was the reflection of the culture which defined it. Dirt is a by-product of a systematic ordering and classification of matter. That which does not fit within the system is rejected and labelled as dirt. Douglas shoes that hygiene is not a matter of mere health, but is a construct that can only be understood in relation to other fundamental social values; cleanliness, order, purity, sacredness, veneration and their corollaries: dirt, disorder, pollution, profanity, and defilement.

Everywhere people have their hygiene rules in terms of a search for health and the avoidance of disease, whether they believe in microbes or not. Arguments about the natural consequences of unhygienic aces are roped in to uphold existing belief about disease, whether they spring from pre-scientific, quasi-scientific ort scientific understanding of disease causation. To elicit the emic (inside) view of hygiene in any society we have to scratch beneath this rationalist surface, to find out the cultural and psychological foundation of hygiene.

Social Significance and Functions of Hygiene

Hygiene springs from a need for individual and social order; good order creates harmony and health. Religion, natural philosophy and science have contrived to offer satisfactory post-rationalisation for what is a fundamental need for order. If we want to promote safer hygiene therefore, we do not need to confine ourselves to arguments about disease avoidance. For example, In India one could build on the existing idea that water possesses the power of purifying, revivifying, and regenerating, to encourage hand washing.

Hygiene and pollution rules are found in each society and are to be understood in the social framework of ideologies, underpinning forces and rationality behind them. In India, the religious conception of the pure/impure dichotomy subtends the whole hierarchical order of society. In his classic work "Homo Hierarchicus" (1966) Dumont states that the fundamental institution in India is caste. Caste is based upon a hierarchical opposition of the pure and the impure, the superior and inferior. If the ritual and purity of the Brahmins helped to set them apart from society, this would have also contributed to the legitimisation of the Brahmins' position at the top of the hierarchy. Eventually Brahmin religion become dominant throughout India among Hindus as did a rigid hierarchical ordering of society based on degrees of purity. Nowhere is it clearer that social rule which are founded on, and justified by, scriptural prescriptions about pollution and purity help to keep each group in their allotted rank in the social hierarchy. The relationship of one group to another is defined by their ritual purity with Brahmins at the top of the purity scale and 'untouchable', who traditionally have the polluting professions (leather work, garbage and night soil collection) at the bottom of the scale (Dumont: 1980). Social sanctions, which work all the way up the edifice of caste, keep the system in place (Curtis: 1998). In other countries, secular morality often plays a similar role (Curtis: 1998) for example elaborate cleanliness, fresh clothes and perfume are not only more available to the rich, but serve to reinforce the distinction between rich and poor and thus perpetuate the inequality. If poverty and oppression can be justified on the grounds of a lack of hygiene, then we are dealing with a potentially explosive concept. Efforts to promote hygiene that are founded on the notion of the ignorance of the peasant or the shanty down dweller, are still the rule rather than the exception in India, Africa and Latin America. If hygiene is intimately related with power, rank and caste, then no effort to promote hygiene can afford to be dealing with a purely scientific issue.

Hygiene keeps society in order because of the threat of diseases. But for this order society has to believe in it. Society provides two categories of explanation of natural phenomena such as birth, growth, the changing of the seasons, or disease, calamity and death. The first is the agency of some external forces deriving its power from religion, magic or symbolism. The second is the agency of properties that are intrinsic to the natural world and designated as naturalistic or scientific. While it is commonly thought that societies have evolved away from mystical explanation and towards the scientific, the two categories cannot be separated so easily. The ancient Hindu science of health, Ayurveda does not separate the divine from the earthly. It gives a central role to the balance of the humors. Disease is but one consequence of offences against the natural order. Burkert (1992) suggests that to try to separate the divine from the earthly in early societies is wasted efforts: "In archaic societies the social and physical ills were not clearly differentiated… the administration of justice and healing can be seen to fuse…An offence is the source of illness, illness is the result of an offence, be it in the personal, the social or the religious sphere. Even the Greek word 'Nosos' embraces both the physical and the social ailments and disturbances."

Throughout history people have been advised, exhorted, and ordered to conform to certain rules of hygiene behaviour. The explanations offered have included factors such as public and private morality, religious purity and the preservation of health. As the scientific understanding of disease transmission has advanced, so the case for hygiene for health reasons has come to dominate in our supposedly scientific societies. However, motivations for domestic hygiene lie not in the avoidance of specific diseases, but in subtle social forces. On the other hand health scientists ignore the social forces in the path of disease transmission.

Meaning of Sanitation

Sanitation is the hygienic which means of promoting health through prevention of human contact with the hazards of wastes as well as the treatment and proper disposal of sewage wastewater. Hazards can be physical, microbiological, biological or chemical agents of diseases. Wastes that can cause health problems include human and animal feces, solid wastes, domestic wastewater (sewage, sullage, grey water)), industrial wastes and agricultural wastes. Hygienic means of prevention can be by using engineering solutions (e.g. sewerage and waste water treatment), simple technologies (e.g. latrines, septic tanks), or even by personal hygiene practices (e.g. simple hand washing with soap).

World Health Organisation (2000) states that: "Sanitation generally refers to the provision of facilities and services for the safe disposal of human urine and feces. Inadequate sanitation is a major cause of disease world-wide and improving sanitation is known to have a significant beneficial impact on health both in households and across communities. The word 'sanitation' also refers to the maintenance of hygienic conditions, through services such as garbage collection and wastewater disposal.

Sanitation and Public Health

The importance of the isolation of waste lies in an effort to prevent disease which can be transmitted through human waste, which afflict both developed countries as well as developing countries to differing degrees. It is estimated that up to 5 million people die each year from preventable water-borne diseases (Gleick: 2002). Sanitation is necessity for a healthy life.

There are two schools of thought: the "miasmatists" who regarded miasmas as being responsible for disease; and the "contagionists" who regarded that disease came from bodily contact, sharing of substances such as food and water, or proximity. Edwin Chadwick (1800-1890), the great sanitary reformer explained that epidemic fevers sue to miasmas arising from decaying animals and vegetable matter. In the wake of industrialisation and urbanisation came the concern that urban population concentrations were the breeding ground for filth, epidemic and vice; all of which threatened the social order. In pre-revolutionary Paris Joseph Guillotin proposed the setting up a health committee in 1790 to look into health conditions of the urban masses. Social unrest in England led to the Edwin Chadwick's of the Sanitarian movement and the Public Health Act of 1848. Boards of Health were set up in Philadelphia, Boston and New York and Public Health legislation was enacted throughout Europe. DeSwaan suggests that a collective effort to pacify the urban poor was required to maintain the social order in the interest of elites (1988). But the stated concern of sanitarians was that "epidemic disease was the product of dirt and decomposing matter". Pickstone points out that the 'expert' explanation of disease did not coincide with what the masses perceived; their emic vies was that fevers and other diseases were due to privation and the high price of corn (1992). The elite used new theories about disease to explain their fear of the threat of the poor; the poor saw their disease as a consequence of their property.

New Culture of Urban Sanitation

Bombay is India's largest and fastest growing city and exemplifies many of these problems as traditional, rural culture clashes with the reality of conditions in the modern megacity. Over half of Bombay's residents live in poorly serviced slums marked by overcrowding, pollution, poor sanitation and a host of other problems shared by the urban poor the world over. Of particular concern in Bombay is the problem of human waste. The lack of clean and adequate toilet facilities, the lingering rural custom of relieving oneself outdoors, and deeply entrenched attitudes and taboos preventing most slum dwellers from cleaning up human society.

Bombay's Community of Resource Organisation (CORO) is working to provide sustainable, community run sanitary facilities in the city's low-income settlements. In the congested slum areas, stationary toilets have proven difficult to build and nearly impossible to maintain, but in July, 1992, CORO took over the management of government constructed toilet facilities in several locations throughout the city. Building a unique partnership between their new sanitation project and their longstanding literacy program, CORO combined community library facilities with their sanitary facilities. Local groups manage the toilets on a co-operative bases, sometimes finding sponsors for the poorest areas where the toilets cannot pay for their own upkeep. The maintenance activity is providing monthly pay for 500 workers, while community members who are happy with clean facilities and adequate water are willing to pay (Palnitkar: 1988).

The introduction of on-site sanitation systems is much more than the application of simple engineering techniques - it is an intervention that entails considerable social change. If sanitation improvements in rural and urban areas are to be widely accepted, the relevant social and cultural factors have to be taken into consideration during planning and implementation. It is, therefore, necessary to understand how a society functions, including the communities and households within it, and what factors promote change.

Social Structure

Social structure determines the nature of individuals which reflect cultural beliefs and practices, about sanitation and disease and attitudes towards hygiene. These function as forces of change and in response to these forces we can analyse the change. Therefore, social and cultural considerations are important to understand the institutional functioning of sanitation.

Consideration should be given to the institutions of a political, economic and social nature that are operating at the national and/or local level, such as government, the civil service, religious institutions, schools and colleges, and the family, and to the forms of leadership and authority that are generally accepted by the majority of the people. It is also important to consider the various roles and patterns of behaviour of individuals and social groups, and to determine who is traditionally responsible for such areas as water supplies, environmental hygiene, family health and children's defecation habits, etc. For example, Caste sanctions and strictures still govern all social, religious and economic activities of an average Indian in the villages and to a decreasing extent the towns and cities. Hence, socio-cultural considerations based on caste, marriage, family and other social institutions establish the beliefs and practices which determine the nature of sanitation.

Consideration should be given to the institutions of a political, economic and social nature that are operating at the national and/or local level, such as government, the civil service, religious institutions, schools and colleges, and the family, and to the forms of leadership and authority that are generally accepted by the majority of the people. It is also important to consider the various roles and patterns of behaviour of individuals and social groups, and to determine who is traditionally responsible for such areas as water supplies, environmental hygiene, family health and children's defecation habits, etc.

Cultural Beliefs and Practices

Group and community identity, gender roles, the relative importance attached to different forms of authority and the ways in which it is exercised are all influenced by culture, i.e., all that is passed down by human society including language, laws, customs, beliefs and moral standards. Culture shapes human behaviour in many different ways including the status attached to different roles and what is deemed to be acceptable personal and social behaviour. In many cultures, for example, the elderly command traditional authority and influence within the family and community.

As regards sanitation behaviour, defecation is often a private matter which people are unwilling to discuss openly, while the burying of faeces is widely practiced to ward off evil spirits. Contact with faecal matter is unacceptable to certain individuals in societies where it is the responsibility of low-income or low-caste groups, while taboos may dictate that separate facilities should be provided for particular social groups.

A particular cultural practice to be considered, which has direct technical consequences, is the method of anal cleansing used by the community. Whether water, stones, corncobs or thick pieces of paper are used will affect the design of the sanitation system. Culture also influences how people interpret and evaluate the environment in which they live. Investments in sanitation seek to improve health by providing a clean physical environment for households. There is a logical series of technical questions that need to be asked in order that acceptable technical solutions can be found. It may be confusing, therefore, when sanitation behaviour is found to vary widely between communities within the same physical environment. Predetermined rules cannot be applied. However, the sanitation behaviour of individuals usually has a rational basis, and people are often aware of the environmental causes of ill-health. Many societies have a detailed knowledge of the physical environment as a provider of resources for curative and preventive medicine and as a cause of illness. More than this, they have an understanding of the environment, not only in its physical sense, but also in relation to social and spiritual factors. This holistic view of the environment permeates many of the cultural beliefs and customs that impinge on both water use patterns and sanitation behaviour. Some illustrations of these beliefs are given below.

Concepts of Hygiene

Although communities may lack knowledge of modern medical explanations of disease, they often have concepts of what is pure and polluting. Of the water resources available to particular households for domestic purposes, running water may be most acceptable for drinking because it is exposed to the sunlight; it is considered to be "alive" and therefore "pure", while water in shallow wells, which does not have these attributes, is deemed suitable only for washing and cooking. Communities have been observed to use the environmental resources available to them, such as bamboo, to bring fast-flowing river water to their villages in preference to more convenient well water that is unacceptable in taste, colour and smell.

Concepts of clean and dirty, pure and polluting, are well developed in the major world religions, and have a ritual and spiritual significance as well as referring to a physical state. When people are told that new sanitation facilities will make their environment "cleaner", it is their own interpretation of this concept that will be used. "Clean" may have quite different meanings to project promoters and recipients. Thus "it is essential to look into traditional categories of cleanliness and dirtiness, purity and pollution before embarking on a campaign to motivate people to accept a project in improved... sanitation or to change their behaviour to comply with new standards of "cleanliness" (Simpson-Hebert, 1984).

Beliefs about Sanitation and Disease

Evidence of the value attached by communities to cleanliness and, by implication, environmental sanitation is found in studies of diarrhoea. People's perceptions of its causes may be divided into three categories, physical, social and spiritual. In many cases, physical causes are identified and, although the germ theory is not explicitly stated, the faecal oral transmission routes of diarrhoea appear to be understood. Households may associate diarrhoea with a polluted environment including uncovered food, dirty water and flies. Graphic descriptions of pollution have been quoted (de Zoysa et al., 1984):

- "We have to drink the dam water where animals and children bathe and the dirty water makes us ill."
- "Flies sit on dirt which they eat then they come on to uncovered foods and spit on to foods which we eat."

As on-site sanitation involves improving the physical environment, it may therefore be readily accepted as one means by which to reduce the incidence of disease.

Equally, social and spiritual causes are perceived to be important, and include, for example, female social indiscretions and witchcraft. But these three apparently unrelated causes of diarrhoea should not be interpreted as mutually exclusive or divergent approaches to disease. They are often closely interrelated in practice, within a holistic interpretation of the environment.

Efforts should be made to determine how a community's beliefs, knowledge, and control over the environment can be harnessed in a positive way. Careful judgment is required to distinguish between those beliefs and ritual behaviour that are conducive to good sanitation practice and those that need to be changed.

Forces for Change

All societies undergo adjustments in their social structure and culture over time. This may result from contact between societies or from alterations in the physical environment such as prolonged drought. Further, changes in development practice and in international aid influence national goals and priorities with respect to different sectors and regions. How change is brought about and what it is that changes are important issues that need to be addressed. The profound impact of forces for change on diverse societies finds expression in patterns of apparently increasing uniformity between countries and cultures. In demographic terms, these include rapid rates of national population growth, and internal migration of people from rural to urban areas coupled with urban expansion.

Responses to Change

The responses of individuals and groups to urban life, to factory employment or to new technology are a product of the values, experiences and behaviour patterns that they have assimilated over time as members of particular communities and societies. Some groups and individuals are more open to change and more able to adapt to it than others. Decisions are taken to accept or resist an innovation on the basis of characteristics peculiar to the individual, household or group within the context of the local physical, social, economic, cultural and demographic environment.

Access to education may increase awareness of the health benefits of improved sanitation technology, while income will influence the ability of a household to acquire particular facilities. Personal experience and demonstration of alternative technologies may help to convince people that the benefits of the investment will outweigh any costs incurred. Community organisations and influential leaders can assist in marketing the concept by emphasising factors valued locally. These may include the status attached to possessing a facility, or its functional value in terms of comfort. Equally, factors such as rapid increase in population which limits privacy may heighten the perceived need for innovations in sanitation.

People resist change for many reasons. There may be resentment towards outside "experts" who know little of local customs and who are perceived to benefit more from the innovation than local people. Leadership may not be united within a community. For example, those with traditional authority who fear a loss of power and status may oppose innovation strongly supported by political or educated elites. New technologies may be aesthetically unacceptable or conflict with established patterns of personal and social behaviour. Furthermore, households vary widely in the resources of money, labour and time available to them and have their own priorities. For those with limited resources, the costs in the short term of an apparently "low-cost" system may be too great when set against their need for food, shelter and clothing. In addition, in terms of capital investment latrines may be very costly for households if they take a long time to clean, are difficult to use or involve radical changes in social habits (Pacey, 1980). There may also be seasonal variations in the availability of money and labour. Thus the timing of the promotional aspects of a project in relation to, for example, agricultural seasons may be important in determining the local response.

The demographic composition, economic characteristics and attitudes to sanitation of individual households change over time. Experience shows that once people start to improve their houses their interest in latrines is likely to be aroused. Thus some households may be encouraged to install a latrine as one aspect of the modernisation process. Projects should be flexible enough to allow households to invest in on-site sanitation not only when they feel motivated but also when they have the resources to do so. Indeed it may be most appropriate to introduce a range of on-site technologies within a particular community from which households can make a choice according to their own changing needs and priorities.

Terming manual scavenging as "despicable", Lok Sabha Speaker Meira Kumar called on society to cleanse its mindset to get rid of such practices. "The caste system and untouchability in the country has given rise to such practices. Unless the society cleanses its mind of all the ills, no amount of effort can rid us of such practices," she said. The speaker added: "Parliament should also rise to the occasion to meet the expectations of the nation and the house should be allowed to function to conduct its business."

Barrier to Implement Sanitation

Why does 40 per cent of the world's population still have no basic sanitation? Many people do not realise the health benefits to the individual, the community and to society from improving sanitation. The high cost of improving sanitation is often cited as a barrier to implementing sanitation projects. However, to decrease the proportion of people lacking basic sanitation and water supply by 50 per cent worldwide by the year 2015, it is estimated that US$ 23 billion per year would be needed - about US$ 7 billion a year more than is currently spent (WHO, 2000; WHO, 2001b). On a global basis this is truly a small sum of money. Improving sanitation is often low on the list of priorities. There are so many other pressing needs for the attention of governments: food supply, education, medical treatment and dealing with war and conflict. Most people are aware that poor sanitation has a health impact, but there is a lack of awareness of the extent of ill-health that it causes.

Empowering People

There needs to be a political will for - and in investment in - sanitation, and those in need of such services need to exert sufficient pressure to bring about change. WHO's strategy for improving access to sanitation focuses on targeting the highest risk communities. Success depends on:

- identification of the communities at highest risk from diseases related to insanitary conditions;
- giving higher priority to sanitation in national planning for health and investment in infrastructure;
- community involvement in planning, implementing and maintaining the services;
- the development of sanitation technologies suitable for difficult geographical and residential conditions;
- taking into account cultural beliefs and habits;
- sanitation should be integrated with other aspects of development, e.g., hygiene promotion, child survival, maternal and child health, essential drugs, and agricultural development;
- Allowing for long-term ecological and financial sustainability.

The question of who pays for improvements often arises. The set up costs have to be considered: but public investment would lead to substantial returns in the form of better health for these communities and the associated economic benefits for the community and nation as a whole. To offset costs and ensure greater sustainability of sanitation systems, considerable community involvement and self-help are needed (WHO, 1997).

The Cultural Factor: Throw away Societies Versus 'Waste-not-want-not' Societies

People have evolved different ways of thinking and behaving about waste: this affects behaviour and also affects the way messages about health effects or sensible re-use will be received. Human society has developed very different sociocultural responses to the use of untreated excreta. This ranges from deep disgust to practical preference. While determined partly by survival economics, these cultural differences apply to many water poor countries, as well as to water rich areas of the north. For example, in Africa, the Americas and Europe, excreta use is generally regarded as culturally unacceptable, or at best with indifference. This result from the strongly held view that human excreta, especially faeces, are repugnant substances best kept away from the senses of sight and smell. Products fertilised with raw excreta are regarded as tainted or defiled in some way. These views are less rigid in the case of using excreta in compost and sludge for agriculture, but still pose a barrier to use of waste.

In contrast, both human and animal wastes have been used as fertilisers in agriculture and aquaculture in, for example, China, Japan, and Indonesia for thousands of years. Some countries such as China, India and Japan have used wastewater and excreta for irrigation for over 100 years. In China over 1.3 million hectares are irrigated with wastewater. This practice reflects the high social importance of frugality: a waste not, wants not approach. It also relates to a deep ecological, as well as economic, appreciation of the way soil fertility and enrichment with waste is related. In such societies intensive cultivation practices have evolved in response to the need to feed a large number of people with only limited land available. All resources have to be carefully conserved, included excreta. This does not mean that the excreta are always used safely. There can be strong cultural barriers in changing practices to make them safer. For example, excreta are safer if stored long enough for worm (helminth) eggs to be inactivated. Introducing the use of stored rather than fresh excreta is likely to be culturally acceptable: but persuading people not to eat raw fish from contaminated waters is much more difficult. In some cultures, consumption of raw fish is a major element of the diet and it may be hard to persuade them that raw fish pose an increasing hazard, because of rising pollution of marine and freshwaters (Mara and Cairncross, 1989).

Waste as a Resource

Reducing the adverse health effects associated with inadequate management of wastewater, sludge and excreta is possible but takes sustained effort at the individual, community and national levels. Additionally more emphasis must be placed on finding sustainable approaches for reducing health hazards associated with wastewater, sludge and excreta, and at the same time, closing the nutrient cycle from waste to agriculture and aquaculture and protecting limited fresh water sources and the environment.

If waste is to be used safely then:

- Wastewater and excreta need to be treated in such a way as to reduce pathogen concentrations and facilitate the use of nutrients;
- application of wastes should be done safely;
- exposed workers should wear protective clothing;
- wastewater and excreta application to crops should be restricted based on the degree of treatment it receives and the type of crop to be grown (e.g., food eaten raw, food normally cooked or industrial crops);
- Industrial wastes need to be treated separately to avoid contamination of drinking water sources and the environment by toxic chemicals.

Wastewater - and human excreta - is used in many countries and in some places this dates back thousands of years, for example in the cultivation of fish. In urban communities, use of wastewater may supplement an otherwise insufficient water supply (Table 1).

Table 1

Setting for wastewater use	Type of use
Coastal/ river banks	Aquaculture (fish cultivation), aquifer recharge to prevent saline intrusion.
Rural communities	Irrigation, Aquaculture.
Urban	Car washes, toilet flushing, irrigation of recreational areas, and street cleaning

Use of Wastewater and Excreta

The goal of safe wastewater and excreta use is to ensure that wastewater, sludge, and excreta are managed, treated and used so that the adverse health effects are controlled and the water and nutrients can be reclaimed for beneficial use.

Treated municipal sludge has long been used by individuals and communities as a fertiliser and soil amendment. In the United States of America, some wastewater treatment facilities sell treated sludge to farmers and home owners for use as a fertiliser. This activity helps defer some of the cost of wastewater treatment. However, it is important that sludge is treated to a high degree before it is used in this manner. Most of the pathogens and toxic chemicals are concentrated in the sludge. Therefore, sludge is often composted or dried at high temperatures to kill pathogens that might be present. Care also must be taken to reduce the amount of toxic substances that might initially appear in the wastewater. This can often be accomplished by treating industrial wastewater separately from municipal wastewater.

Aquaculture, the cultivation of fish, shellfish, and aquatic plants, has been practiced for thousands of years in many different regions. Fish and plants grown in wastewater and excreta fed ponds still account for a large percentage of the world's aquaculture production. In Calcutta India, for example, 10 - 20 per cent of the region's fish is supplied by a network of wastewater fed fish ponds to the east of the city. In many areas, untreated wastewater and excreta are directly used for pond fertilisation. However, this practice can have adverse human health effects. The use of untreated wastewater or excreta to fertilise fish ponds has been associated with the transmission of many diseases - particularly those caused by trematodes or flukes. Wastewater and excreta should be properly treated before they are used in aquaculture and products grown in this manner should be thoroughly cooked before they are eaten.

In many areas of the world, particularly in water scarce regions, treated wastewater has been used for numerous activities in urban settings including: irrigation of golf courses and public parks, creation of recreational lakes, street cleaning, environmental restoration, car/train washing, fire protection, and for toilet flushing. In many urban areas non-potable uses require larger amounts of water than potable uses. Using properly treated wastewater for these purposes is one way of extending water supplies. This could allow communities to protect high quality water sources, reserving them exclusively as drinking water sources.

Aquifers that supply drinking water may be used faster than they recharge. Moreover, in coastal areas saline intrusion of aquifers occurs as water is withdrawn faster than it can be naturally replaced. Increasing salinity makes water unfit for drinking and other purposes such as irrigation. In several countries where arid conditions exist and advanced wastewater treatment techniques are available, treated wastewater is used to augment ground water, creating a barrier to saline intrusion.

When treated wastewater is used to replenish ground water sources that serve as drinking water sources, important safe guards must be put in place. For example, after conventional secondary treatment, chemicals may be added to the water to help remove particles, the water may be filtered through several different types of filters, it may be processed through a membrane, and may be disinfected at several different stages of the process. Additionally, it is important to monitor the health of the exposed population through epidemiological studies to ensure that no adverse health effects occur because of this wastewater reuse practice. Highly treated wastewater has been safely used to supplement drinking water supplies in Windhoek, Namibia since 1968 (Box 1). The State of California, USA also has safely used highly treated wastewater to augment water supplies in aquifers for nearly 30 years.

Box 1: Use of treated wastewater for drinking water in Namibia

Windhoek, Namibia is located in an arid region characterised by chronic freshwater shortages. In the late 1960's, all available freshwater sources were being used at the maximum rate to supply the city with drinking water. During prolonged droughts, the only alternative water supply the city could turn to was treated wastewater. In 1968, Windhoek became the first city in the world to directly augment its drinking water supplies with treated wastewater.

To ensure the safety of the water supply Windhoek has developed a comprehensive treatment process that relies on primary, secondary and tertiary treatments. It also includes extensive chemical, bacteriological, virological and epidemiological monitoring. Potentially toxic industrial wastewater is prevented from entering the municipal waste stream and is treated separately (Haarhoff and van der Merwe, 1995).

Since 1973, epidemiological studies of Windhoek residents have shown no adverse health effects associated with drinking reclaimed wastewater (National Research Council, 1998).

The Role of WHO

The use of waste and wastewater has to be carefully controlled to prevent risks to health. In 1989, following extensive collaborative activity with the World Bank and others, WHO with UNEP published Guidelines for the Safe Use of Wastewater and Excreta in Agriculture and Aquaculture. These guidelines outline the health basis for guideline derivation and describe the practices necessary to protect public health. Other WHO reports relevant to sanitation include the Technical Report Control of Foodborne Trematode Infections (1995) and the Technical Report Food Safety Issues Associated with Products from Aquaculture published in conjunction with the Food and Agriculture Organisation of the United Nations and the Network of Aquaculture Centres in Asia - Pacific. WHO is supporting UNEPs "Global Plan of Action" for the protection of the marine environment against land-based sources of pollution through the coordination of the "Sanitation Connection" web-based resource (Box 6) as a mechanism to increase access to information on sanitation in general and sewage in particular. The WHO has also made prevention of trachoma a priority, through its worldwide campaign to eliminate the causes of preventable blindness.

Sanitation Connection

Sanitation Connection is an internet-based resource intended to facilitate access to information on sanitation. The site brings together a number of ongoing initiatives in sanitation information management, to ensure that the best information is widely available, and brings together important institutions working in sanitation into a single wide-reaching information initiative. Sanitation Connection functions as a virtual partnership with a range of sector players taking responsibility for the provision and maintenance of state-of-the-art information on selected issues. Sanitation Connection is administered by a core group of partners and coordinated by WHO.

The core Sanitation Connection Partners include, the Water and Sanitation Program for South Asia (World Bank), the International Water Association, the Global Programme of Action for the Protection of the Marine Environment from Land-based Activities (GPA) of the United Nations Environment Programme, the Water Supply and Sanitation Collaborative Council, and the World Health Organisation (For more information please visit Sanitation Connection at http://www.sanicon.net)

Campaigns

Things are getting better in the villages, however slowly. Only 40 per cent had access to sanitation facilities in 2002. This increased to 51 per cent in 2008-009. More than 60 per cent of homes in Bihar, Jharkhand, Madhya Pradesh, Orissa, Rajasthan, Tamil Nadu and Uttarakhand states were still without toilets. There are other interesting behavioural and cultural pointers: Sikh and Christian households had the highest - over 70 per cent - access to improved sanitation. Hindus - at 45 per cent - had the least access [Biswas, Soutik (Delhi Correspondent of BBC News in India):2012].

India provides subsidies to construct toilets and runs sanitation and hygiene campaigns. Federal spending on sanitation was increased nearly three-fold in 2005. In 2003, the government kicked off a scheme to award village councils which are able to eliminate open defecation. Kerala has been the best performer with 87 per cent of its village councils picking up the award. Only 2 per cent of councils in dirt-poor Bihar won in a dismal commentary on the state of its sanitation.

India could take the lead from the tiny states of Himachal Pradesh and Haryana. Both have used and empowered local people to tackle open defecation, build toilets and adopt good waste management. Haryana provides subsidies to poor households to build toilets, and enlists women to run campaigns in what is a largely patriarchal and less progressive state.

Volunteers visit homes, encouraging people to build toilets. All homes in Himachal Pradesh have a toilet today, say government surveys. The plan is to get rid of open defecation by the end of this year. But until the time its people get rid of curious - and skewed - cultural attitudes to community sanitation and hygiene, India will never have enough toilets.

References

Baum, F. (1995), "Researching Public Health: Behind the Qualitative Quantitative Methodological Debate", *Social Science and Medicine,* 40(4), 459-62

Berman, P et al. (1994), "The Household Production of Health: Integrating Social Science Perspective on Micro-level Health Determinants", *Social Science and Medicine,* 38, 2, 205-215.

Biswas, Soutik (Delhi Correspondent of BBC News in India (2012): *'Is India's lack of toilets a cultural problem?'* 16 March 2012.

Burkert, W. (1992), *The Orientalising Revolution: Near Eastern Influence on Greek Culture in the Early Archaic Age,* Cambridge USA: Harvard University Press.

Cairncross, C. et al. (1996), "The Public and Domestic Domains in the Transmission of Disease", *Tropical Medicine and International Health,* 1, 27-34.

Carey, J.W. (1998), "Linking Qualitative and Quantitative Methods: Integrating Cultural Factors into Public Health", *Qualitative Health Research,* 3(3), 298-318.

Curtis, Valerie (1998), *The Dangers of Dirt: Household Hygiene and Health,* Wageningen: Grafish Service Centrum.

Curtis, Valerie, S.Cairncross and R.Yonli (2000), "Domestic Hygiene and Diarrhoea, Pinpointing the Problem", *Tropical Medicine and International Health,* 5: 22-32.

Curtis, Valerie and S.Cairncross (2003), "Effect of Washing Hands with Soap on Diarrhoea Risk in the Community: A Systematic Review", *The Lancet Infectious Diseases,* 3: 275-281.

DeSwaan A. (1988), *In care of the State: Health Care, education and Welfare in Europe and the USA in Europe and USA in Modern Era,* Oxford: OUP.

Dongre, A.R. et al., (2007), "An Approach to Hygiene Education Among Rural Indian School Going Children", *Online Journal of Health and Allied Sciences,* Vol.6, 4, Oct-Dec.

Douglas, M. (1966), *Purity and Danger: An Analysis of Concepts of Pollution and Taboo,* London: Ark

Dumont, L. (1980), *Homo Heirachicus: The Caste System and Its Implications,* Complete revised English edition, Chicago: University of Chicago press (First published in 1966).

Gleick, Peter H. (2002), "Estimated Deaths from Water-related Diseases 2000-2020". *Pacific Institute Research Report,* Pacific Institute for Studies in Development, Environment and Society.

Goering, P ad D.L.Streiner, Reconcilable Differences: The Marriage between Qualitative and Quantitative Methods", *Canadian Journal of Psychiatry,* 41, 491-497.

http://www.sanicon.net

Hasan, K.A. (1979), *Medical Sociology in Rural India,* Ajmer: Sachin Publications.

McLaughlin, T. (1971), *A Social History as Seen Through the Uses and Abuses of Dirt,* Dorset Press.

Mukhopadhyay, Prianka et al., (2012), "Identifying Key Risk Behaviours Regarding Personal Hygiene and Food Supply Practices of Food Handlers Working in Eating Establishments Located within a Hospital campus in Kolkata", *Al Ameen Journal of Medical Science,* 5 (1): 21:28.

Nagla, Madhu.(2015) Social Construction of Hygiene and Sanitation in Haryana, *in Bindeshwar Pathak (ed). Sociology of sanitation, Delhi kalpaz publication.*

Nakkash, R. et al., (2002), "The Development of a Feasible Community-Specific Cardiovascular Disease Prevention Programme: Triangulation of Methods and Sources", *Health Education and Behaviour,* 10, 405-421.

Nichter, M. et al., (2002), "Using Qualitative Research to Inform Survey Development on Nicotine Dependence Among Adolescents", *Drug and Alcohol Dependence,* 68, S41-S56.

Palnitkar, Sneha (1988). *New Culture of Urban Sanitation* (CORO), Th, e Mega-Cities Project, Publication MCP018F *Mumbai (Bombay), India,*

Pickstone, J.V. (1992), "Dirt, Dearth and Fever Epidemics: Rewriting the History of British Public Health, 1780-1850", in T Ranger and P.Slack (eds.), Epidemics *and Ideas: Essays on the Historical Perception of Pestilence,* Cambridge: Cambridge University Press.

Reddy, B. Suireh and M. Snehlata (2011), "Sanitation and Personal Hygiene: What does it mean to Poor and Vulnerable Women?" *Indian Journal of Gender Studies,* Vol. 18, No. 3, pp. 381-404.

Report on Environmental Sanitation in Rural India (1957), Government of India: Ministry of Health.

Roberts, et al., (2002), "Factors Effecting uptake of Childhood Immunisation: A Bayesian Synthesis of Qualitative and Quantitative Evidence", *The Lancet*, 360 (9345), 1596-1599.

World Health Organisation (2000), Global Water Supply and Sanitation Assessment 2000 Report, Geneva.

5

Social Structure and Sanitation

Along with the concept of culture, social structure is a crucial defining concept for sociology as a way of thinking about social life. Hence, social structure determines the nature of individual which develops through socialisation process of different social institutions like marriage, family, caste etc. They form cultural beliefs and practices. We have already discussed social structure, cultural beliefs and practices in the fourth chapter on culture of sanitation of this book. In this chapter, first we would like to discuss the social institutions like family, marriage, caste etc. Taking the ideas from the formation of these institutions, we would analyse the following things to understand the social structure and sanitation:

1. Practice of Scavenging
2. Caste and class of scavengers – Origin, nature and functions, socio-economic conditions, historical deprivation, social and religious disabilities, contemporary Scenario.
3. Gender and sanitation – Health, hygiene, education and employment, gender equality
4. Children and sanitation – Health and Hygiene

I
Practice of Scavenging

Who is Scavenger?

Scavenger is one who is partially or wholly engaged in the

obnoxious of manually removing night soil and filth. The dependents of a scavenger is one who is a member of his family or is dependent on him irrespective of the fact whether he is partially or wholly engaged in the said occupation. The scavenger community is distributed all over the country. Here, I enumerate the description of scavengers which I inferred from my article on, Scavenging and Scavengers in the State of Haryana' (Nagla: 2011).

The scavengers in Haryana are also called valmiki/Balmiki, Chuhra, Bhangi, Lalbegi, and Khaqrobe. Chaudhary and jamadar are two titles of this community; the latter is normally used for the working class. Locally, they are called Chuhra. They claim to be the descendants of Saint Balmiki. One of the Chuhra *Gurus,* is another name for Bal Mik, a hunter of the Karnal district, who was converted by a holy Rishi, and eventually who wrote the epic Ramayana. The Rishi wished to prescribe penance, but reflected that so vile a man would not able to say RAM RAM. So, he set him to say MRA MRA which, if you say it fast enough, comes to much the same thing. Their other Guru (teacher) is Lalbeg and it is after this guru that they are also called Lalbegi; and they still call their priests Lalgurus (Ibbetson: 1974:294).

Scavenger Castes

On the basis of census data, Risley, the Commissioner for 1901 Census, classified castes into seven main categories according to their social standing and ranked the Jatis in the local hierarchy and varna affiliation of each. The scavenging castes which were known by different names in different States like Bhangi, Balmiki, Chuhra, Mehtar, Mazhabi, Lal Begi, Halalkhor etc. in northern India; Har, Hadi, Hela, Dom and Sanei etc. in eastern India;Mukhiyar, Thoti, Chachati,Pakay, Relli etc. in Southern India ;and Mehtar, Bhangias, Halalkhor, Ghasi, Olgana, Zadmalli, Barvashia, Metariya, Jamphoda and Mela etc. in Western and Central India,also made an effort to get united and have a common name. In 1911 census some of them started returning as Adi Dharmi, Adi Dravida, Adi Karnataka and Adi Andhran (Srivastava:1997:178).

Ibbetson (1974) included Chuhra, Dhanak, and Khatik in the scavenger castes. These castes are numerically and economically one of the most important in the province. For the Chuhras do the Jat, Rajput, and Brahman exceed the only in number, while they occupy a very prominent position among the agricultural labourers of the Punjab? But socially they are the lowest of the low, even lower perhaps than the vagrant Sansi and the gypsy Nat, and as a rule can hardly be said to stand even at the foot of the social ladder, though some sections of the clan have mounted the first one or two steps. Their hereditary occupation is scavenging, sweeping the houses and streets, working up, carrying to the fields, and distributing manure, and in cities and in village houses where the women are strictly secluded, removing night soil. They alone of all classes keep those impure animals, pigs and fowls; and they and the leather-workers alone eat the flesh of animals that have died of disease or by natural death. Together with the vagrants and gypsies they are the hereditary workers in grass and reeds, from which they make winnowing pans and other articles used in agriculture; and like them they eat jackals, lizards, tortoises, and pigs. Many of them have abandoned scavenging and taken to leatherwork and even to weaving, and by doing so have mounted one or two steps in the social grades, as in the later case they pass over the leather-workers. But to secure the full benefit of this change of occupation they must relinquish the habit of eating carrion.

Bhangi

The term Bhangi has been derived from the Sanskrit word bhangi meaning hemp; it seems to be an illusion to their drinking habits. The Bhangi was described as a representative of the Chandala of manu, who is said to heve descended from the union of Sudra and a Brahman woman. The Bahngi were traditionally associated with scavenging, sweeping, basket making, etc. In the colonial period they were brought into urban areas to perform the first two roles and became an urban community. With the widespread use of septic latrines and other modes of public conveniences, the practice of carrying head load of night soil has perceptibly declined now in many parts of urban India. The national Scheme of Liberation and Rehabilitation of Scavengers and their Dependants (1991-92) seeks to liberate them from their existing 'hereditary obnoxious and inhuman occupations of manually removing night soil and filth' and to provide for and engage them in 'alternative and dignified occupations' over a period of five years. (Annual Report 1991-92, Ministry of Welfare, Government of India, New Delhi). The Bhangi have now taken to other occupations as well.

Chura

The Chura or Bhangi of Hindustani is the sweeper and scavenger *par excellence* of the united Punjab and the present Haryana, is found throughout the province. They are also called Churha, Chruhe, Bhangi, and Khakrobe. The major occupation of the Churhas is the removal of dead animals and night soil and scavenging. Of late, some of them have acquired land and taken to agriculture. A few of them are engaged in sharecropping. Traditionally, the Chuhra are linked with other communities through economic relationships. They used to receive polluted clothes at the time of birth or death and on ceremonial or ritual occasions like the solar and lunar eclipse. They are also given leftover food while seeking alms. They accept both kachcha and pucca food from other communities, but no other community accepts any food from them. In urban centres there are no restrictions on the sharing of common water sources. The Chuhras' attitude towards various development programmes is positive. They avail of educational and medical facilities.

Lalbegi

Lalbegi is a class of Mohammedan sweepers supposed to have come from upper India, some with sepoy regiments, others as wanderers in search of work. Though styled Mohammedans, they neither practise circumcision nor abstain from pork. The Lalbegi are employed as sweepers in European households, and are always addressed as *jamadar* by the other servants.

They eat the leavings of Europeans, and drink any sort of wine or spirits. They will not, however, eat with the Raut, who in their turn pride themselves on abstaining from food that has come from a European table. Nor will they touch a dead body. The religious rites of the Lalbegi are partly Hindu, partly Muhammadan. As with Mussulmen generally, marriages are arranged by an old woman who acts as matchmaker. No *cabin* or marriage settlement is drawn up, but an *ikrair* or bond is executed, in which both promise to love one another, and in the bridegroom undertakes not to bring a second wife into his house. Previous to the wedding day the Khanduri ceremony is observed, as well as other Muhammadan customs, but the services of the *Acharji* Brahman are not required. Should the marriage be celebrated in the bridegroom's house, a fee of twenty annas is paid to the panchayat; if in the bride's only five annas.

A few of the Lalbegi keep the fast of Ramazan, although they dare not enter a public mosque. Their funeral ceremonies are peculiar. The dead may not be buried in Mussulmen cemetery, but are consigned to the ground in some waste and jungly spot. The corpse is wrapped in five shrouds, a handkerchief is placed under each arm and in each hand, a *kasawa* or napkin is bound round the head and a *khirqa* or blouse is put on the body. After the grave has been filled in, a cloth cover (*phul ka chadar*) is laid over it, while four pieces of "Agar" wood are inserted at the corners and set fire to. The rest of the funeral ceremonies are strictly Mohammedan. For four days after a death a fire is not allowed to be lighted in the dwelling-house of the deceased, the family in the meantime receiving food from their neighbours; but on the fifth day a tray laden with betel-nuts and adorned with flowers is placed in front of the hut, and a feast is given to the whole tribe.

The Lalbegis follow many Hindu customs, observing the Diwali and the Holi as the greatest festivals of the year. On this occasion a mud image of a mosque with five domes is made, supposed to be a model of one still existing at Ghazni, in Kabul, which belonged to lal beg, the eponymous ancestor of the tribe. In front of the image a cook is sacrificed, and offerings of *pilao, sherbet* and sweetmeats, are made in his name. Lal Beg is identified by Sir H.Elliot (supplemental Glossary, I, 32) with Lal Guru, the same as the Raksha Aronakarat; but in Benares (Sherring, Hindu Tribes of Benares, p.397) he is confounded with Pir Zahr, perhaps the famous Chishtiya saint sayyid Shah Zuhur. In the Punjab, again, Mihtars adore Lal Pir or Baba Faqir, as the dyers do Pir Ali Rangrez, and the blacksmiths Hazrat Daud. It seems not only improbable, therefore, that the Lalbegi, like many other tribes converted to Mohammedanism, have adopted a Mohammedan saint as their common ancestor (Risley: 1981:3-4).

Thus, the word lalbegi is derived from lalbeg, 'the eponymous ancestor of the tribe' (Risley, 1891). Their surnames are begi and balmiki. They are found in Bihar, Uttar Pradesh, Arunachal Pradesh, Delhi, Meghalaya and Mizoram. The Lalbegi are landless. Most men, women and grown-up children work in municipalities as sweepers. Their oral traditions recall that they were earlier balmiki, but after taking initiation from Saint Kabir, have become Lalbegis. They also claim that their original homeland was Rajasthan.

The scavengers earn their livelihood by scavenging working in the fields and at the construction sites. They are also engaged in animal husbandry, poultry, and piggery. A few of them have land. The community's traditional primary occupation is scavenging including removal of night soil from the houses and offices. Their secondary occupations include manual work, playing the band, petty trade, hawking, vending of fruit and vegetables, selling of meat and eggs. Some also own small tea stalls and restaurants. They depend on the local market for their day-to-day needs. In towns and cities they transact business in cash, but in villages, there is the barter system. However, now in the villages of Haryana, we do not find scavenging work. Some families engage scavenger for the care of animals. In small towns, Brahmin, Baniya, Punjabi (ethnic community) employs some persons for scavenging work. In the old areas of the cities, we still find pit latrines in the houses where scavengers are employed by paying RS.20 per month for cleaning the latrine from the pit. They carry human excreta on their heads and throw at the garbage centre where corporation will come to carry away excrement.

Scavengers are mostly landless, hence work as labourers in agriculture, plantation and industries. Many of them have to try their luck with the old traditional low yielding occupations such as leather work, flaying dead cattle, scavenging, weaving, dyeing, bamboo craft, fishery, wild herbs and fruit gathering. These occupations, being in the unorganised sector, require more labour, full day's work and the total employment of the family with low returns. Their social status is considered low because of the involvement in disagreeable unclean work. Children below the age of 15 years also do the scavenging work. They get their payment in cash or kind.

Working Hours and Payment Pattern

Working hours of scavengers vary in formal and informal organisation. They work 8 hours in formal organisations like in Municipal committee, hospitals, schools, colleges, universities, banks and other Government jobs. Generally females do scavenging of roads and males clean gutters as assigned by the municipalities. They work 6.00 to 11.00 AM in the morning and 2.00 to 5.00 PM in the evening. Normally, they get RS. 3,000 to 4,000 per month salary in the formal organisations. The scale of a Safai-worker is equivalent to the class IV employee i.e. RS. 2,550-55-2650-EB (efficiency bar)-60-3200 in municipality and other government organisations. However, everyone gets DA (40 per cent of the basic pay), medical allowance, HRA (house rent allowance), Conveyance allowance, CCA (city compensatory allowance), uniform and washing allowance along with the basic pay. In the unorganised sector, they work generally from 7.00 to 11.00 AM and in exceptional situation they work up to 4.00 PM as reported by the sweeper respondents. They visit 30-40 houses daily for cleaning the flush and sweeping work in the household.

Tools of Trade: Scavenging-related Tensions

Their tools of scavenging occupation are broom (small and big), mops (duster on big stick), bamboo basket, shallow pan, shovel, ash etc. There is no problem for getting jobs for scavengers. 95 per cent scavengers are either in private or public jobs. There is no competition of their work from other communities. Traditionally this occupation is meant for them because of Hindu social order. For example, something wrong in the safety tank or sewerage, it will be repaired by the scavengers only. Therefore, they have always private earnings. Moreover, all the members of the family are engaged in the work. Nevertheless, they quarrel each other with their own community members sometimes taking the division of area claiming that these are my households. I have been working in these houses from long time so that others cannot do even sometime household wants to change the person. There will be quarrels for such matters.

Generally Women scavengers do household work. They take help of daughters in scavenging because ultimately daughters have to do same work. Earlier, women scavengers used to do only scavenging work in the household. Now they do other work like cleaning the utensils, cloths etc. They do not have any type of leave. There is no rest. Thus, they work every day. They do work even they are ill. They have fear to lose their work if they are not regular. They are threatened by their owners that they (owners) would do work themselves if they (scavengers) were not regular. This is a major tensions related to the scavenging. On the contrary, owners generally complaint that women scavengers miss their work 4-8 days' work in a month in various types of pretences. They give them kinds occasionally also besides monthly fixed payment in cash. Scavengers quarrel sometime with their household employer for timely payment or when they do not get suitable gifts as desired by them on certain occasions particularly on marriage, birth of a child or something extra on festivals like Holi Diwali etc.

Women have a role in agricultural operations, scavenging and in social, religious and political spheres. Their traditional occupation is scavenging. They are also engaged in labour work of various types. Some of them are engaged in animal husbandry, poultry, piggery, playing musical instruments in a concert, vending fruits, vegetables, meat eggs, etc.

According to the 1981 Census 29.37 per cent is returned as workers (48.62 per cent males and 7.69 per cent females). Of them, 56.63 per cent are returned as agricultural labourers and only 3.10 per cent are cultivators; 3.40 per cent of the workers are engaged in livestock, etc.; 23.20 per cent in "other services" which indicates their traditional occupation of scavenging; the remaining 13.67 per cent workers are engaged in household or other-than-household industries, construction, trade and commerce, etc.

However, this community has few entrepreneurs, scholars or creative artists or administrators. Some members of the community work as teachers, engineers, and doctors. Some have white-collar jobs. Some members also serve in defence, police and railway services. Political leadership has emerged at the village level only. Cultivator labour relationship does exist and so does the employer-worker relationship.

Life-Styles of Scavengers:

Habitat and Civic Amenities

Scavengers live in Kachha-Pucca houses but not in slums. Drinking water is available in their localities. They have tap water, hand pumps and wells. Cinema, radio, television facilities are available. Road, water and electricity facilities are also available for them. Every house has electricity but not tap water. They get water from community hand pump or community pipeline. They also fetch water from community wells. They use firewood/fuel wood, dung-cakes, coal, and kerosene oil and liquefied petroleum gas for cooking. They also use organic manure. They make use of chemical fertilisers and insecticides. Integrated Child Development Schemes are available and facilities of public distribution system exist. They get sugar, kerosene, rice and coarse cloth through the fair price shops. However, scavengers complaint that they do not have facilities likes general population except reservations in jobs.

Social Inter-mixing

Caste Hindus do not accept water from the scavengers. Many scheduled caste communities accept water from the scavengers if they good personal equations. Similarly, *kachcha* or *pucca* food is not accepted from them. They accept sidha food from all the community except sikligars and dehas. Putative kinship-based relationship exists. They share wells with *Chamar* and the *Dhanak*. Road facilities are shared with other and so are railways, schools and cremation grounds. But sometime they also have their separate cremation grounds. They share *panchayat ghars* (community halls) with all other communities. *Jajmani* system has been reported to exist. Community members working as scavengers in some areas get one and a half or two quintals of cereal and some cash biannually.

Food-Habits and Use of Intoxicants

The community members eat non-vegetarian food almost regularly. They eat pork, chicken, fish and mutton. They consume wheat, rice, jowar (minor millet), bajra, maize, and barley. They prefer roti to rice. Among pulses, they eat gram, urad (black gram), moong (green gram), peas, moth (lentil), arhar (red gram). Ghee or mustard oil is used for cooking purposes. Among the scavengers, onion, garlic and egg-eaters are considered vegetarians. They consume all seasonal vegetables and fruit. They are fond of cane sugar juice, tea, milk, coffee, and fruit juice and milk products. They are equally fond of alcoholic drinks, even though liquor is considered a vice. They buy liquor from the local market.

They beat their wives after drinking and ask more money from their wives for drinking. Hence, a large number of wives beating cases are found among scavengers. Females go outside the house for doing work and males start playing cards most of the time in the temple where police does not go. Therefore, they have a vice of gambling. They do quarrel each other for very small issues. For example, one claims: "I drink more than you; I have a bigger house than you." Many of them are also drug addicts. They eat meat of pigs, which is not considered as a good food. Generally, there are a people saying that as you eat food, as you will have heart and mind. Children do learn such habits in the association of parents.

Social Milieu

They are Hindus. They have separate Balmiki temples. They accept food from all the communities, though very often it is not reciprocated. They share wells and crematoria with the Chamar, Dhanuk, etc. They utilise modern Medicare, family planning and rural employment programmes.

Customs and Rituals

Scavengers are Hindus in Haryana. They have village and regional deities in common with others. The Balmikis share major sacred centres and centres for pilgrimage with other Hindu communities. Besides, they have their separate temples- the Balmikis temples. They are also staunch believers of Mata Masani. This deity can be worshipped anywhere, but is normally put up at some crossing. There are also holy men in this community. Some of them have opened ashrams (hermitage). One such ashram is at Modinagar in Uttar pradesh. Sacred specialists are also exorcists. They perform pooja (worship) and preach on religion. They also perform birth, marriage and death rituals. There is another ashram at Rohtak. This is called "Sadanath kA Dera". Bhajan-kirtans (religious songs) are sung and arranged here. With its income schools are being run. The gaddi (enthrone) system is followed. Disciples inherit the gaddi.

They celebrate all festivals of the Hindus and have fairs in common with them. They celebrate Balmiki's birthday with great zeal. Festivals are of economic, social and religious importance.

Their old traditions are similar to those of other communities. Both men and women sing folksongs. Folktales are also recited but only few remember them. The common musical instruments are damroo, dhol, dholak, ek tara, harmonium, banjo, chimta, khartal. Both sexes take part in dance. The scavengers speak the Haryanvi dialect in different parts of the state, at their homes and with other communities. They also speak Hindi with other communities. The community members wear the common attrie of the state; that is, men wear dhoti-kurta or kurta-pyjama and khes (blanket) in winter. Elderly men also wear a turban. Women wear lehnga, kurta and odhni the young wear salwar-kameez and chunni.

Marriage

Small social divisions in the form of gotra have been reported. The exact number of Balmiki gotras is not available, but there are about two dozen such as Pihwal, Dugalgach, Tank Saudde, Baid Marholia, Tanwar, Chauhan, Pathak, Rajput Chauhan, Jingalia, Panche, Kunjinwal, Gaichand, Bagdi, Lohat, Luchare, Lohaye, Chandalia, Athwal, Khekhra, and Bhooranda.

Marriage rituals are performed at the bride's and bridegroom's residences. The bride's parents give a feast. Marriage is consummated at the house of bridegroom. They generally marry by *phera.* Marriage between the same gotra is prohibited. One cannot marry within one's mother's or paternal grandmother's gotras. The community has a number of exogamous clans (gotras) like Pihwal, Tonk, Baid, Tanwar, Jingalia, Chindalia, etc. Their clan names, which are also used as surnames have undergone a change: e.g. Dugalgach to Duggalm, Chanwaria to Chawla, Sudde to Sood, Chandalia to Chaddha, Pihwal to panwar, etc.

Some scavenger community members consider themselves inferior to other Hindu communities, while affluent ones consider themselves of equal status. They do not recognise the Varna system, because they think that it leads to "untouchability". They also do not consider their place in the Sudra category.

The scavengers are an endogamous community having village and gotra exogamy. In cities and towns, they marry in different mohallas (localities). Dewar-bhabhi (husband's younger brother and elder brother's wife) and jija-sali (sister's husband and wife's sister) can marry. Jeth (husband's elder brother) may also keep his younger brother's wife after her husband's death or on his becoming invalid. One may also marry wife's elder sister, if she is a widow and gives her consent. There are few child marriages.

Adult and negotiated marriage is the norm. The normal marriage age for the boy is 20 years and for the girls is 18 years. The boy and the girl do not meet each other before marriage. Monogamy is the rule but there are certain exceptions. Sindur, cosmetics and glass bangles are considered marriage symbols. Bride price was prevalent about 40-50 years ago, but now it has almost vanished. If anyone is found accepting a bride price, he/she is excommunicated. Bride price has yielded to dowry, which is both in cash and kind and according to the bride's parent's capacity. Patrilocal form of residence is practised. Frequency of divorce is very low. Mostly it is the biradari panchayat that deals with the cases of divorce. It is always in writing. Sometimes a marriage is dissolved through judicial approval and in such cases compensation/alimony to the wife is decided by the court of the law. When a marriage is dissolved with the intervention of biradari panchayat the divorcing husband has to return the dowry to his wife. Both husband and wife can divorce. Children are the father's responsibility, but small children can live with their mother. Common grounds of divorce are adultery, impotency, and maladjustment. The widow or widower can remarry. A widow can undergo phera ceremony again. Such pheras are called punna pheras and these consist of two and a half pheras. Men or women who are divorced can also get remarried. The marriage age has increased and marriage symbols are observed strictly. Adult and negotiated marriages are in vogue. Levirate and sororate are permitted. Divorce is permitted on grounds of adultery, maladjustment and impotency. Sometimes two and a half rounds around the sacred fire (punna pheras) perform the remarriage of a widow.

Family

Among the scavengers extended families still exists, but they are breaking into nuclear ones. Usually, relations between family members are cordial, but sometimes conflict and confrontations do arise. These are on account of property, check on the freedom of youngsters and challenge to the authority of elders. It can also be due to lack of adjustment on the part of the daughters-in-law. Conflicts and confrontations are resolved through a familial compromise, or biradari panchayat, failing which the parties seek redress with the court of law. They rarely go to court. Daughters do not take a share in the property of their father, in spite of the provisions in the existing law of the state. Even in the absence of brothers, they may leave their share in the ancestral property to their cousin and nephew, who in turn discharge their social obligations towards their cousins. The eldest son succeeds as head of the family on the death of the father. Inter-family linkages are strong as much as they cooperate with each other in happy times as also in adversities.

Status of women

They claim to give equal status to women. Women have an important role in agricultural operations. They have a role in such social functions; rituals/religious spheres political activities such as lecturing and canvassing in election days. The women bring potable water and collect fuel and fodder. Some women also contribute to the family income by way of doing scavenging work.

II
Caste System

India's caste system is a unique method of social ordering dividing society into high-caste and low-caste people on the basis of birth. The persons belonging to lower caste occupying a very lowly position in society are socially, economically, educationally and culturally backward. They had been subjected to various discriminations and disabilities resulting in their dehumanisation and degradation. India's constitution came as a redeemer to the socially excluded sections of the society, declaring prohibition of untouchability and has led to enactment of laws relating to several affirmative action programmes to bring the low caste people (scheduled castes and scheduled tribes) into the mainstream of society by initiating policies and programmes for their economic, social and political up-gradation, welfare, development and empowerment, with the result, that profound changes are taking place in the hereditary caste system and its pernicious practices that have led to the disability and degradation of such people. Today, the old discriminations and disabilities of the untouchables do not have social approval, nor do they have the old oppressive strangle-hold. Many profound social, economic, and technological changes have weakened the caste system to a great extent and there is much greater social intercourse amongst different caste groups.

However, there still remains a class of persons belonging to the scavenging castes, who were traditionally ordained in Indian society to clean and carry human waste. Their appalling hardship, humiliation and savage exploitation have to parallel in human history. Living in the filthiest of surroundings under most trying circumstances, scavengers are hated even by those whose excreta they carry on their heads. Reduced to the depth of degradation as untouchables and forced to lead a sub-human existence, they are the worst victims of a cruel caste-based social order. Their story is the sordid story of utmost violation of human rights. Their heart rending plight stretching over centuries is a blot on India's person to take up the scavengers' cause as he was deeply moved by their plight, in his lifetime, though, he could not succeed in making India a scavenging-free country.(See, New Princes of Alwar:2009:xxii)

Caste and Class of Scavengers

In their study on, "Manual Scavenging as Social exclusion: A Case Study", Singh and Ziyauddin (2000) viewed that caste based occupational groups in India, like that of manual scavengers, constitute one group which is socially, economically, psychologically and politically marginalised section of the society. Although manual scavenging was banned twice (in1952 and 1993), this practice still continues in various pockets of the country under different names. Manual scavengers in India, who are caste-based occupational groups, constitute one such excluded class.

The evil of manual scavenging is directly related to the lack of availability of sanitation facilities. Like food, clothing and shelter, proper sanitation is one of the basic requirements of mankind. Poor sanitary conditions lead to water-borne diseases like diarrhoea, dysentery, etc. While the lack of sanitation facilities affects all individuals, children and women are particularly vulnerable. As per the World Health report, 1999, only 49 per cent of the urban population (in 1997), and merely 14 per cent of the rural population (in 2000) have adequate facility for excreta disposal. The problem is more conspicuous in developing countries like India, where manual removal of human excreta, defecating in the open place etc. exists.

Manual scavenging is the removal of excreta (nigh soil) manually from "dry toilets", i.e. the toilets without modern flush system. The system of building public toilets and employing people to remove excreta was introduced during British rule in India, when municipalities were constituted. That time, often containers were used in such toilets that needed to be emptied daily. After the invention of flush type toilets, all other types of toilets disappeared from the western world. However, this inhumane practice continues in many developing countries including India.

In India, manual scavenging is a caste-based occupation carried out by dalits. The manual scavengers have different names in different parts of the country: Bhangis in Gujarat, Rajasthan and Uttar Pradesh, Phakis in Andhra Pradesh and Sikkaliars in Tamil Nadu. These communities are invariably placed at the bottom of the caste hierarchy as well as dalit sub-caste hierarchy. Refusal to perform such manual task leads to physical abuse and a social boycott. Manual scavengers are exposed to the most virulent forms of viral and bacterial infections that affect their skin, eyes, limbs, respiratory and gastro-intestinal systems. Tuberculosis is rife in the community. A 2002 report prepared by the International Dalit Solidarity Network (Including Human Rights Watch US), Navserjan (Ahmadabad, Gujarat) and the National Campaign on Dalit Human Rights (NCDHR) estimates the number of Dalit manual scavengers at one million.

A random survey conducted by Action Aid in 2002 in six States- Madhya Pradesh, Andhra Pradesh, Orissa, Uttar Pradesh, Rajasthan and Bihar- claimed that manual scavengers were found working on at least 30,000 dry toilets. The survey also pointed out that, these scavengers face severe discrimination even from other dalits. The National Commission for Safai Karmchari, a statutory body, has pointed out in its reports that the use of dry latrines and continuing employment of manual scavengers by various departments of the government of India, particularly in the departments like the railways, defence and ministry of industry. The Employment and Manual Scavengers and Construction of Latrines (Prohibitions) Act, 1993 punishes the employment of scavengers or construction of dry non-flushed latrines with imprisonment for up to one year and or the fine of Rs. 2,000. Offenders are also liable to prosecution under the Scheduled Castes and Scheduled Tribes (Prevention of Aristocracies) Act, 1989. Given the high prevalence of the illegal practice, the government of India launched a national scheme in 1992 for identifying, training and rehabilitating Safai Karmchari and allotted substantial funds for this purpose.

The Rajiv Gandhi Mission for sanitation and Water Supply Scheme introduced by the Ministry of Rural Development aims at converting dry latrines into wet water-borne sanitary latrines and rehabilitating the liberated scavengers in alternative occupations. However, it has been noticed that, even though scavengers are trained and assisted for taking up alternative occupations, some of them again come back to manual scavenging.

Causes for continuing the Work of Scavenging

- Scavenging does not require any skill and provides some additional income with no competition, investment and risk. These features couples with the need for cleaning dry latrines and a lack of alternatives force the scavengers, particularly women, to continue in this occupation. It has also been found that I certain cases, scavengers also face a difficulty in taking up other occupations like running shops due to the prevailing social prejudices.

Causes and Consequences of Manual Scavenging

Singh and Ziyauddin (2009) have analysed the causes and consequences of manual scavenging in Ghazipur district of Uttar Pradesh. The study is based on the pilot survey that was conducted from July to September 2007 with the help of local NGO the community Development Society. The study found that scavenger system was closely associated with the caste and religious structure of society. Nearly all scavengers belonged to Mehtar caste, which is on the lowest rung of the social hierarchy. The houses of these scavengers situated outside the main residential area and they dwell in very poor and unhygienic conditions. They are not allowed to dine and interact with the people of higher caste. The prevalence of alcoholism and drug addiction is very high among the Mehtar community. This results in most of the scavengers being involved in this practice as women; have also to play the part of the bread-earner. However, in some cases this occupation was carried forward by the next generation as their parents or forefathers do not want to lose their patrons. The tendency of hiring manual scavengers is more prevalent among the middle class Muslim. This is because of the evil of purdah system apart from the absence of modern flush system toilets. It is shocking to note that nearly 90 per cent women are working as scavengers for more than 15 years, and nearly 50 per cent of them had worked more than for 20 years. They have inherited this job from their forefathers and now younger generation of the family (especially, daughter-in-laws, and sons) is helping them in this task. The day of these women starts at 5 am and most of them continue it up to 11 am without having any meal. Some scavengers have tried to challenge their social and economic status by changing their jobs. But finally, they have to return to their original profession because of a social boycott and the lack of support from both private and governmental agencies. The law and order machinery has also proved inefficient.

The study concludes that there is no consonance between theoretical formulation of the welfare programmes for the upliftemnet of the scavengers in India and real life conditions. This may be attributed to the dominant nature of the social structure as well as India's emerging social formation, particularly since independence. A big hiatus between the communicative and the motivational structure on the one hand, and the opportunity structure on the other (Atal: 1998). No doubt that the state has talked about palliatives for the improvement of this segment of society but because of the conditioned psychological make-up of the scavengers or the equivocation expressed by the state, the exploitation is continuing. The state has largely reflected the expression of a handful of the dominant sections, where not only caste, but also some of the feudalistic remnants of the system are responsible (Beteille: 1969). It is also because of this element that the scavengers are constrained to remain in this status. The scavengers have become totally conditioned to remain satisfied with their life style (Singh: 1994).

III
Gender and Sanitation

Gender refers to the culturally and socially constructed differences between males and females found in the meanings, beliefs, and practices associated with feminity and masculinity. Gender is important in defining what females and males are, what they should do, and what sorts of relations do or should exists between them. Gender organises social relations in everyday life as well as in the major social structures. Sanitation refers to the principles and practices relating to the collection, removal or disposal of human excreta, household waste water and refuse as they impact upon people and the environment. Good sanitation includes appropriate health and hygiene awareness and behaviour, and acceptable, affordable and sustainable sanitation services. A lack of adequate sanitation or inadequately maintained or inappropriately designed systems can therefore constitute a range of pollution risks to the environment, especially the contamination of surface and ground water resources.

There are many gender issues in sanitation which need to be taken into account to improve development efforts. Many scholars deal with the different tasks men and women have, in fact all tasks related to sanitation are women's duties. And sanitation issues also relate with gender ideology as a major obstacle, blocking change.

The following are the gender issues related to sanitation:

Women are responsible for water in the House

Even though the responsibility for cleanliness and hygiene should be with all, in reality it is women of households and also of villages who are seen as the cleaners of the yard, the house, the kitchen, the bathroom and the toilet facilities. IN these situations women are usually also responsible for getting water to the house, from far away, from less far or from close by. Both the cleaning and fetching of water take a lot of time. Women are responsible for the hygiene of themselves, their children and men folk; women have to do the work for all of them; and women suffer when they themselves have negative influence of bad hygiene, by getting ailments and diseases, but also of their children are ill, which means extra work for them. When their men folk and parents are ill that also gives them extra work, and more water to carry. So women are at the centre of hygiene for all. Either way, with or without diseases, it means a lot of work for them. Not all women are in the same position; the younger women in household have more duties than the senior ones.

Women are Responsible for the health of family, especially of Children

Both men and women can get ill, but women are the caretakers per se. Hygiene becomes doubly important when there are sick family members who could infect the others. Extra water is needed, and lot of extra work needs to be done. Gender ideology prescribes that women do all this; there is no other real reason. The same is true for the elderly, with the difference that sick people in the house should be an exceptional situation, whilst to get ill will happen to all who are healthy and lucky.

Women Menstruate, get Pregnant and give Birth

Women in their menstruating period are generally seen as unclean. They should clean their blood themselves, and that is one of the reasons that women always have to clean everything. Not according to reason, but according to the prevailing gender ideology. During the time of being pregnant, giving birth and breast feeding, the risk of getting infections is high. All women will try to avoid that by giving lots of attention and spending extra energy in hygiene. The direct relation with the quality and quantity of water available during that time, and the fact that she will not always be able to get it, makes her very vulnerable. Maternal mortality is directly related to hygiene, and hygiene to sanitary facilities and their cleanliness.

Gender Issues of Toilets

In both rural and urban areas, women without toilets only go out to relieve themselves in the dark, because their gender ideology tells them that they cannot take the risk to be seen. They often face risks, by snakes, scorpions, or other creatures, but also by men. Three are endless stories of women getting harassed and even raped when going out in dark. For men and children this is no problem, they can go anywhere and anytime. For them urinate or to defecate has no relation to sex at all, but women who go out in the daylight are seen as light or fallen women who ask for trouble. This is again gender ideology, and even discrimination. Furthermore to wait till the dark results in constipation and adapted diet and drinking habits, which give serious health problems? In densely populated urban areas, public toilets, if available, are to be cleaned by women only. They often cannot be locked, and here again women suffer from violence.

Why is Gender Issues Important in Sanitation Sector?

Gender issues are important in sanitation sector for the following four important reasons:

(i) Improving Gender Equality

Proper sanitation facilities with toilets help to achieve the social status of women. It is known that parents will not marry their daughter to a household without toilet. The economic value of clean sanitation facilities ensure women fewer days of illness and therefore more days to work and more income: less unpaid work in caring for the sick, daughters with higher education so with more income.

(ii) Improving Women's Health and Livelihood

Proper sanitation facilities are essential for fewer infections for women, for less sexual harassment, for security and physical dignity, sanitation will empower women. Time savings also have a considerable impact on women's livelihood. There is an economic benefit of hiving water close to home so that the saved time can be used to generate some income.

Securing good sanitary facilities to meet family needs has direct bearing not only women's health but also on their access to education and employment.

In rural areas fetching water takes more time which keeps girls out of school and limits the economic productivity of women. Globally, more than one in five girls of primary school are not in school, this is imparted attributable to a lack of clean water and sanitation facilities available at the community level and schools. Girls like their mothers must often walk miles to fetch the daily water supply. Girls who reached menstrual age may also be deterred from school by inadequate sanitation in public places. Simple measures such as providing schools with water and latrines, and promoting hygiene education in the classroom can enable to get an education.

(iii) Health of Families

Improved sanitation facilities with regular and safe water supply, good latrine facilities enhance only the health of women, but also the health of entire family. The time saved from fetching water from places can be best used to maintain the health of the family members. In this connection gender differences is of particular importance with regard to hygiene and sanitation initiates and gender balanced approaches should be encouraged in plans and structures of implementation. Access to adequate sanitary latrines is a matter of security, privacy and human dignity, particularly for women. Access to adequate and clean, near water is a matter of women's health, their access to education, employment, livelihood and their empowerment.

Keeping this in mind the following initiatives should be taken to improve sanitation programmes.

At the national Governmental level: The ministries of health, water resources and social services are key actors and have important roles to play in ensuring that sanitation, hygiene promotion education and gender are incorporated into water resources and health policies. The line ministries should be motivated and willing to address gender in sanitation policies and legal frameworks.

(iv) Community Level

Hygiene and sanitation are considered to a women's issue, but they impact on both genders. The societal barriers continually restrict women's involvement in decision regarding sanitation improvement programmes. Thus, it is important that sanitation and hygiene promotion and education are perceived as a concern of women, men and children and not only of women. Separate communication channels, materials, and approaches have to be developed to reach out to men and boys. It is also important to target community leaders for gender sensitisation; this would facilitate mainstreaming gender in sanitation and hygiene promotional activities.

Attention and Funds should be focused on sanitation and hygiene in schools, in order to reduce transmission of water-related diseases and implement hygiene and health education. School children are key change agents because they can influence their parents and will be tomorrow's adults. When they learn sanitation- related behaviours, such as hand-washing, they can bring about change in their families and communities, leading to health improvements and higher school attendance of girls. It is critical that school sanitation and hygiene programmes address both boys and girls.

One problem that has been observed is that the latrine designs, especially for primary and secondary schools, are mainly prepared by male persons. The tendency therefore has been to construct latrines which are not sensitive to the special needs of girls. This has resulted in girls staying away from schools when they are menstruating, even when their schools have latrines. In the case of small boys too, the urinals are often too high. Moreover, it is important that separate sanitary latrines are constructed for boys, in order to prevent boys for taking over the latrines that are meant for girls. And toilet blocks for girls and boys should not be constructed next to each other. Sanitation design needs to be sensitive to physically challenged girls and boys too. In India, a survey carried out among school children revealed that about half the ailments found were carried out among school children revealed that about half the ailments found were related to unsanitary conditions and lack of personal hygiene (UNICEF and IRC: 1998).

Gender and Sanitary Facilities

Poor sanitation is something that not only affects the health of the people of the country, but also affects the development of the nation. In fact, women are most affected by the hazards of lack of proper sanitation. For instance, in India majority of the girls drop out of school because of lack of toilets. Only 22 per cent of them manage to even complete class 10. On economic grounds, according to the Indian Ministry of Health and Family Welfare, more than 12 million rupees is spent every year on poor sanitation and its resultant illnesses.

Women and marginalised populations are mostly affected by lack of water and sanitation in rural India (Ahmed: 2005; Coles and Wallace: 2005).

- Women may not be able to access water due to religious beliefs or patriarchy.
- Women may not able to access toilets because men do not encounter similar hardships to pen defecation

Women in Bawana and Bhalswa localities have reported their problems while accessing toilets and sanitation facilities (Panda and Agarwal: 2012) finds that various policies and schemes pertaining to urban water and sanitation in India can be categorised as 'gender blind' since these do not recognise the gender-based disadvantages in accessing safe water and sanitation, sewage and drainage. The paper also confirms that the overall budgetary allocation for water and sanitation in the resettlement colonies for Juggi Jhopri (JJ) clusters (slums) is grossly inadequate and in sync with neither the needs nor the effective level of service delivery. Confusion and lack of effective sanitation and consultation among various agencies remain part of the problem.

School Sanitation and Girls

School sanitation facilities across the country remain woefully inadequate. Despite government efforts to improve the situation, a report by the Right to education Forum (2011) 40 per cent of schools in India still lack a functional common toilet. A further 40 per cent lack separate toilet facilities for girls. Without a functioning toilet at school, many girls are forced to use nearby open spaces. The risk of harassment is real, and reports of sexual assaults are increasingly common. As girls approach puberty, the lack of school toilets and the related fears around safety cause many mothers to remove their daughters from the education system altogether. A National Study by A C Nielsen and NGO Plan for India revealed as many as 23 per cent of girls in India drop out to school when they hit puberty. In many cases when girls remain in school a lack of facilities causes widespread absenteeism each month, with the report showing that girls miss an average of 50 days of school each year because of menstruation. When puberty kicks in that has a massive impact and it's been evidenced that is preventing a lot of young girls from going to school. It is the taboo of having a period in India, not having facility to deal with that when you are at school in highly problematic.

Schools that have water and sanitation attract and retain students, particularly girls. One in four girls does not complete primary school, compared with one in seven boys. Girls bear the burden of water collection, which can take many hours a day, leaving them with no time or energy for school. Secondly, girls particularly those old enough to menstruate, are reluctant to attend school without toilets, and their parents are reluctant to send them. In general healthy children attend school more and get more out of it. The WHO estimates that 194 million schooldays, resulting from fewer incidents of diarrhoea, would be gained annually if the Millennium Development Goals of water and sanitation were met. Studies have shown that children with intense worm infestation perform poorly in learning ability tests, cognitive function and educational achievement that heavy infestations can result in a six-month delay in development. Some infected children attend school only half as much as their uninfected peers.

Sanitary Napkins and Girls

Commercial sanitary towels rain out of reach for many in India. They are too expensive for young girls to buy each month. During menstruation girls have little alternative than to use bundles of cloth, usually stripped from old clothing. In other areas, it is ash or sand rapped in leaves or newspaper.

Without facilities at school to allow girls to wash, dry, and change these clothes, many are embarrassed to attend lessons while menstruating. "Obviously having a situation where you had a leak at school and your menstrual blood was visible to others was just abhorrent to girls", explains Zelda Yanovich, technical officer at the water Supply and sanitation Collaborative Council (WSSCC). "It points to the fact that the facilities are just not fit for purpose. The idea of using facilities to change materials was just not an option".

Sanitation: The Hidden Gender Problem

Case Study

Munni sits holding a plate laden with three large rotis topped with a generous helping of spicy dal. She is hungry, but will not eat it yet. Covering the food with another plate, she quietly put is away, while her husband and two teenage sons quickly finishes the same.

"Yes, I am hungry. I have not eaten since morning, but if I eat now I will have to go to the toilet by the time food is digested- and there is always a long line at the washroom. We have just two toilets for women in this camp. So I eat only one meal a day, to minimise the number of visit to the toilet", she says. Munni and her family are getting used to living in makeshifts transit accommodation, on the outskirts of Bangalore, after their house got burnt down along with those of 57 other families in the neighbourhood. The women suffer an additional dimension of cruel handicaps that do not apply to the men- that of attending to nature's calls and bodily functions."

The lack of sanitation facilities compounds the trauma of displacement and loss. As some of the women affected by the limited access to toilet facilities confess, the only solution available is to ensure that their need to use a toilet is educed as far as possible. Some of them say that this means they hesitate to drink water even when they are thirsty. This in turn means that their health suffers, because denying the body sufficient fluid intake can result in kidney problems and other illnesses, some of them serious. These health hazards are in addition to those that both men and women, as displaced persons in relief camps, face in terms of unsatisfactory living conditions.

Given the existent cultural constraints on women, women do not relieve themselves in public the way men do. Educated and well-dressed men will get out of a car and urinate by the roadside without felling abashed- a state of mind few women, rich or poor, young or old can reach. Women tend to hold on, control and force their bodies into punishing (and often harmful) restraints because that is what socio-cultural norms decree.

Gender bases Disadvantage in Accessing Sanitation, Sewerage and Drainage:

- Incidents of sexual harassment while availing sanitation facilities at Community Toilet Complexes (CTCs)
- Poor and faulty designs of CTCs which put women at the risk of being harassed.

- CTCs are not open for the entire day which causes inconvenience to women to meet their sanitary needs.
- Inadequate and unsafe sanitary pubic infrastructure causes loss of dignity and privacy to women who are forced to resort to pen defecation.
- Inadequate infrastructure raises vital safety concerns for women as they are sexually assaulted or attacked when they resort to pen defecation.
- Women have to wait until dark to defecate and urinate in the open, so tend to drink less water during the day, resulting in all kinds of health problems such as urinary tract infections (UTIs).
- Poor maintenance and design of drains leading to conflicts that put women at risk physically.
- Loss of dignity and privacy while disposing menstrual waste.
- Hygienic conditions are often poor in public defecation areas, leading to worm infestation and water-borne diseases.
- Girls, particularly after puberty, miss school due to lack of proper sanitary facilities for dealing with menstrual hygiene.

IV
Children and Sanitation

Sanitation and hygiene are key to child survival, development and growth. Improved sanitation has to reach 2.6 billion people in the developing world- almost 980 million of which are children under 18 years old. The result is not surprising and yet it is shocking that millions of children die each year from preventable diseases.

Expected Impact of Improved Sanitation:

- Lowe morbidity in the population
- Lower mortality rates due to diarrhoea
- Better nutrition among children
- Cleaner environment
- Safer food and increased impact of improved water supplies
- Better learning and retention among school children

- Moe dignity and privacy for everybody especially women and girls
- Increased awareness of the importance of sanitation and hygiene and the need to develop a more permanent strategy.

Sanitation is Vital for Children

Of the approximately 120 million children born in the developing world each year, half live in households without access to improved sanitation, at grave risk to their survival and development. Poor hygiene and lack of access to sanitation together contribute to about 88 per cent of deaths form diarrhoeal diseases, accounting for 1.5 million diarrhoea-related under five deaths each year WWW.sanitationyear2008.org

Sanitation is a Good Economic Investment

Research shows that for every 10 per cent increase in female literacy, a country's economy can grow by 0.3 per cent. Re-educated girls are more likely to raise healthy, well-nourished, educated children, to protect themselves from exploitation and AIDS and to develop skills to contribute to their societies. Children weakened by frequent diarrhoea episodes are also more likely to be affected by malnutrition and opportunistic infections such as acute respiratory infections, the three major child killers. The WHO Commission established that reducing infant mortality is key to economic growth. Lowering infant mortality is associated with greater abilities to invest in health and education, in fewer dependents per worker and overall increase in per capita GNP and economic growth.

Conclusion

To identify a demand for improved sanitation is more positive than to initiate a supply of technology that is deemed to be good for communities. The former depends upon cooperation between providers and beneficiaries which comes through dialogue and the exchange of information. Individual users are the ultimate decision-makers in the acceptance or rejection of new technology. It is they who determine the success of a project, since the value of the investment depends not only upon community support but, more particularly, on the consent of households and individual users. They need to be convinced that the benefits of improved sanitation, and the new technology with which it is associated, outweigh the costs. Equally, it is for providers to appreciate the social context and the constraints within which individual decisions are made. They must learn from communities about why improved sanitation may elicit negative responses and also the positive features of community values, beliefs and practices which can be harnessed to promote change. (Franceys, R., J. Pickford & R. Reed: WHO: 1992:245).

References

Action Aid Report (2003), New Delhi.

Atal, Yogesh (1998), *The Changing Frontier of Caste*, New Delhi: National Publishing house.

Betéillé, André (1969), *Social Inequality*, New Delhi: Penguin Books.

Brown, A.L. (2010), *Empowerment and Gender Equality for water and sanitation in Rural India: Two case Studies*, Nov. 8

Ahmed, S. (2005), "Flowing upstream: Towards Gender Just, Equitable, and Empowerment Water Management", in S. Ahmed (ed.) *Flowing Upstream: Empowering Women through Water management Initiatives in India* (1-50), Ahmadabad: Centre for Environment Research.

Coles, A. and R.L.Wallace (1999), *Introduction*, in A.Coles and Wallace (eds.), Gender, water and Development, Oxford.

Franceys, R., J. Pickford & R. Reed (1992) *A guide to Development On-Site Sanitation, Geneva:* World Health Organisation (WHO) p. 245.

Nagla, B.K. (2011). 'Scavenging and scavengers in the State of Haryana', in Makwana, M. H. and Richard Pais (eds.) *Backward Classes and Social Justice*, Jaipur: Rawat Publications.

Panda, G.R. and Trisha Agarwal (2012), "Gender responsive Budget Analysis in Water and Sanitation Services in the Resettlement Colonies of Delhi", *Social Science Research Network.*

Singh, Rajeev Kumar and Ziyauddin (2000), "Manual Scavenging as Social exclusion: A Case Study", *Economic and Political Weekly*, Vol. XLIV, Nis 26 and 27, pp. 521-523.

Singh, Yogendera (1994), *Modernisation of Indian Tradition*, Jaipur: Rawat Publications.

Srivastava, B.N. (1997). *Manual Scavenging in India: A Disgrace to the Country*. Concept Publishing Company (P) Ltd. p. 178.

World Health Organisation, Annual Report, 2000.

WWW.sanitationyear2008.org

6

Toilet as a Tool of Social Change

The situation of toiletlessness in India and around the world is a very important human development issue which the global community will have to desperately address. This has drawn the attention of national and international organisations engaged in the promotion of sanitation-related programmes and activities. Toilet is a central subject of health and hygiene in India and other developing countries, which has become a tool for changing the structure of Indian society. This revolution has touched social, cultural, health, hygiene and sanitation related issues, leaving its powerful impact on the pace and progress of a wide variety of current initiatives aimed at breaking the barriers of caste and changing its old traditional structure and system of Indian society.

Indian society is an inert society which has many ills of this type. We elect governments every 5 years 'in the name of democracy' and none of our leaders, planners and administers have so far seriously pondered over this vital issue. Leaders must be forced to prioritise our basic needs of sanitation, water, electricity, good roads and food availability without wasting any time. India needs quality healthy population and not the numbers.

When the Governments don't see sanitation and hygiene for the people as a high priority, the situation would continue to prevail as it did since independence. The greatest cause of loss of life in India, in all ages, is preventable infections born out of poor sanitation and ignorant hygiene practices. Nation's considerable budget is spent on treating infected people while preventive measures would have saved lives and the nation's treasury. It is a sad reflection on the nation's leaders and policy makers. Those policies need to include providing with needed lavatories and amenities to the public at large as well as introducing as a subject in the primary school level creating early awareness in the growing children. Subsidies and technical advice are to be offered to rural population and a nationwide campaign with the help of Cricket and Movie stars would get people to cooperate and make changes in their behavior. This an eminent need and one can't waste any time anymore.

Defecation in the rural areas is done in woods or near fields, where the excreta is always covered by soil and quickly converted to land nutrient in the presence of the sun. So it is a nature friendly method of recycling since ancient times. The same cannot be said about open defecation in slums and cities, where it is definitely unhygienic. But this is a failure of governments and town planners who allow hordes of immigrants from rural India to take over public spaces, because they represent votes to politicians and hafta for the local dons and authorities. If this is taken care of, all the ensuing problems of sanitation and health will be taken care of automatically. This will take time, so in the meantime, Sulabh or public toilets offer an immediate solution, which should be implemented without delay.

The World Bank study is right that the majority of our population still defecate in the open area. It is a sorry state of affairs that many people still defecate near the railway tracks making very difficult to sit beside the train windows particularly in the morning. The Railway authorities just can't do anything except to raise the fares all the time in the year. The state government has no time to look into this problem even after more than sixty seven years of independence. This is the time to think about our country and sanitation in the interest of promoting better tourism in India. This chapter highlights two things:

1. First the origin of toilet and its benefits
2. Second, toilet and social change

I

Historical Development of Toilets

A toilet is a sanitation fixture used primarily for the disposal of human urine and feces. They are often found in a small room referred to as a toilet/bathroom/lavatory. Flush toilets, which are common in many parts of the world, may be connected to a nearby septic tank or more commonly in urban areas via "large" (3–6 in or 7.6–15.2 cm) sewer pipe connected to a sewerage pipe system. The water and waste from many different sources is piped in large pipes to a more distant sewage treatment plant. Chemical toilets are used in mobile and many temporary situations where there is no access to sewerage, dry toilets, including pit toilets and composting toilets require no or little water with excreta being removed manually or composted in situ.

Ancient civilisations used toilets attached to simple flowing water sewage systems included those of the Indus valley Civilisation, e.g., Harappa (Mohenjo-Daro, Sindh. "Bathing Area") and Mohenjo-Daro (Yadav: 2004) which are located in present day India and Pakistan(Jutti and Wallenius: 2005) and also the Romans and Egyptians who invented a version of the flowing water toilet. Although a precursor to the modern flush toilet system was designed in 1596 by John Harington, such systems did not come into widespread use until the late nineteenth century (Praeger: 2007). Thomas Crapper was one of the early makers of toilets in England.

Diseases, including cholera which still affects some 3 million people each year, can be largely prevented when effective sanitation and water treatment prevents fecal matter from contaminating waterways, groundwater and drinking water supplies. Infected water supplies can be treated to make the water safe for consumption and use (Praeger). There have been five main cholera outbreaks and pandemics since 1825. In London alone, the second killed 14,137 people in 1849, and the third took 10,738 lives in 1853-54. In 1849 the English physician John Snow published a paper *On the Mode of Communication of Cholera*, in which he suggested that cholera might be water born. During the 1854 epidemic, he collected and analysed data establishing that people who drank water from contaminated sources such as the Broad Street-pump died of cholera at much higher rates than those who got water elsewhere.

According to *The Global Water Supply and Sanitation Assessment 2000* by the World health Organisation, 40 per cent of the global population does not have access to "good" "excreta disposal facilities"—they live mostly in Asia and Africa. There are efforts being made to design simple effective squat toilets for these people (WHO: 2010). Usually, they are made by digging a hole, then installing a premade plastic squat toilet seat atop this hole, covering the walls with canvas (Retrieved September 16, 2011).

Threat to Human Capital

Nobody liked the smell of truth, more so since it concerned the tetchy aspect of toilets in India. India's Federal Minister of Rural Development Jairam Ramesh was accused last year of hurting Hindu religious sentiments by the opposition Bharatiya Janata Party for saying the country needed "more toilets than temples" (Spotlight News).

Cleanliness may be next to godliness, but India - with 1.2 billion people - is far from achieving it. Less than one-in-three households in Indian villages have toilets. Urban areas have more toilets but nevertheless suffer from poor sanitation and disposal mechanisms. The lack of public toilets for the urban poor and in rural areas leads to alarming rates of water-borne disease and affects women and children most, campaigners say.

India also carries the shame of having manual labourers, mostly marginalised people who belong to a community formerly called "untouchables" or Dalits, to clean human excreta from open lavatories, even today in the 21st century. Inder Salim, Delhi based artist says: "you can find public urinals for men, but women suffer most as Indian cities and villages do not make space for women's basic needs. Gender gets the worse off this shitty business."

While a 1961 census by the government said there were more than 3.5 million "faeces scavengers", recent reports have said the number is down to 64,000. This is contested by NGOs saying these workers still suffer the ignominy of cleaning human excreta, suffer illnesses and social ostracisation. A few years ago, "Shit of the Other" - a show by Inder Salim - displayed human faeces in a bottle. Some contended it was not scatological but a telling artistic statement of the state of the poor and disadvantaged, who are compelled to defecate in public in Indian cities. "Toilets are not just confined to sanitation in India," Salim says. "They contain layers of oppressed people, Dalits, our inability to deal with this basic human need."

Mahatma Gandhi, India's "Father of the Nation", had in the early part of the 20th century branded the practice of engaging manual scavengers to clean latrines as a social evil. Gandhi preferred to clean his own toilet to set an example - something that shocked many. Gandhi's call to make sanitation a hygienic issue 67 years ago seems to have gone down the drain.

II
India's Toilet Problems

We are giving here the census data to know the toilet statistics in India. The latest Census data of 2011 reveals that half of India's population still defecates in the open. In fact, the percentage of households having access to television and telephones in rural India exceeds the percentage of households with access to toilet facilities. Only 46.9 per cent of the 246.6 million households have lavatories while 49.8 per cent defecate in the open. The remaining 3.2 per cent use public toilets. Census 2011 data on houses, household amenities and assets reveal that 63.2 per cent of homes have a telephone. The economic impact of inadequate sanitation is about Rs. 2.4 trillion ($38.4 million), or 6.4 per cent of India's gross domestic product, according to the Water and Sanitation Programme. The states of Jharkhand and Odisha rated lowest with 78 per cent of households lacking toilet facilities. - More people in India have mobile phones than toilets.

Open defecation lies at the root of many development challenges, the 2013 World Bank report said. "Open defecation continues to be a big concern for the country as almost half of the population do it," Registrar General and Census Commissioner C Chandramouli said while releasing the latest data. India's sanitation and toilet statistics continue to raise a stink. The World Health Organisation and United Nations Children's Fund (UNICEF) estimate that there are more than 620 million people practicing open defecation in the country; over 50 per cent of the population.

Analysts say the data show the complex contradictions of the Indian system. They say the census reveals a country where millions have access to cutting-edge technology and consumer goods but a larger number of poor who lack access to even basic facilities. About 77 per cent of homes in the eastern state of Jharkhand have no toilet facilities, while the figure is 76.6 per cent for Orissa and 75.8 per cent in Bihar. All three are among India's poorest states with huge populations which live on less than a dollar a day.

Here's the stinking truth. More than half of 1.2 billion people in India live without toilets. They squat on roadsides, in agriculture fields or at railway tracks and defecate in the open. This, despite the Indian government spending close to Rs1, 250 billion on water and sanitation projects in the last 20 years. This fiscal, the UPA government has mounted the sanitation budget to Rs 15,260 crore against the revised estimate of Rs 13,000 crore. Obviously, all that money is going down the drain, literally.

"Cultural and traditional reasons and a lack of education are the prime reasons for this unhygienic practice. We have to do a lot in these fronts," Chandramouli said. The data also reveal that Indians now largely live in nuclear families with 70 per cent of homes consisting of only one couple - a dramatic change in a country where joint families were always the norm. The census figures also show changes in how people access information and entertainment. More than half the population - 53.2 per cent - have a mobile phone. There has been a 16 per cent rise in the number of homes with television sets, while the use of radios has declined by 15 per cent . The data show that 47.2 per cent of households have a television while only 19.9 per cent have a radio. And the reach of computers with internet access is still minuscule, with only 3.1 per cent of the population connected (BBC News India: 14th march 2012). It is necessary toconsider these facts

According to a World Bank Report (2013), access to improved sanitation can increase cognition among children. Further, Indian households defecating in the open, absence of toilet or latrine is one of the important contributors to malnutrition. According to UNICEF, hand washing with soap particularly after contact with excreta, can reduce diarrheal diseases by over 40 per cent and respiratory infections by 30 per cent. Diarrhea and respiratory infections are the number one cause for child deaths in India. With 638 million people defecating in the open and 44 per cent mothers disposing their children's faeces in the open, there is a very high risk of microbial contamination (bacteria, viruses, amoeba) of water which causes diarrhea in children. Children weakened by frequent diarrhea episodes are more vulnerable to malnutrition and opportunistic infections such as pneumonia. About 48 per cent of children are suffering from some degree of malnutrition.

"Our research showed that six-year-olds, who had been exposed to India's sanitation programme during their first year of life, were more likely to recognise letters and simple numbers on learning tests than those who were not," said Dean Spears, lead author of the paper 'Effects of Early - Life Exposure to Sanitation on Childhood Cognitive Skills.'

The paper studies the effects on childhood cognitive achievement of early life exposure to India's Total Sanitation Campaign, a national scale government programme that encouraged local governments to build and promote use of inexpensive pit latrines. "This is important news - the study suggests that low-cost rural sanitation strategies such as India's Total Sanitation Campaign can support children's cognitive development," Ms. Spears said (The Hindu, New Delhi: November, 19, 2103).

The results also suggest that open defecation is an important threat to human capital of developing countries and that a program accessible to countries where sanitation development capacity is lower could improve average cognitive skills. The sorry state of affairs has been confirmed by the latest baseline survey under the Nirmal Bharat Abhiyan, earlier Total Sanitation Campaign, under progress across the country at the moment. The survey figures, collected so far, mention that 54.7 per cent households in the country are without toilets. The number is likely to go up sharply, considering that data is still being collected. So far, only a fraction of the total 252,824 gram panchayats in the country has been covered under the survey. According to Nirmal Bharat Abhiyan, government's programme to solve 'toilet crisis' in India, by 2022 the country will be declared as free from open defecation (The Hindu, New Delhi: November, 19, 2103).

Right to Dignity

"We need to view services – such as the availability of functional toilets – as a part of the right to live a life of dignity and equality," says Subhadra Menon, director of Health Communication at the Public Health Foundation of India. But she adds: "Having said that, the provision of toilets to 1.2 billion people is far more complex than making mobile phones available, so in a sense, it isn't right to compare apples and oranges. But yes, the kind of social and other marketing that can be utilised to influence choices and behaviours is not being done optimally in the case of the use of toilets."

Sulabh International is an NGO promoting sanitation across the country. Its founder, Bindeshwar Pathak, bemoans that "India lacks a culture of sanitation." The royal rajas - erstwhile rulers - might have had slaves to evacuate their "thunder boxes", but much of India has had a late start to "toilet training", Pathak says. "Even the rural rich in the 1950s did not have toilet facilities in their mansions. Women went to the open for their ablutions as did the men." While he says India has made progress from a no-toilet scenario to providing nearly half of its population with latrines, "implementation of rural sanitation must be made priority and speeded up", says Pathak. Sulabh is seeking ways to accelerate the installation of toilet facilities. These programmes include training youth in both rural and urban areas on health and sanitation; pressing the government for fund allocation, and encouraging alternative livelihoods for caste groups that manually scavenge toilets.

According to Reuters, the provisional of Census 2011 data had revealed a grim picture, mentioning that less than 31 per cent of Indian population has access to sanitation facilities. The figures had caused huge embarrassment to the Government of India as the Ministry of Drinking Water and Sanitation had claimed more than 57 per cent sanitation coverage. It is pertinent to mention here that the country has also signed the UN resolution on the right to water and sanitation and thereby committed to take steps to realise that everyone has an access to water and sanitation facilities, be it people living in tribal area or people with physical challenges.

"The government is mechanically releasing the money and targeting toilet construction without paying any attention to community involvement. As a result most of the toilets, especially in rural areas, are lying non-functional. People use these toilets for storing fodder or cow dung cakes," says Ran Singh Parmar, who is working with a community-based organisation in Madhya Pradesh.

Nevertheless it is not that the government is not committed. Rather, the government has made big commitments at national and international platforms time and again, to achieve complete sanitation by eliminating manual scavenging and open defecation practices. Commitments have been made at global level through the Millennium Development Goals (MDG) and at regional level during four South Asian Conferences on Sanitation, since 2003. Besides, the high level political leaders have been attending the SAARC Summits and have agreed to work collectively to address water and sanitation challenges in the country. Rebutting these hollow commitments, the MDG report confirmed that over 75 per cent of Scheduled Caste and Scheduled Tribe households do not have access to safe sanitation. In rural areas, even today poor and low caste families are living on the mercy of the powerful and rich upper castes. The social divide restricts SC/ST to use the community facilities whereas their women face exploitation. The barriers these excluded communities face are much bigger and stronger than technology, design and monitoring or access issue.

Even a UNICEF report mentioned that the national Indian average of sanitation, hygiene and water safety is mere 34 per cent. For the urban population it is 58 per cent whereas for the people in the rural area it is just 23 per cent. The situation is endorsed by the Joint Monitoring Programme report, which establishes the fact that at least 40 per cent of the people from poorest background have barely benefited from sanitation facilities meant for them in the last decade.

On failing to keep its promises made in the past, the government of India extended its deadline to achieve the targets. Now under the Nirmal Bharat Abhiyan the government has kept 2017 as the year to declare the country free from open defecation and for ensuring hundred per cent safe disposal of faecal waste. Concerned by the situation, about 40 odd civil societies, working on various issues, have come together on a joint platform to demand the government to 'keep its promises'.

A pressure group is emerging through the campaign to press the government to look at the marginalised population of the country which is still not getting any sanitation facilities.

"The government gives a subsidy for the construction of toilets but the same does not reach the real beneficiary, be it a Dalit, tribal or extremely poor population or women, children and physically challenged people. There is a need to build a momentum and remind the government of its promises to provide safe and complete sanitation to all," says R Murali, the convener of Fresh Water Action Network South Asia, which is a major partner in the regional campaign on sanitation. The World Health Organisation (WHO) finds inadequate sanitation as a tool to ensure a significant beneficial impact on health, both in households and across communities (TCS: 2011).

III
Toilet and Social Change

Excreta Disposal

Human excreta are a source of infection. It is an important cause of environmental pollution. Every society has a responsibility for its safe removal and disposal so that it does not constitute a threat to public health. The health hazards of improper excreta disposals are:

- Soil pollution
- Water pollution
- Contamination of foods
- Propagation of flies

The resulting diseases are typhoid and paratyphoid fever, dysenteries, diarrhoeas, viral hepatitis and similar other intestinal infections and parasitic infestations. These diseases are not only burden on the community in terms of sickness, mortality and a low expectation of life, but a basic deterrent to social and economic progress. Proper disposal of human excreta, therefore, is a fundamental environmental health service without which these cannot be any improvement in the state of community health.

Extent of Problem in India

In many areas of the world, including India, excreta disposal is a problem of grave importance. Nearly 70 per cent of India's population live in rural areas and the majority of them go to the fields for defecation and thereby pollute the environment with human excrement. The situation is in no way better in urban areas.

Social Aspects of Excreta Disposal

India is land of villages and nearly 70 per cent of our population lives in villages. The problem of sanitation therefore is one of rural sanitation. According to WHO-UNICEF, surveys have shown that 58 per cent of population to the open fields for defecation , among them 18 per cent of urban India still defecates in the open while in the rural areas it comes to 69 per cent (WHO-UNICEF: 2010). This habit of indiscriminate fouling of surroundings with human excrement is generations' old, and rooted firmly in the cultural behaviour of the Indian village people.

In urban areas, the latrine is considered a necessary part of a house. In rural areas, by and large people have not accepted latrines with any enthusiasm, and even when installed only a few used them regularly. The problem in rural sanitation is how to overcome the resistance of the village people and induce them to use sanitary latrines. Research studies have indicated that there is only one way to solve the problem, i.e. through health education. Social scientists have listed the reasons why villagers do not accept latrines. Some of the reasons found in the surveys are:

1. Latrines are associated with bad smell
2. They are the breeding places of flies
3. They are something foul and dirty so that one should not have them close to houses
4. Latrines are costly and beyond their means to install
5. They do not know how faecal borne diseases are spread.

In short people have a bad image of latrines in their minds. Secondly using a latrine goes against a DAILY habit pattern of going to the fields. The use of latrines involves a drastic change in the day to day behaviour of a large number of people.

The solution of the problem lies in teaching the people first the reason why latrines are important. The teaching should be undertaken by all known methods of health education: direct discussion, group discussion, larine demonstration, and use of visual aids and above all service facilities. The ultimate goal of health education will be to motivate the rural people towards acceptance and use of sanitary latrines.

Bindeshwar Pathak founded Sulabh International Social service Organisation in the year 1970, an organisation exclusively engaged in promoting low-cost sanitation technology, eradication of manual scavenging and liberation and rehabilitation of scavengers. The toilet revolution that Sulabh International and its accompanying social movement – called Sulabh Sanitation and Social Reform Movement – ushered in the country has been a tool of social transformation that Pathak envisaged and worked for with the cooperation of friendly voluntary workforce of over fifty thousand people working whole time for a mission. Thus, Sulabh became a catalytic agent for sanitation and non-caste oriented transformatory social change.

The Sulabh International Service Organisation has engineered an innovative, affordable, and environmentally-friendly toilet that has helped over one million marginalised people in India. This group of society in India, known as Balmikis, is condemned to cleaning and manually transporting human waste. The Balmikis have suffered institutionalised discrimination for centuries and require advanced strategies for integration into mainstream society.

The Sulabh toilet is not only a unique technology for sanitation and preventing environmental pollution, but also for social reform. Required to remove human waste by hand, the Balmikis suffer occupational hazards of poor hygiene and health in addition to being callously marginalised by society for their unclean work. To change this, Sulabh founder Dr Bindeshwar Pathak created a technology to convert bucket latrines into two-pit pour-flush toilets. These new toilets were soon being utilised across India.

To coincide with this, Sulabh provided alternative jobs to the Balmikis, who had lost their jobs due to the large-scale conversion of privy latrines into Sulabh toilets. Sulabh prioritised skill development, improving literacy, and vocational training for Balmikis, including the community's children. It has set up many centers and institutions across the country to provide vocational training in many market-friendly trades.

Understanding that traditions take time to evolve and require initiative from all members of society, Sulabh has implemented the concept of 'social adoption.' The non-profit encourages citizens to formally and publicly adopt a Balmiki family. The pair of families closely interacts and visits each other's homes. At times, the adopting family helps the adopted family to overcome social adjustment problems. Adopters are typically persons of high social standing and prestige, and so their approach and interaction become an example for others to reinforce the integration of the Balmikis into mainstream society.

Today, 1.2 million Sulabh household toilets have been constructed and 54 million government toilets constructed based on the Sulabh design. There over 8,000 Sulabh community toilet blocks in the country and 10.5 million people use toilets based on the Sulabh design daily. As a result, Balmikis are not condemned to their traditional role in 640 towns. Sulabh has also constructed 200 biogas plants all over the country. The simple production of biogas from public toilets and recycling and reuse of waste is a breakthrough in the field of sanitation and community health.

It is important to support social enterprises and encourage the business community to continue working to improve the health of society, which is why Women Deliver has organised a Social Enterprise Challenge. Through this "challenge," Women Deliver convened a group of social entrepreneurs to showcase their projects and solutionsat the Women Deliver 2013 Conference (Hettige: 2013).

Some of the major social reform endeavours of Sulabh International, like its social up-gradation programme in which upper caste elite closely interact with a family of a scavenger community as part of their social obligation, running Sulabh Public School (wherein children of both high caste and low caste people study under one roof and share meals), and social mainstreaming programmes (wherein efforts are made to prepare scavengers to get connected with mainstream society) have made a dent on the rigidities of the caste system.

Sulabh International recently has undertaken a micro-level programme for the development/ empowerment of women from the scavenger community. Through this the social status of those women is upgraded by providing them vocational education in economically rewarding occupation. Consequently, the eatables prepared by these women of the scavenger community are being purchased by the so-called touchable of high caste groups.

The wide variety of programmes and activities of Sulabh organisation are exclusively focused on social activities inspired and informed by secularist mandate of the Constitution of India which seeks to abolish all forms of caste and cred based discrimination. The organisation has successfully pursued its agenda to include India's excluded castes in the social mainstream of society. One outstanding example of this has been to visit to a Hindu temple which disallowed the entry of the so-called untouchable persons.

In reference to toilets, several varieties of social changes can be attributed to the invention of toilets, promotion of toilets and toilet-centred sanitation practices:

- The liberated women scavengers were invited to the United Nations in New York to put on July 2, 2008, a cultural programme, where they walked the ramp with Indian models in dresses embroidered by them. The show highlighted the social transformation process undertaken by Sulabh for liberating, rehabilitating and mainstreaming women scavengers into society and providing them sustainable livelihood, thus fulfilling the dream of Mahatma Gandhi and B. R. Ambedkar.

New Princes of Alwar: Shame to Pride (2009): Liberation of Scavengers

A class of people has been condemned as scavengers and treated as untouchables from generation to generation in India. Such was the collective myopia of society that hardly any-one ever paused and wondered what could be done to help them until Gandhi and Ambedkar raised a war cry against their suffering in the late 20th century. India banned untouchability and the construction of dry latrines to obviate the need for scavenging. But the evil which had continued for centuries could not be ended overnight. Bindeshwar Pathak launched Sulabh movement, the main purpose of which is the liberation of scavengers from their ignoble calling. With his efforts millions of scavengers have been freed from the task of carrying night-soil as head-load. All over the country over one lakh people, mostly women, are still engaged in the demeaning profession. What is their life? What are their sufferings? What are their hopes and aspirations? Interviews with women scavengers hailing from Alwar in Rajasthan blow the lid off the searing experiences of these wretched women unfolded in 'New Princess of Alwar: Shame to Pride'

The book *"New Princes of Alwar: Shame to Pride"* is a documentation, which throws light on the practice of human scavenging in the caste-ridden Indian society. It is an effort to wipe off the blot on the face of Indian society that boasts to be egalitarian in nature. It comprises articles, which elucidate the traumatic lives led by women scavengers. They manually clean excreta from households and carry it physically, at times even as head-load, for disposal elsewhere. The work is demeaning, degrading, humiliating and deprives them of their rights. They have been practising scavenging as profession for centuries...

Scavenging has been present since the *Pauranic* days and prevailed during the Buddhist and Medieval periods. The horrendous practice continued from the days of the Mughals till the time of British rule. Tragically, the practice continues to hold roots in our society. When Gandhi came to India from South Africa, he drew everyone's attention towards this problem. The Indian Government constituted a number of committees to look into this social problem but offered no solution. Gandhi dreamt of a society free from the shackles of scavenging, but his dream remains unutilised during his life. When Bindeshwar Pathak entered the sanitation scene in 1968, he too was confronted with the existence of the practice of and problems posed by scavenging.

In order to study them in depth and to be acquainted with their problems intimately, Pathak went to and lived in a colony of scavengers in Bettiah, an outlying district of Bihar in India. What awaited him there was a depressing and revolting scenario, and he resolved to wipe off the blot of scavenging forever. Two episodes stirred further Pathak's conscience and strengthened his resolve. The first incident related to his seeing a newly wedded bide, reluctant to take up the work of scavenging, being forced and driven by her in-laws to clean bucket toilets. The initiation was met with unsuccessful resistance and heart-rending cries and sobs of the bride. Pathak's intervention with a view to persuading the in-laws to desist from forcing the daughter-in-law to take to scavenging was met with the rude counter question whether Pathak would be willing to take the responsibility of feeding the daughter-in-law. Obviously, his remonstrance melted. The second episode related to a boy being gored by a bull and none of the spectators gathered at the site was willing to intervene to rescue him and take him to a hospital. The boy ultimately died. The reason of non-intervention, Pathak was told, was the fact that the boy was from a scavenger's family.

The experience of living in a scavenger's colony and the two illustrative episodes narrated afore made Pathak to think about methods and solutions lay in replacement of the bucket toilet system. This led him to devise and implement the two-pit, pour-flush, compost toilet system technology for individual households and operating and maintaining public toilets linked with biogas plants attached to Sulabh Effluent Treatment (SET) device, leading to liberation of scavengers from their demeaning profession. With this effort, Bindeshwar Pathak is proud to say that it has been possible to do so and thereby bring about Social Transformation.

After being liberated, it was noted that the scavengers were able to find employment elsewhere and if unable to do so, were provided training by Sulabh in market-oriented trades, whereby they could secure gainful employment or be self-employed. Social transformation has been to the extent that the locals now consume eatables made by them, a fact which until a couple of years ago was unthinkable. They acquired self-confidence to participate in a show where they walked the ramp in New York. Their grit and toil has helped them gain self-esteem and enhanced their social status.

In fact, the very purpose behind terming erstwhile women scavengers as new princess of Alwar is to lend them dignity and enhance their social status. Moreover, it is very much in keeping with the tradition where a father lovingly addresses his daughter as *Rani Bitiya*.

Pathak has taken the help of media and journalists to promote the social cause. The journalists have interacted with the erstwhile women scavengers; talked to them, heard their real life experiences and written stories of their sorrows, the humiliations they suffered from social ostracisation they faced living as scavengers. The book 'New Princess of Alwar: Shame to Pride' is an effort of members of the media and others who associated themselves in this endeavour.

'No toilets, No Marriage'

It's easier for modern Indian women in the metros to walk into a shopping mall and find a loo. But it is not so for their underprivileged sisters who are poor or live in villages with no toilet facilities. Women and girls often defecate in public, harming their health and also inviting molestation and unwanted attention from men in both rural and urban areas.

Police in the state of Bihar have admitted violence against women could be contained if more public toilets were provided.

Ramesh, who has campaigned zealously for the need for toilets, last year invoked a "no toilet, no bride" campaign. He exhorted women to not marry men whose family homes did not come equipped with toilets.

Some instances have occurred where brides have left the home of the groom after finding the household did not have a proper toilet. It has forced some men to pose in photos beside toilets in their home before seeking a bride in their villages. Priyanka Bharti returned to her husband's home only when a proper toilet was built (AFP)

A "right to pee" campaign was also launched in April 2012 by a group of non-profit organisations in Mumbai. They fought for the use of free toilets for women who were until then charged a fee to use toilets, while men could use them for free. India's Supreme Court ruled in 2011 that every government school must provide toilets, especially for girls. Inability to do so would mean closing the schools down.

"Once political support – across party lines – builds up for an issue, chances are it gets addressed satisfactorily," says Menon. "Therefore, it is more about how all our politicians and elected representatives can take up the issue of toilets being provided.

"The critical issue is this – each and every day, young, adolescent girls and young adult women [and men actually] need to expose themselves to multiple vulnerabilities," Menon says. "This makes even more serious the ignominy that these girls and women face – including not having a clean and functional toilet that they can use with a guarantee of privacy." (Source: Al Jazeera)

Benefits of Toilets

An exhibitor demonstrates the use of a toilet tap where water is recycled and reused, during Reinvent The Toilet Fair in New Delhi, India. Scientists who accepted the Bill & Melinda Gates Foundational s challenge to reinvent the toilet showcased their inventions in the Indian capital with the primary goal to sanitise waste, use minimal water or electricity, and produce a usable product at low cost. (Tsering Topgyal/AP Photo) (Daigle, Katy: 2014).

Who would have expected a toilet to one day filter water, charge a cellophane or create charcoal to combat climate change?(Daigle:2014).

These are lofty ambitions beyond what most of the world's 2.5 billion people with no access to modern sanitation would expect. Yet, scientists and toilet innovators around the world say these are exactly the sort of goals needed to improve global public health amid challenges such as poverty, water scarcity and urban growth.

Scientists who accepted the Bill & Melinda Gates Foundation's challenge to reinvent the toilet showcased their inventions in the Indian capital Saturday. The primary goal: to sanitise waste, use minimal water or electricity, and produce a usable product at low cost.

The World Bank estimates the annual global cost of poor sanitation at $260 billion, including loss of life, missed work, medical bills and other related factors. India alone accounts for $54 billion — more than the entire GDP of Kenya or Costa Rica.

India is by far the worst culprit, with more than 640 million people defecating in the open and producing a stunning 72,000 tons of human waste each day — the equivalent weight of almost 10 Eiffel Towers or 1,800 humpback whales.

Pooping in public is so acceptable that many Indians will do it on sidewalks or in open fields. Gaze out the window of any Indian train and face a line of bare bottoms doing their business on the tracks. Meanwhile, diarrheal diseases kill 700,000 children every year, most of which could have been prevented with better sanitation." In the West, such things are a nuisance, but people don't lose their lives," said Christopher Elias, president of global development at the Gates Foundation. "People don't immediately realise the damage done by infections coming from human waste."

India has been encouraging rural communities to build toilets, and last year launched a $1.6 billion program to help. But building sanitation systems in developing countries is not easy. Flush toilets are not always an option. Many poor communities live in water-stressed areas. Others lack links to sewage pipes or treatment plants.

To be successful, scientists said, the designs being exhibited at Saturday's Toilet Fair had to go beyond treating urine and feces as undesirable waste, and recognise them as profit-generating resources for electricity, fertiliser or fuel." Traditionally, people have gone into communities and said, 'Let's dig you a pit.' That's seen as condescension, a token that isn't very helpful. After all, who is going to clean that pit?" said M. Sohail, professor of sustainable infrastructure at Loughborough University in the U.K.

All the designs are funded by Gates Foundation grants and in various stages of development.

Some toilets collapsed neatly for easy portability into music festivals, disaster zones or illegal slums. One emptied into pits populated by waste-munching cockroaches and worms.

One Washington-based company, Janicki Industries, designed a power plant that could feed off the waste from a small city to produce 150 megawatts of electricity, enough to power thousands of homes.

The University of the West of England, Bristol, showcased a urine-powered fuel cell to charge cellophanes overnight.

Another team from the University of Colorado, Boulder, brought a system concentrating solar power through fibber optic cables to heat waste to about 300 degrees Celsius. Aside from killing pathogens, the process creates a charcoal-like product called bio char useful as cooking fuel or fertiliser." At the core are really interesting scientific principles, so translating this into scientific advances that people can relate to is really exciting," said one of the project leaders, Karl Linden, professor of environmental engineering in Boulder. "Bio char is an important subject for scientists at the moment, since it can be used to sequester carbon in the soil for 1,000 years or more."

A team from Beijing Sunny breeze Technologies Inc. also brought a solar-bio char system, but with the solar panels heating air that will dry sludgy human waste into nuggets that are then heated further under low-oxygen conditions to create bio char." We are trying to build a system simple enough to be fixed in the village," technical adviser John Keating said.

One company from the southern Indian state of Kerala was not as concerned with providing toilets as with cleaning them. Toilets are more common in Kerala than they are in much of the country, but no one wants to clean them, said Bincy Baby of Eram Scientific Solutions."

There is a stigma. The lowest of the low are the ones who clean the toilets," Baby said. Eram's solution is a coin-operated toilet with an electronic system that triggers an automated, self-cleaning mechanism. With 450 prototypes now looped into sewage systems across India, electrical engineers are lining up for jobs as toilet technicians. "Now, they're proud of their jobs."

Conclusion

Toilet is so mundane and innocuous that many people may be loath to talk about it. Dr Pathak has talked extensively about how toilet as a simple invention of tremendous civilising impact has played a vital role in enhancing the quality of life and in resolving some of the intricate social problems, like the practice of untouchability and the rigidities of India's caste system. In view of this, the sociological implications of toilet revolution around the world, especially in India, have been most profound.

History of the evolution of toilets from 2000 BC to date suggests many notable changes that have been brought about by this supposedly innocuous but realistically important invention. History shows how an ordinary invention like that of toilet has stirred human mind, evoked passion, inspired imagination and kindled hope and vision of many a social crusader around the world. In this context, the invention of toilet as one of the winning ideas. This winning idea of toilet invention, evolution, propagation and action oriented has demonstrated the power and potential that the toilet has had in course of human history. While discussing toilet, one ends up discussing virtually everything – society, culture, economics, technology and even history and geography. Toilet is one single small time invention that has made us civilised. This makes us feel that toilet is one of the important achievements of mankind. Toilet revolution around the world today has made its mark on the modern civilisation, the advances of which have been truly amasing, inspiring and, at times, terribly horrifying.

Hundreds of millions of people in India have no access to a toilet at home. Nearly half of India's 1.2 billion people have no toilet at home, but more people own a mobile phone, according to the latest census data. There is a structural problem in it. The infrastructure which is needed really need government intervention. Sulabh shochalya is one solution. Can we run a campaign as we had run for Polio? This directives need to come from the government. But Indian government is busy in distributing Bharat Ratana and discussing who should get it and who should not. Please wake up and make India more beautiful and hygienic for all. (Matrubhumi Yearbook 2014).

There is a need of moral sanitation education. The little book, entitled, 'Moral Sanitation' written by Groves belongs to a class of literature which is constantly becoming more abundant and which emphasises a very healthy attitude on the part of the people who read them, namely a desire for some real knowledge about themselves which will be helpful in the practical problems of living. Groves hardly claims to have written a treatise on Moral Sanitation. His book is more of a running commentary or a collection of thoughts, designated as chapter headings, tied together by the comments of a man who has read widely and thought much over the problems of human conduct and believes profoundly that in a scientific study of man's behaviour ought to be found the principles upon which efficient living must be based and that these principles are to find their way into the highways and byways of social life, into the factory and be applied by the workman at his task, into the family and be applied by the parents in the education of their children, into the church, mosque temple, Gurudwara etc. and provide moral sanitation.

If everyone uses toilets, does India have enough water? It is the western closet that pollutes by converting drinking quality water to sewage! One of the implications of the above news is that, besides the difficulty in carrying out their daily function in privacy and comfort as and when they need to, something one might truly term a HUMAN RIGHT, girls and women remain exposed to attack, rape and worse, as they are forced to venture out to attend to nature call.

References

Daigle, Katy (2014). *"Could a toilet reinvention help save $260 billion worldwide?"* Associated press. Posted on Internet on 03/24/2014

Groves, Ernest R. (1916). Moral Sanitation, New York: Associates Press, pp. Viii + 128; see also *The Psychoanalytic Review*, (1917), 4:124

Harington, John (1956), *A History of the Flush Toilet,*

Hettige, Harshi 2013), *Women Deliver: The Toilet as a tool for Social Change,* posted on Internet on February 25th.

Jutti, Petri S. and Katri J. Wallenius (2005). Kaivot Ja Kaymalat: Johdatus Historian Esimerkkina Sumoi (A Brief History of wells and Toilets – The case of Finland), Tempere University press, ePublications, Tampere.

New Princes of Alwar: Shame to Pride: Startling Stories of Untouchables Scavengers (2009), Authored by 50 Journalists, concept and vision by Bindeshwar Pathak, New Delhi: Sulabh International Social Service Organisation.

Praeger, Dave (2007), *Poop Culture: How America is shaped by its Grossest national product*

Yadav, Anurag (2004), *"Loo and Behold! — A Toilet Museum!"* April, .The-south Asian.com.

World Health organisation (WHO), *"Cholera vaccines: A Brief summary of the March 2010 position paper"* (PDF).

WHO-UNICEF (2010), Progress on sanitation and Drinking Water, Who-UNICEF: Joint Monitoring Programme for Water Supply and sanitation

7
Environmental Sanitation

Context

V.S. Naupal in his book, 'An Area of Darkness' repeatedly referred to the Indian women and men defecating in the open air generally and on the roadsides flanks specially. After 65 years of Independence, the phenomenon is still not quite out of sight to a motorist who drives in the wee hours of the morning or during the hours after dusk and switches on his headlights to encounter the bizarre scenes. The human excreta are thus exposed for being trampled by a pedestrian and for throwing an obnoxious smell all around. On the other hand, the concept of ecological sanitation which aims at protecting ecosystems treats excreta as a valuable input if scientifically recycled for generation of power and production of organic manure. Environmental sanitation calls for interventions aimed basically at improved management of excreta.

Providing environmentally safe sanitation to millions of people is a significant challenge, especially in the world's second most populated country. The task is doubly difficult in a country where the introduction of new technologies can challenge people's traditions and beliefs (CUSS : 2010). The World Health Organisation (WHO) finds inadequate sanitation as a tool to ensure a significant beneficial impact on health, both in households and across communities (TCS: 2011). Therefore, efforts should be made at the all levels of sanitation, namely, individual, household, community, waste management and finally sanitation to all. In this chapter, we would like to discuss the following things:

1. Problems of Environmental Sanitation in India
2. Concept of Environmental Sanitation
3. Environmental and Social Sanitation
4. The Environmental Burden of Disease:
5. The Scope and Subjects of environmental Hygiene and sanitation:
6. Promoting Sanitation:
7. Water and Sanitation:

I

Problems of Environmental Sanitation in India

The problems of environmental sanitation in India is universal both in rural and urban areas. The difference of the problem is related to the nature and extent of the environmental sanitation in rural and urban areas. Park and Park (1977:94) highlight the problem rural environmental sanitation in India which deals:

1. Disposal of human excreta
2. Disposal of Waste
3. Water Supply
4. Housing

Besides these there is another solution to deal with environmental sanitation i.e. Public toilets. In the ensuing section we would discuss all these to analyse the problems of environment.

1. Disposal of human excreta

The most important problem in rural sanitation in India today is the disposal of human excreta. The bulk of India's population lives in rural areas: surveys in different parts of the country have revealed many people still defecate in the open areas. This practice is time honoured, and is not considered harmful. A popular belief among the village folk is that the excreta of children are harmless. Children are permitted to defecate in the backyards close to the houses. Womenfolk in the villages also go the fields for defecation, but they go in small intimate groups. In this they get an opportunity to meet their friends and renew social contacts, thus combining a physiological function with social function.

Sociologists have found several reasons why an average Indian villager does not accept a latrine:

- The first and foremost reason given is that a latrine close to the house is considered unhygienic because of the bad small. They maintain that the latrines are meant for city-dwellers, where there are no field for defecation;
- Going to the fields give them an additional advantage of a morning walk;
- The houses are small, and there is no space to locate a latrine;
- Going to the fields is cheaper;
- Latrines are only meant for females and invalids;
- Total ignorance that faeces is infective; it is considered as only something that is impure.

Thus the problem of excreta disposal is bound up with numerous customs and beliefs. The health hazards associated with improper excreta disposal are soil pollution, water pollution and transmission of diseases by flies, unclean hands and polluted food.

2. Disposal of Waste

The waste water from the houses is permitted to collect in ditches and overflow into the streets, as there is usually no drainage system in the country-side. The average villager is not aware that mosquitoes breed in collections of dirty water. In regard to household refuse, it is invariably thrown in front of the house and permitted to accumulate and decompose. Periodically, it is removed to the fields and used as manure. The animal dung (cow/buffalo dung) is allowed to accumulate and when a sufficient quantity is reached, it is pressed into cakes, sun dried and used as fuel. These heaps of dung cakes are sources of fly-breeding.

3. Water Supply

The well/ponds/rivers occupy a pivotal place in the cultural environment of a village. It is place where people go not only to draw their supply of water, but also a meeting place where people bathe, and wash their clothes. It is also a place where the animals are sometimes washed and given a drink. Tanks and ponds are used for washing, bathing, ablution and sometimes even as a source of drinking water. Some rivers are considered hold. People go on pilgrimage to have a dip in the holy rivers. They not only bathe and wash their clothes in the river, but also drink the raw water, which they consider sacred. Samples of holy water are bottled and carried over long distances for distribution among friends and relatives. Epidemics of cholera and gastro-enteritis have been due to this.

4. Housing

Rural houses are practically the same all over country. They are usually kachha and damp, ill-lighted, and ill-ventilated. For reasons of security, no windows are provided, and if at all one is provided, it is merely a small hole. Absence of a separate kitchen, latrine, bathroom and drainage are characteristic features of an average rural house. Animal keeping is very common in villages. Infrequently, human beings and animals live under one roof. Houses are generally kept clean inside, regularly white-washed or plastered with mud and cow dung.

In developing countries, waste management often emerges as a problem that endangers human health and the environment. To make matter worse, waste management usually has a low priority on the political agenda of such countries, as they are struggling with other important issues such as hunger, health problems, water shortage and unemployment. In such situations, it is easy to understand why waste problems have tendency to grow steadily. Several past researches have focused on investigating the cost benefits of providing safe and convenient living conditions to households in developing world, especially on housing conditions, notably on the relationship between water, sanitation and disease. Citing from different sources, Yongsi, Herrmann, Ntetu, Sietchiping, and Herrmann (2008:220-228) state that water supply, sanitation, and health are already related. It is also evident that each year, poor hygiene, mismanagement of liquid or solid waste, and lack of sanitation facilities contribute to death of millions of the world's poorest people from preventable diseases. Considering the nexus of cleaning/sanitation and health, empirical evidence points to their close linkages. In particular, the relationship could be outlined as follows:

1. As cities continue to grow, the management of solid waste is becoming a major environmental and public health concern in urban areas of many developing countries.
2. Lack of sanitation and unsafe disposal or shortage of waste in/around houses and streets and in undersigned containers may provide habitats for vectors of that cause various infectious diseases including amoebiasis, typhoid fever and diarrhoeas.
3. Uncontrolled landfills are a huge danger for the surrounding environment and are a health risk to the population, causing contamination of the drinking water and soil.
4. More than 5 million people die each year from diseases related to inadequate waste disposal system (WHO; 2007).

It is estimated that 1.8 million people die worldwide every year from diarrhoeal diseases (including cholera). Among them, 90 per cent are children under 5 mostly in developing societies. An estimated 88 per cent of this burden is attributed to unsafe drinking water supply, inadequate sanitation, and poor hygiene. These risk factors do not evenly threaten urban districts as slums and informal settlements are more vulnerable to communicable diseases (Yongsi et al: 2008).

As per estimates, inadequate sanitation costs, India almost $54 billion or 6.4 per cent of the country's GDP in 2006. Over 70 per cent of this economic impact or about $38.5 billion was health related, with diarrhoea followed by acute lower respiratory infections accounting for 12 per cent of the health-related impacts. Evidence suggests that all water and sanitation improvements are cost-beneficial in the sub-regions of the developing world. Sectoral demands for water are growing rapidly in India owing mainly to urbanisation and it is estimated that by 2025, more than 50 per cent of the country's population will live in cities and towns. Population increase, rising incomes, and industrial growth are also responsible for this dramatic shift. National Urban Sanitation Policy (2008) was the recent development in order to rapidly promote sanitation in urban areas of the country. India's Ministry of Urban Development commissioned the survey as part of its National Urban Sanitation Policy in November 2008.

In rural areas, local government institutions in charge of operating and maintaining the infrastructure are seen as weak and lack the financial resources to carry out their functions. In addition, no major city in India is known to have a continuous water supply and an estimated 72 per cent of Indians still lack access to improved sanitation facilities. Besides this, 63 per cent of urban population in India is without proper sanitation. The 11th Five-year Plan envisages 100 per cent coverage of urban water, urban sewerage, and rural sanitation by 2012. Although investment in water supply and sanitation is likely to see a jump of 221 per cent in the 11th Plan over the 10th Plan, the targets do not take into account the quality of water being provided or sustainability of systems being put in place (Kumar, Kar and Jain:2011).

India is still lagging far behind many countries in the field of environmental sanitation. According to Pandve (2008), most cities and towns in India are characterised by overcrowding, congestion, inadequate water supply, and inadequate facilities of disposal of human excreta, wastewater and solid wastes. Most of the problems in the country are due to defective environment, which in turn rob people of their health, destroy their livelihoods, and undermine their overall development potential. The environmental sanitation is still an ignored issue in India. To raise the overall of standard of living, the issue of environmental sanitation must be tackled seriously. It is essential to take some stricter steps to raise the current state of environmental sanitation in India. For example in Nigeria, the state government of Lagos has set up a sanitation court, which will prosecute offenders arrested for violating the state environmental sanitation. Moreover, there is a need to provide facilities to the people such as **public-toilet** which would be a step for the environmentally safe sanitation.

5. Public Toilets

A public toilet (also called a bathroom, restroom, comfort room, powder room, toilet room, washroom, water closet, W.C., public lavatory) is a public toilet facility — in contrast to a private usually residential toilet room, which may be a standalone water closet, or part of a bathroom. At a minimum, a public toilet can be a single unit featuring a toilet and hand basin for hand washing. Public toilets can also be larger facilities, which may include bathing facilities or showers, changing rooms and baby facilities. Thus, Public toilets may be standalone buildings or installations, or be contained within buildings such as railway stations, schools, bars, restaurants, nightclubs or filling stations. Public toilets can also be found on some public transport vehicles, for use by passengers. Public toilets are usually fixed facilities, but can also refer to smaller public portable toilets, or larger public portable toilets constructed as portable buildings.

Public toilets are commonly separated by gender into male and female facilities, although some can be unisex, particularly the smaller or single occupancy types. Both male and female toilets may incorporate toilet cubicles, while many male toilets also feature urinals. Increasingly, public toilets incorporate accessible toilets and features to cater for people with disabilities. Public toilets may be unattended or be staffed by a janitor (possibly with a separate room), or attendant, provided by the local authority or the owner of the larger building. In many cultures it is customary to tip the attendant, while other public toilets may charge a small fee for entrance, sometimes through use of a coin operated turnstile. Some venues such as nightclubs may feature a grooming service provided by an attendant in the toilet

II

Concept of Environmental Sanitation

The term 'environmental sanitation' has been given various interpretations in different countries and at different times. In its most restrictive sense, sanitation has been equated with the safe disposal of human excrement. Environmental sanitation is a major public health issue in India. Recent interventional studies on environmental sanitation in India highlighted the importance of prioritising control strategies. Research related to the appropriate cost-effective intervention strategies and their implementation in Indian context is a big challenge.

Environmental sanitation means the control of all those factors in man's surroundings, which may or may not cause adverse effects on his health. The sanitarian makes an effort towards hygiene of water supply and food supply, hygiene disposal of human and animal wastes, hygiene of housing, and control of rodents and other vectors (RSHB). The WHO defines 'environmental sanitation' as the 'control of all those factors in man's physical environment which exercise or may exercise a deleterious effect on his physical development, health and survival'. Environmental/ hygiene includes all the activities aimed at improving or or maintaining the standard of basic environmental condition affecting the well-being of people. These conditions include the following:

- Clean and safe water supply
- Clean and safe ambient air
- Efficient and safe animal, human and industrial waste disposal
- Protection of food from biological and chemical contaminants
- Adequate housing in clean and safe surroundings (http://www.healthizen.com.blog.index.phb/general/environmental-sanitation/)

According to Mmom and Mmom (2011), environmental sanitation comprises disposal and treatment of human excreta, solid waste and waste water, control of disease vectors, and provision of washing facilities for personal and domestic hygiene. It aims at improving the quality of life of the individuals and contributing to social development... It has defined by the Water Supply and sanitation Collaborative Council as 'Interventions to environment in which to live, with measures to break the cycle of disease.

Environmental sanitation comprises both a change in behaviour and facilities to form a hygiene environment. However, it is truism that a significant number of people worldwide lack access to adequate water, sanitation, drainage, and solid waste disposal services. The latest statistics reveal that 1.1 billion people do not have access to safe drinking water and 2.4 billion people do not have access to adequate sanitation. (WHO/UNICEF/WSSCC, 2000, cited by Kawachi and Berkman: 2003)

Furthermore, in many urban areas of developing countries, less than 50 per cent of the municipal solid wastes are collected and only an insignificant fraction is disposed appropriately...

This not only increases the rate of diseases and mortality, but also slows down the economic progress of hundreds of millions of people in developing countries. At the same time, the world's natural supply of fresh water is subject to increasing environmental and economic pressure. Mmom (2003) noted that urban environment condition is deplorable in many cities of the developing world. In fact, the problems associated with providing environmental sanitation considered one of the most serious and pressing urban environmental problem. Most cities focus on simply getting rid of their waste 'out-of-sight' and fail to recognise its potential danger when not properly disposed, treated, or managed.

Options for Controlling Excreta

For practical purposes sanitation can be divided into on-site and off-site technologies. On-site systems (e.g. latrines), store and/or treat excreta at the point of generation. In off-site systems (e.g. sewerage) Excreta are transported to another location for treatment, disposal or use. Some on-site systems, particularly in densely populated regions or with permanent structures, will have off-site treatment Components as well.

Safe disposal of excrete is of fundamental importance, not only for the health of the community, but also because of the social and environmental benefits it brings. However, for many low-income communities, particularly in developing countries, installation of a sewerage system, with its high cost and need for a piped water supply, is not a feasible option. For such communities, on-site disposal - dealing with excrete where they are deposited - offers a hygienic and affordable solution.

On-site disposal

In many places, particularly in areas with low population densities, it is common to Store and treat wastes where they are produced - on-site. There are a number of technical options for onsite Waste management which if designed, constructed, operated and maintained correctly will provide Adequate service and health benefits when combined with good hygiene. On-site systems include:

Ventilated improved pit (VIP) latrines, double vault composting latrines, pour-flush toilets, and septic tanks. Dry sanitation or eco-sanitation is an onsite disposal method that requires the separation of urine and faeces. Building and operating these systems is often much less expensive than off-site alternatives.

Some on-site systems (e.g. septic tanks or latrines in densely packed urban areas) require sludge to be pumped out and treated off-site. Composting latrines allow waste to be used as a fertiliser after it has been stored under suitable conditions to kill worm eggs and other pathogens.

Based on the authors' experiences(Franceys,R., J. Pickford & R. Reed (1992: 245) in a number of developing countries, the book provides in-depth technical information about the design, construction, operation and maintenance of the major types of on-site sanitation facility, from simple pit latrines to aqua privies and septic tanks, with numerous practical design examples. Recognising that the introduction of on-site sanitation system) involves considerably more than the application of simple, engineering techniques, the authors describe in detail the planning and development processes, and the financial and institutional factors that will need to be taken into account. Particular emphasis is given to the need to involve the community at all stages from planning to evaluation, to adapt projects and programmes to the local situation, and to provide continuing support to the community after the system is installed.

Off-site Disposal

In more densely packed areas sewerage systems are frequently used to transport wastes off-site is that where they can be treated and disposed. Conventional centralised sewerage systems require an elaborate infrastructure and large amounts of water to carry the wastes away. This type of approach may work well in some circumstances but is impractical for many other locations. The cost of a sewerage system (which can be as much as 70 times more expensive than on-site alternatives and its requirement of a piped water supply preclude its adoption in the many communities in less-industrialised countries that lack adequate sanitation. In specific circumstances, cost-effective alternatives to conventional sewerage systems have been developed including small diameter gravity sewers, vacuum and pressure sewers. Simplified sewer systems have been successfully used in Brazil, Ghana and other countries.

Wastewater and Excreta Treatment

Waste needs to be treated to remove or inactivate pathogens before it can be safely reused or disposed of safely. Many on-site waste disposal methods treat excreta by storing it for enough time to kill the pathogens. Most off-site strategies (and some on-site systems) require wastes to be treated at a facility before it can be safely used or released into the environment. In industrialised countries, one approach has been to use mechanical and biological processes (primary and secondary treatment) to remove suspended solids, biological oxygen demanding substances (BOD) and other pollutants. Pathogens and nutrients are typically only minimally removed in these processes. The problem is that these conventional or mechanical processes are expensive to operate: they require energy, skilled labour, infrastructure, and maintenance. To further reduce the pathogens and nutrients requires additional processes, which pushes up the cost still further. In efforts to reduce the cost and complexity of waste treatment, experiments have been conducted with smaller decentralised treatment units. For example in Durban, South Africa local sewerage networks have been connected to small treatment plants (baffled aerobic reactors) to cost-effectively treat more waste. In other areas where offsite treatment is required, and land is available at low cost, waste stabilisation ponds have proven to be cost effective methods for treating wastewater.

How does Sanitation affect the Environment?

In regions where a large proportion of the population is not served with adequate water supply and sanitation, sewage flows directly into streams, rivers, lakes and wetlands, affecting coastal and marine- eco-systems, fouling the environment and exposing millions of children to disease. Particularly in the context of urbanisation, domestic wastewater, sewage and solid waste improperly discharged presents a variety of concerns from providing breeding grounds for communicable disease vectors to contributing to air, water and soil pollution. The results of poor waste management also contribute to a loss of valuable biodiversity. In the case of coral reefs, urban and industrial waste and sewage dumped directly into the ocean or carried by river systems from sources upstream, increase the level of nitrogen in seawater. Increased nitrogen cause over growth of algae, which in turn, smother reefs by cutting off their sunlight. Improved sanitation reduces environmental burdens, increases sustainability of environmental resources and allows for a healthier, more secure future for the population.

III
Environmental and Social Sanitation

Environmental sanitation is a more comprehensive term than soil sanitation; the latter is mostly limited to water supplies and disposal of human and animal wastes. All sources of water are related to soils, as rain which falls on earth must fall and flow on, or percolate, into some soils, and such that in polluted soils, it gets heavily contaminated with materials and, sources of infection. Similarly, all human and animal wastes including excreta and decomposable rubbish in primitive communities are deposited on soils, which in turn contaminate surface water supplies or, soak into sub-soil water sources. Prevention of soil pollution is, therefore, a major issue of soil sanitation, and clean soils in addition to hygienic houses and neighbourhoods, as well as prevention and atmospheric pollution, by and large comprises environmental sanitation. No wonder, therefore, soil sanitation engaged the early sanitarians, so much, that till few decades ago it comprised the major occupations of public health officials, and, therefore, of the discipline of public health. Such concepts of similar terms which considerably overlap in scope, will explain the intimate relationships of physical and biological environments- a clean physical environment is tantamount to a wholesome biological environment as well. It is no wonder that these basic principles of hygiene and sanitation were recognised from ancient times, as all religious persons and places insisted on *'cleanliness as next to Godliness'* long before any specific knowledge of biological causes or carriers of disease was known, as we have today. The percept of person hygiene well known to ancients, is also intimately related to environmental and soil sanitation, as hygiene habits and customs to keep the body clean is but a prelude to cleanliness of the house, neighbourhood or near environments; it is almost impossible to keep one's body and house clean among insanitary conditions of at least close environments. Environmental and soil sanitation is of primary importance, and so is the first line of defence for primary prevention, as it at once promotes and preserves health, as well prevents and protects from diseases, and helps in turn secondary and tertiary preventive methods, as well. The low static level of health in a community, and the overt conditions of disease are always present under insanitary environments; and in such cases immunisation as a specific preventive measure, or even specific treatment becomes temporary and, fails to confer permanent cure and protection.

It is little use inoculating a population every year with anti-typhoid vaccines, if the water supplies are liable to gross faecal contamination, and, it is no use treating people with helminthic drugs against hook-worm or round-worms, if the chances of acquiring these infections are ever present in polluted soils in the community. Even if radical cure is effected, in a hospital or dispensary for hook-worm infection at the times, as soon as the 'cred patients' return back to their environments, they walk on polluted soils to get re-infected, again and again. Similarly, infantile diarrhoeas and dysenteries can be traced to environmental sanitation, while droplet infections are promoted in over-crowded single-room-tenement houses and unplanned towns and villages, as in slums. The more the soil pollution, the greater the chances of accumulated decomposing organic matter which collects on the surface, and soaks into superficial layers of soil, pollutes water supplies, breeds insects, vermin and rodents which are either direct sources of disease, or indirect vectors or act as reservoir hosts. Diseases which relate to soil pollution are water-borne infections and, such protozoal, helminthic and insect borne, as well as bacterial, and viral infections which are incidental to polluted water and soils. All these factors are yet another illustration, that the causal agents of several diseases are found in physical and biological environments, as much as psychological and socio-economic environments; and the former needs grater and primary attention than the latter. This is the essence of permanent prevention; as it attacks the causes of diseases, and hence the old adage 'prevention is better than cure', can often also be cheaper and, more effective than cure, as well. The fact that infant mortality rates are used the world over by all public health officers as the standard measuring rods to assess the sanitary state of a community, indicates how intimately the health and disease status of infants are related to physical environments; and to a less degree with adults as well (Dakshinamurty:*1962:198-202).*

Ecological approach to sanitation which seeks to contain, treat and reuse excreta where possible – thus minimising contamination and making optimum use of resources. The key issue here is that each community, region or country needs to work out what is the most sensible and cost effective way of thinking about sanitation in the short and long term and then act accordingly. Ecological sanitation is sometimes presented as a radical alternative to conventional sanitation systems. Ecological sanitation is based on composting or vermicomposting toilets where an extra separation of urine and feces at the source for sanitisation and recycling has been done. It thus eliminates the creation of black water and eliminates faecal pathogens. If ecological sanitation is practiced municipal wastewater consists only of grey water, which can be recycled for gardening. However, in most cases grey water continues to be discharged to sewers.

UNO states that: whatever humans gather, their waste also accumulates. Progress in sanitation and improved hygiene has greatly improved health, but many people still have no adequate means of disposing their waste. This is growing nuisance for heavily populated areas, carrying the risk of infectious diseases, particularly to vulnerable groups such as the very young, elderly and people suffering from diseases that lower their resistance. Poorly controlled waste also means daily exposure to an unpleasant environment. The build of faecal contamination in rivers and other waters is not just a human risk: other species are affected threatening the ecological balance of the environment.

The discharge of untreated waste water and excreta into the environment affects human health by several routes:

- By polluting drinking water
- Entry into the food chain, for example via fruits, vegetables or fish and shellfish
- Bathing, recreational and other contact with contaminated waters
- By providing breeding sites for flies and insects that spread diseases

IV
The Environmental Burden of Disease

According to a study conducted by Environment and Social Development Unit South Asia Region (Environmental Health in India: Priorities in Andhra Pradesh: 2001), environmental factors account for about 20 per cent of the total burden of disease in Andhra Pradesh (AP). Over 90 Per cent of this is associated with traditional environmental risk, such as lack of access to a protected water supply and sanitation (73 per cent of AP's population has no sanitation facilities) and indoor air pollution resulting from the use of biomass fuels. The largest portion of the environmental burden of ill health is borne by people in rural areas, where access to basic infrastructure services (water, sanitation and commercial fuels) is lower and where baseline infant and child mortality rates are higher than in urban AP. In rural areas, environmental factors account for 22-25 per cent of the burden of disease, significantly higher than urban areas. This burden is almost entirely caused by the lack of access to water and sanitation facilities and by exposure to indoor air pollution (89 per cent) of the rural population relies on wood and dung cakes for cooking fuel) and contaminated drinking water. Thus while modern environmental risks linked to industrial pollution and urban development also exist and are growing, environmental health is still to a large degree, a rural health issue in AP—and will continue to be for quite some time. Urban households have much higher level of access to water and sanitation services and rely less upon dirty cooking fuels. As a result of these and other factors (such as higher levels of income and education), the average burden of disease is significantly lower for the urban population, as is the share of the household environment in the total burden.

V
The Scope and Subjects of environmental Hygiene and Sanitation

Dakshinamurty (1962:198-202) discusses the Scope and Subjects of environmental Hygiene and sanitation. The scope of this subject is clear from the terms of reference of the Environmental Hygiene Committee appointed by Government of .India, 1949; from which the following are adapted:

(a) Town and Village Planning

(b) Housing, Urban and rural

(c) Water Supply

(d) General sanitation, including conservancy and drainage;

(e) Prevention of river, beach pollution, road sides and all open places'

(f) Control of rodent and insect vectors of diseases; and

(g) Regulation of certain trades, industries and occupations dangerous to health and offensive to the community, producing atmospheric pollution, noise and nuisance to the locality.

The factors involved in Environmental hygiene are enunciated as well as in the report of the above Committee, as follows:

(1) Home and Surroundings

The home and its surroundings should provide the family with shelter against exposure to extremes of temperature, sun, wind and rain; with security of person and propriety; with comfort, with privacy and company of fellow beings when desired; with architectural and aesthetic satisfaction; and with protection against infection contagious and physical hazards. The fulfilment of this purpose is to be achieved through town and village planning and, housing of residential areas.

(2) Water Supplies

People should have the facilities to obtain an adequate supply of safe, potable and pleasant water to sustain life and to keep clean. This is to be achieved through protected water supplies for domestic consumption and, abundant supply for municipal purposes.

(3) Foods

They should also have the facilities to obtain adequate and nutritious food, milk and beverages, prepared and served under hygienic conditions. This is to be achieved through the sanitation of food and drink establishments, markets, slaughter houses, public eating places, cattle-sheds and diaries.

(4) Atmosphere

They should live and work in a comfortable atmosphere free from hazards to their health, such as dust, smoke, odours, fumes, and microbes of disease. They should have adequate light and ventilation, quiet and peace to carry on their duties efficiently. This is largely achieved through the control of dangerous and offensive trades and, through industrial hygiene engineering of factories and mills.

(5) Wastes

The waste products of the family, the community and the factory should be collected and disposed of, so as not to endanger the health of the pubic by any chance. This is achieved through efficient pubic cleansing and sewerage, through hygienic disposal of excreta and refuse, and through controlled pollution of wells, tanks, lakes, rivers, beaches, roadsides and all open spaces.

(6) Infections

The risk of transmitting infections from one person to another are particularly great at places where people congregate, as at schools, markets, fairs and festivals, places of amusements, public transport vehicles, and railway stations, vigilant control has to be exercised over the sanitation of the environment in these places.

(7) Seeds of Disease Control

The environment should be unfavourable to the growth of the seeds of disease both physical and biological. Hence cleanliness and facilities to keep clean are important. Sunlight, dryness and other natural agencies discouraging microbic life should be taken advantage of with discretion. Rat, flies, ticks, fleas and mosquitoes should find the environment unsuitable for their feeding, breeding and resting places.

(8) Rapid Recovery

When a person falls ill, he should be treated in an environment favourable to rapid recovery. This will be partly achieved through the construction of hospitals, sanatoria, nursing homes and asylums, designed for their particular function, far away from industrial areas, and near to residential areas, in 'silent zones' where horning of motor vehicles is prohibited (Dakshinamurty:*1962:198-202).*

VI
Promoting Sanitation

Many diseases are spread from person to person by germs in faeces. According to Jeff Conant (2005), some experts believe health from poor sanitation can be prevented only if people change their personal habits, or 'behaviours', about staying clean. But this idea often leads to failure because it does not consider the barriers that people face in their daily lives, such as poverty or lack of access to clean water. Then when behaviour does not change, people are blamed for their own poor health. Other experts look for technical solutions, such as modern toilets that flush water. Technical solutions often come from outside a community and may not fit the traditions or conditions of the community. Sometimes they create more problems than they solve! The disease caused by germs from poor hygiene and sanitation will not be prevented if people are blamed for their own poor health, or if only technical solutions are promoted. To improve health in a lasting way, health promoters must listen carefully and work together with people in the community. When communities use hygiene and sanitation methods that fit their real needs and abilities, they will enjoy better health.

The poor sanitation leads to more healthy problems. Illnesses caused by germs and worms in faeces are a constant source of discomfort for millions of people. These illnesses can cause many years of sickness and can lead to other health problems such as dehydration, anaemia, and malnutrition. Severe sanitation related illnesses such as cholera can spread rapidly, bringing sudden death to many people.

Children have a high risk of illness from poor sanitation. While adults may live with diarrhoea diseases and worms, children die from these illnesses. It is important for children to have toilets that are safe and that feel safe. When children feel safe using the toilet and have an easy way to stay clean, they get less sick. Many children especially girls, leave school because safe toilets and healthy conditions are not provided for them. Allowing children to help build toilets and teaching them about illness caused by poor sanitation are some ways to help them develop healthy behaviours (Akram: 2014:170-171).

Social Mobilisation: Social Mobilisation is an essential pre-requisite for the success of any intervention for the development of environmental sanitation and hygiene. It is also essential that for identifying the needs, raising the awareness of and ascertaining the demands for sanitation and hygiene, all feasible social partners and allies must get together to face the emerging challenges and carry out the well-defined tasks. Or else, the governmental and non-governmental interventions alone would not suffice.

VII
Water and Sanitation

Water is the most essential and basic ingredient for any effort towards development of hygiene and sanitation. In a large number of villages of India, the supply of piped water continues to remain a distant dream. According to a source, 240crores of people the world over live under highly unsanitary conditions and, due to their unhygienic behaviours; they are exposed to the risk of falling prey to diarrhoea and other infectious diseases. The share of the Indian population facing similar situations must be quite substantial. Several schemes have been launched by the central and state governments for the construction of latrines, but the requirements have been rather insurmountable.

Drinking water supply and sanitation service quality in India is generally poor, although there has been some limited progress concerning continuity of supply in urban areas and access to sanitation in rural areas. In fact, it continues to be inadequate, despite longstanding efforts by the various levels of government and communities at improving coverage. The level of investment in water and sanitation, albeit low by international standards, has increased during the 2000s. Access has also increased significantly. For example, in 1980 rural sanitation coverage was estimated at 1 per cent and reached 21 per cent in 2008 (UNICEF/WHO: 2008; Census: 2001; and Planning commission in India: 2010). Also, the share of Indians with access to improved sources of water has increased significantly from 72 per cent in 1990 to 88 per cent in 2008 (UNICEF/WHO: 2008; Census: 2001). At the same time, local government institutions in charge of operating and maintaining the infrastructure are seen as weak and lack the financial resources to carry out their functions. In addition, no major city in India is known to have a continuous water supply (Panning Commission in India: 2010) and an estimated 72 per cent of Indians still lack access to improved sanitation facilities.

A number of innovative approaches to improve water supply and sanitation have been tested in India, in particular in the early 2000s. These include demand-driven approaches in rural water supply since 1999, community-led total sanitation, and public-private partnerships to improve the continuity of urban water supply in Karnataka, and the use of micro-credit to women in order to improve access to water. (Development Policy review: 2010)

Hon'ble Mr. Bharatsinh Madhavsinh Solanki, Minister of State (independent charge), Department of Drinking Water and Sanitation, speaking on the occasion named sanitation and drinking water as the basic needs of society. We have to gear up and streamline our efforts at the national scale to make provision for their availability for all, we will seek the active participation and cooperation of all, especially the nongovernmental organisations in these endeavours, he added. Hon'ble Mr. Jairam Ramesh, Union Minister for Rural Development started his address with drawing attention of the audience to the sanitational situation in the country with provision for sanitary toilets still to be made on a large scale, especially in the villages, where even now, about 25 lakh scavengers are engaged in cleaning toilets. The government has taken a pioneering step by constituting Mahila Swayam Sahayata Samooh. The effort is to provide what has been termed as Aajeevika to sponsor self-help activities arranging bank loans for the purpose. 25,000 such Samoohs have been constituted targeting to reach 75,000 in a year. The Department of Drinking Water and Sanitation has initiated Nirmal Bharat Abhiyan. So far 2,500 Panchayats have become Nirmal, whereas their total number is 2.5 lakh. It has been planned to reach all of them in ten years' time. There is a bill before Parliament to make prohibitory provisions against manual scavenging stricter, since the existing Act preventing the practice has not been effective. The Minister said, "I shall request the Hon'ble Speaker to use her good offices to get the proposed bill through to be enacted soon. Only one state so far has been able to totally prevent defecation in the open that is Sikkim. Kerala is expected to be the second such state, to be followed, hopefully by Maharashtra. Efforts are to be concentrated on states like Bihar, U.P., Madhya Pradesh, which are big states to be taken care of. The issue of sanitation is too important and big to be left as a governmental mission. NGOs are to be associated on a large scale in the drive for cleanliness; Sulabh's work in the field has been really pioneering".

Conclusion

At present, each year more than 200 million tones of human waste- and vast quantities of waste water and solid waste- go uncollected and untreated around the world, fouling the environment and exposing millions of children, women and public at large to disease and squalor. Improved sanitation leads to less environmental degradation, increased sustainability of environmental resources and a more secure future for not only to the women and children but also to the whole society.

References

Akram, Mohammad (2014). 'Sanitation and Environment' in *Sociology of Health,* Jaipur: Rawat Publications, Pp. 163-172.

Conant, Jeff (2005). *Sanitationand Cleanliness for a Healthy Environment,* USA: Hesperian Foundation

Chhattisgarh Urban Sanitation Strategy (CUSS):2010: CG. Govt-2011

Dakshinamurty, Sonti (1962), *Introduction to preventive and Social medicine: An Epidemiological and Social Medicine,* Kakinada: Educational Enterprises.pp.198-202.

"Development Policy Review".World Bank.http://web.worldbank.org/WBSITE/EXTERNAL/COUNTRIES/SOUTHASIAEXT/0,,contentMDK:20980493~pagePK:146736~piPK:146830~theSitePK:223547,00.html. Retrieved 19 September 2010.

Environment, Water and Sanitation, Irish Aid Key sheet, Environmental Policy for Sustainable Development. Available on line at: www.irishaid.gov.ie.

Environment health in India: priorities in Andhra Pradesh (2001). Environment and Social Development unit South Asia region, October.

Franceys, R., J. Pickford & R. Reed (1992).A guide to Development of On-Site Sanitation, Geneva: World Health Organisation (WHO) p.245.

Kawachi, I. and Berkman, L.F. (2003). Neighbourhoods and Health, New York: Oxford University Press.

Kumar, G.S., Kar, S.S. and Jain, A. (2011). 'Health and Environmental sanitation in India: issues for prioritising Control Strategies', *Indian Journal of Occupational and Environmental Medicine',* September 15 (3): 93-96.

Mmom, P.C. (2003). 'Willingness of Port Harcourt City residents to relocate their residence; implication for urban decongestion', J.

Pedagogy Dev., Special Ed., and Pp: 78-89. Cited in Mmom, P.C. and Mmom, C.F. (2011).

Mmom, P.C. and C.F. Mmom (2011). 'Environmental sanitation and Public health challenges I a rapidly Growing City of the Third world: The case of Domestic waste and Diarrhoea Incidence in greater Port Harcourt Metropolis, Nigeria' *Asian Journal of Medical Sciences*3 (3).

Pandve, H.T. (2008). 'Environmental Sanitation: An Ignored Issue in India', *Indian Journal of Occupational and Environmental Medicine,* 12 (1): 40.

Park, J.E. and Park (1977), *Text book on Social and Preventive and Social Medicine*, Jabalpur: Banarsidas Bhanot Publishers. P.94 (old book)

Planning Commission of India."Health and Family Welfare and AYUSH : 11th Five Year Plan". http://planningcommission.nic.in/plans/planrel/fiveyr/11th/11_v2/11v2_ch3.pdf. Retrieved 19 September 2010. p. 78.

UNICEF/WHO Joint Monitoring Programme for Water Supply and Sanitation estimate for 2008 based on the 2006 Demographic and Health Survey, the 2001 census, other data and the extrapolation of previous trends to 2010.

Yongsi, H.B.N., Herrmann, T.M., Ntetu, A.L., Sietchiping, R. and Herrmann, C.B. (2008). 'Environmental sanitation and Health Risks in Tropical Urban Settings: Case Study of Household Refuse and Diarrhoea in YaoundeCameroon', International Journal of Human and Social Sciences, 3:3, 220-228, Available at www.waste.org/journals/ijhss/v3/v3-3-29.pdf

WHO (2007). Available at: http://www.who.int/whr/2007/en/index.html

http://www.healthizen.com/blog/index.php/eneral/environmental-sanitation/whqlibdoc.who.int/publications/a38153_(ch21).pdf, en.wikipedia.org/wiki/sanitation.

8

State and Sanitation in India

In contemporary India, the endeavours made by the Government and the civil society to liberate scavengers from the suffocating situation have not been able to bear fruit, and therefore, the long shadow of institutionalised discrimination, stigmatisation and marginalisation has still refused to fade out. The atrocious behaviour and treatment meted out to scavengers because of their low social positioning in the caste hierarchy caused deep anger and resentment. Bindeshwar Pathak hated to endorse the entrenched injustice of the Indian Caste System, especially against the so-called untouchables, who have been the worst victims of the system. In this context, the present chapter deals with the three things related to the State and sanitation In India:

1. Sanitation in the policies and programmes in India and its critique
2. Implementation and utilisation of sanitary programmes in rural and urban communities
3. Liberation and Rehabilitation of scavengers

1. Sanitation in the Policies and Programmes in India and its Critique

Sanitation is a broad term that includes disposal of human waste, waste water, solid waste, domestic and personal hygiene etc. the lack of sanitation has a detrimental effect on health status ad negates developmental efforts. It has become a yardstick of socio-cultural and economic development of a nation. Lack of sanitation and hygiene is the primary cause of almost all infectious diseases. There is a direct relationship between availability of water, sanitation, health services, nutrition and human well-being. The burden of disease linked to water and sanitation conditions is enormous. According to the global total (UNDP: 2006:45), human excreta alone cause many infectious and parasitic diseases such as cholera, dysentery, typhoid, paratyphoid, infectious hepatitis, hookworm, diarrhoea, polio etc. (www.Sulabhenvis.in:1). It is estimated that one gram of faecal contains about 1 crore virus, 10 lakh bacteria, 1000 parasites cyst and 100 parasitic eggs and with 65 per cent of rural India defecating in the open, the daily faecal load is estimated to be about 2 lakh metric tonnes (www.undop.org:homepagge). According to Health Information Statistics of India, about 25 per cent of deaths in the country are attributed to infectious diseases (HII: 1998-2000). Over half of all polio cases in the world are reported in India whereas this crippling disease has virtually been wiped out in the developed countries. India alone accounts for about one-fourth deaths out of 25 lakh deaths in the world every year due to diarrhoea (htpp://www.who.int). Jaundice, viral hepatitis, gastro-enteritis and cholera outbreaks is almost an annual feature in many villages. High levels of malnutrition (national average being 41 per cent) are also attributed to poor sanitation. Water borne diseases and intestinal worm leads to loss of nutrition as these parasites consume nutrients and aggravate under nutrition from the already insufficient diets of the rural people and consequently result in deficiency diseases like night blindness, poor growth, vitamin deficiencies, low immunity etc. and retard child's physical development. Not only this, certain maternal health conditions are also the manifestations of the cycle of infectious diseases. Further, various kinds of skin diseases are also attributed to lack of water, sanitation and hygiene. At the root of the most public health problems is poor sanitation and hygiene. Studies have shown that sanitation alone can reduce the incidence of infectious diseases by up to 80 per cent by inhibiting disease generation and interrupting disease transmission (WHO: 1986:6).

Access to sanitation is also critical to social and economic progress. It should also be noted that over a billion people in the world do not have access to safe water and over 2 billion lack adequate sanitation. Out of this, about 636 million reside in India alone. The lack of toilet facilities and open defecation at such a large scale in the rural areas of contaminates the soil and water bodies with pathogens (GOI: 2002:39). This a key causative factor behind the high prevalence of soil and water borne diseases in rural India. Therefore, proper sanitation is important not only from the general health point of view but it has a vital role to play in our individual and social life too. Sanitation is one of the determinants of quality of life and human development Index. Further, its availability can be linked to women empowerment as they are more adversely affected by the lack of sanitation facilities in terms of their dignity and privacy.

It is generally believed that the provision and coverage of water, sanitation and hygiene increases with increase in income. It is guided by the argument that these services have to be financed out of household budget. However, the global snapshot reveals that in many countries, wealth and provisional of water and sanitation has not much correspondence. For example, Philippines, as compared to Sri Lanka and India in comparison to Bangladesh have much higher income, yet heir citizens have lower access to sanitation coverage (UNDP: 2006:36). In case of India also, one finds that sanitation, hygiene and sewerage facilities (generally associated with the poor economy, low purchasing power, low levels of literacy and other such social indicators) are poor in many economically developed states such as Maharashtra and Haryana (35 per cent each) Gujarat and Tamil Nadu (45 per cent each). On the other hand, the states of Kerala and Assam have 80 to 84 per cent of households provided with sanitation (toilets) facilities (Census: 2001). Further, what is more disturbing is the fact that in economically developed states, the gap between provision of water and sanitation is quite high. Sanitation provision basically lags far behind access to water. These gaps matter not just because access to sanitation is intrinsically important, but also because the benefits of improved access to water and to sanitation are mutually reinforcing. The Haryana state has exhibited above average performance in all sectors which is reflected in its high per capita income as compared to national average (Government of Haryana: 2006:6). Not only this, the state also has the distinction of having all kinds of physical infrastructure i.e. roads (length and coverage), connectivity of villages with pucca rod, public transport, villages supplied with electricity, postal network, potable drinking water supply, schools, health centres and likewise. With this pattern of development, there should have been better sanitation conditions and smooth epidemiological transition in the state. But the sanitation in the state is not found satisfactory and it has a direct bearing on the disease pattern (Rajeshwari: 2008:81).

Sanitary Policy

Before the 1860s sanitary arrangements for the civilian population were hardly discussed. For example, in 1810, when some Dacca citizens proposed local improvements, such as the removal of filth, or the repair of wells and drains, the governor-general rejected the proposal out of hand (Ahmed:1980: 134-135). By 1823 the governor-general allowed the surplus from town taxes to be spent on urban improvements; but in Dacca, at least, most efforts went into widening rods, draining marshes, and clearing land for (among other things) a race-course (Ahmed: 1980:147-148). Efforts depended on the individuals officials appointed to improvements committees, all of which were abolished in 1829 as a measure of economy (Ahmed: 1980: 159). More concern for the health of the army; for example, after 1835 medical officers were encouraged to submit details of the climate; geography, and medical statistics of districts in order to guide military campsites and cantonments to healthy places (Ramasubban: 1982). However, one measure of civilian preventive medicine predated in 1860s: vaccination against smallpox was supported with fluctuating energy and attempts were made to eradicate the indigenous practice of inoculation (Arnold: 1985).

Preventive health measures in India are usually dated from the Royal Commission appointed to inquire into the sanitary state of the army in India, which reported in 1863. This Commission was established, in part at least, because the deaths of British soldiers from disease during the mutiny greatly exceeded those from injuries received in fighting. It reported that the health of the army could not be separated from "the sanitary condition of the 'native' population" close by, and that 'well-considered measures of water-supply, drainage, paving, cleansing, and general constitution in these towns would be attended with most beneficial results to the health of the troops quartered near them". All the native towns had some system of cleansing and dealing with human excreta and other nuisances, nonetheless, the commission concluded, there was much more to be done (Sanitary Commission 1865:77, 81; Statistical Abstract 1870:53). The priority of sanitary work was thus based on military arguments, and it retained this basis for the rest of the nineteenth century. Sanitary policy was restricted to towns and military areas because the remit of the commission was to consider improvements for the towns "in proximity to military stations (Sanitary Commission 1865:77, 81; Statistical Abstract 1870:53, para 35).

The government of India implemented the proposal of commission's 1863 report of sanitary commissions in each presidency with advisory, but few executive, powers. These sanitary commissions were replaced two years later by single sanitary commissions were replaced two years later by a single sanitary commissioner each, and, by 1868, one for each of the provinces. For twenty years little was achieved, partly because sanitary officers were subordinated to medical ones, and partly because sanitary concerns were restricted to official circles. In addition, technical disputes about the relationship between sanitary measures and medical science hindered the implementation of policy, especially with respect to the role of clean water by preventing cholera (Farrell: 1973: Jaggi: 1979; Hume: 1984).

The Indian System of Medicine was unconvinced of the need to separate sanitary from medical work. In 1866 Gordon argued that the sanitary commissioners would unnecessarily limit the functions of army medical officers, and the Indian Medical Gazette also waged a fierce war against the appointment of major G.B.Malleson, a layman, to be head of the Bengal Sanitary department (Jaggi: 1979: 98-99). Indian authorities had little training in epidemiology as was then understood in Britain, which helped to render the sanitary commissioners' work almost valueless. For example, in the 1870s the Bengal Sanitary Commissioner was attacked in the London press for apparently doing little beyond collating vital statistics which he was unable to analyses to any effect.

Further criticisms came from international concern with cholera. In 1866 an International sanitary Conference in

Constantinople concluded that India was the source of Cholera epidemics, and that the Indian government had failed to control them. The measures proposed to deal with cholera were progressively implemented for the army and cholera mortality dropped to three deaths per 1,000 in the 1870s. But when medical men came to deal with civilian cholera, they hid behind "Orientalist" excuses: Indians were inferior, and one sign of their inferiority was their relentless attachment to superstition, which made it impossible to tamper with religious customs such as pilgrimages, widely agreed to be a major route of cholera transmission (Ramasubban 1982: 21-23).

Sanitary commissioners were expressly excluded from any concern with the cantonments and the European civil lines themselves; these remained the responsibility of the army (Harrison: 1980: 173). Increasingly, towns had local municipal committees, with some elected members. Initially, these committees focused mainly on conservancy- the removal of faces from residential areas. In Allahabad in 1870, 280 sweepers were employed to collect sewage and 90 drivers to remove it for burial. In Calcutta in 1867, a municipal railway was built to deal with the transport problem (Harrison: 1980: 182-183). But the financial limits of these committees prevented them from making much impact on sanitation. Thus, in 1883, when Ranchodlal Chhotalal, the first nonofficial Indian to be made chair of the Ahmedabad Managing Committee, proposed better water supplies and drainages, better hospitals, and more planning controls over housing, his vehement opponents attacked the increased taxation needed to pay for the proposed improvements (Gillion: 1968: 136-138). Eventually, in 1891 an improved water-supply scheme was implemented: but it was not until 1903, after the municipality was ordered by the Bombay government to take the advice of experts, that the drainage scheme was completed. Similarly in Allahabad, the water-supply scheme first mooted in 1883 was in operation by 1891, but a drainage scheme for the extra water supplied was not started until 1913 (Harrison: 1980: 186).

This delay in providing drainage systems (common throughout Indian towns because of the extra expenses involved) meant that introducing clean water supplies actually seems to have increased mortality rates. In six north-Indian towns, recorded death rates in the five years following the introduction of filtered water supplies were higher than the five years before (Klein: 1973:651). The surplus water probably formed stagnant pools, ideal breeding grounds for mosquitoes, thus increasing the spread of malaria, though deaths due to dysentery, cholera, and diarrhea probably did decline (Jeffery: 1988:95).

In the late 1880s Florence Nightingale pressed the Indian government to improve sanitary arrangements in the villages which had been almost totally ignored. No rural agency existed to implement the rules established for village sanitation. Decentralisation only reached the provinces in 1872, under Lord Mayo's reforms, and larger towns were given some autonomy in 1882, with the Ripon reforms. A new extension of local government was set up in train with acts in Bombay (1889) and other parts of the country designed to promote district authorities for whom sanitary measures would be a primary concern. Training in hygiene and sanitation was expanded and, over the next years, graduated were brought into sanitary work.

Activity, however, was severely restricted by the shortage of funds available and by the limitations policy makers believed were because by the "ignorance, prejudices, callousness, and superstitions of the people" (Harvey: 1895: 5). This blaming of the poor and sick for their own conditions may have allowed some doctors to escape the responsibility for eradicating the real causes of high rates of morbidity and mortality. But some doctors advanced more sophisticated arguments, suggesting that European methods of disease control was inapplicable in India, because of social (e.g. Caste) and environmental (e.g. the monsoon) barriers (Arnold: 1985: 6). Clearly, medical administrations were uneasy about their record in sanitary work, particularly when challenged to international settings with responsibility for cholera which emanated from Bengal (Jaggi: 1979:103). However, they were undoubtedly right to argue that implementing sanitary improvements throughout rural India would be beyond the financial limits of Britain, let alone of the Indian government. Funding problems were probably exacerbated by linking sanitary reform to local governments with even less adequate sources of finance than the towns had.

Attempts to intervene in the provision of water, the control of sewage, and other aspects of everyday village life would probably have led to great hostility and little success. Vaccinators had to deal with frequent rumors of the dangers of the treatment and general hostility, partly because they were also trying to eradicate inoculation which was a much more accepted form of smallpox prevention (Arnold: 1985:8).. The response to Plague measures after 1896 reinforced this view. Sanitary measures based on little understanding of village life, would probably have been successful, though this does not justify the pathetic attempts that were actually made. Expenditures on preventive medicine were always small, relative to overall public or to medical expenditure. Probably only water supplies and some vaccination programmes made any marked impact on morbidity and mortality before World War II.

Yet medical administrators appreciated the links between providing sanitation and a population's health, especially in urban areas where collective arrangements for waste disposal, water supply and drainage were major concerns. As in Europe, town planning until 1900 was almost entirely a matter of sanitary provision, fueled by demands from the wealthy for protection from diseases of the poor. In India this took on a racial form, with attempts to protect Europeans- civilians and the military- from native diseases. This is obvious in the reports of the sanitary commissioners, but its most notable results lay in the separation of city from cantonment and in other attempts to place physical barriers between Indian and European. The Royal Commission deplored these efforts (Sanitary Commission 1865: 79), but they accorded with the theories of contagion through bad air (Harrison: 1980:174; King: 1966). Thus, conditions in European areas were much better than in Indian areas; roads were paved and swept, water supply and drainage was quickly improved to a higher standard, and these were infinitely less crowding. But sewage removal arrangements in the European areas differed little from those in the rest of the city, at least during the nineteenth century, and provisions for Indians living there (servants, trades etc.) were possibly even worse than in the towns (Harrison: 1980: 182).

After 1900 improvement trusts were established in many larger towns and Patrick Geddes, among others, was asked to advise on the development of urban areas- promoted partly by a concern for the appalling conditions in the slums. The trusts had power to control only new building ran into overwhelming opposition from powerful slum landlords as well as the municipal committees, for whom they were too expensive. Despite Geddes's propaganda, it was only in Hyderabad (where the nizam gave considerable support) that there was any substantial attack on unsanitary conditions (Meller: 1979: 347).

The other impetus to urban renewal came from plague epidemics. Plague was probably common in India before the British arrived and its association with rats was known (Anstey: 1936):72). But it apparently disappeared from India in the early nineteenth century before being reintroduced from China through Bombay in 1896. Since its sign are distinctive and it generated such horror and official inquiry, deaths from plague were probably recorded fairly accurately. If so, the estimates of some 15 million plague deaths in British India and 18 million in the princely states, between 1896 and 1921, cannot be far off the mark (Census: 1921:350). The disease spread quickly to most parts of the country, speeded by railways, trade, and commerce. The urban poor suffered most and then, panic-stricken, escaped into rural areas, taking the disease with them; European were almost immune.

The vital point to note here is that plague reappeared in India when control and prevention measures were understood, and yet the response of the authorities was almost totally ineffective. The Bombay authorities took drastic action; sufferers were compulsorily removed to hospital, the infected were segregated, premises were evacuated, a sanitary cordon was attempted around affected areas, and travelers were medically inspected. These measures were inadequately explained and few people accepted the rationality of what was proposed. Some resisted openly; traders rejected ban on exports or the movement of goods, mill owners rejected steam cleansing, while Jains and others destroyed rattraps. Others concealed infected people and then dumped their dead bodies anonymously in the street, escaped around cordons, or refused to leave infected areas for fear of theft from their unprotected houses (Klein: 1973). When pushed too far, they rioted.

Western medicine's arrogant self-confidence and its failure to deal with the plague is well exposed by the medical authorities' compromises with Indian opinion. Originally, the authorities wanted all patients to be treated by western doctors, but they were forced to accept instead the use by patients of hakims and vaids. They also had to deny that plague inoculation would be made compulsory (Arnold: 1985: 10-11). By 1900 the sanitary commissioner noted, the plague epidemic was treated as political emergency, not as a matter of public health, and he argued that this was because the idea of public health was alien to the sympathies and traditions of the people (Annual Report of the Sanitary Commissioner 1902: 117-21). Dealing with the threat to trade and social order became paramount: treatment and control measures had to follow behind these imperatives, and the imperial government withdrew from active attempts to prevent the spread of the disease, merely responding to calls for medical services (Klein: 1973).

For the purpose of seeing the sanitation effect, a detailed classification of infectious and parasitic diseases has been taken into consideration by Rajeshwari (2008:79-94) in her paper, 'Sanitation Situation and disease Pattern in Haryana: A Spatial Analysis'. Following are the objectives of the present paper:

1. It presents a spatial pattern in the provision and availability of sanitary facilities in rural and urban areas taking district as a unit.
2. It outlines the disease pattern and existing spatial variations in it.
3. It seeks to relate the various infectious and parasitic diseases (water and sanitation borne) to sanitation situation in the state.

The paper is based on the secondary sources. In the present study, a district-wise pattern of infectious and parasitic diseases has been presented and within this broad category, the pattern of a combination of human excreta borne and water contaminated diseases has been analysed. The paper highlights that despite much technical progress, the state has a poor record in terms of availability of toilet facilities. There is wide inter-district variation, which does not correspond with the level of agricultural development in the state. Further, the non-availability of toilet facilities in urban areas suggests that open defecation is not a problem, of rural areas alone. Further, the rural-urban gap within districts is also large, which suggest that the sanitation campaign should be taken on a war footing in the rural areas.

The paper also stresses the need of sanitation due to the fact that even in the developed state like Haryana, water and filth borne diseases still dominate on examining the pattern of disease in Haryana. Hence, in order to break the vicious circle of communicable diseases, improvement in sanitation is need of the hour. These are the diseases which can be reduced through control of flies and increasing awareness towards the hygiene behaviour. The analysis also suggests that in addition to reducing faecal-oral diseases, the availability of water should also be studied while explaining the disease pattern. The findings need to be corroborated with primary data undertaking micro-level studies in the area.

Water sanitation is the most powerful preventive medicine and investment in sanitation and water is as effective mechanism in reducing risks and deaths due to killer diseases like child diarrhoea, as immunisation has proved in reduction of measles meaning thereby that preventive care can eliminate many diseases. Hence, sanitation measures once undertaken will go a long way in improving the environmental health of population and overall health promotion. Though Government of India has introduced Total sanitation campaign and Nirmal Gram Puruskar schemes at village level involving Gram-panchayats through DRDA (District Rural development Agency), district level throughout India, this campaign need to be implemented at war footing and with greater involvement of people from all walks of life. There are few success stories of TSC, but these are few and relates to urban areas only.

The study also suggests that the sanitation problem is both provision of facility and behaviour change. (As the paper shows that it is not only the economically backward states and districts that lag behind in its provision, economically better districts and states are equally poor in terms of sanitation and hygiene.) Hence, until the need for and benefits of sanitation are realised and internalised, mere provision of facilities will not provide the expected results.

2. Implementation and Utilisation of Sanitary Programmes in Rural and Urban Communities

National Policy on Sanitation

The Environmental Hygiene Committee (1948-49) appointed

by the Union Government was the first agency of its type charged with an overall assessment of the country wide problems in the entire field of Environmental Hygiene. The Committee recommended a comprehensive plan to provide safe water supply and adequate sanitation services for 90 per cent of the population within a period of 40 years. In 1954, when the first national water supply programme was launched as part of Government's health plan, sanitation was mentioned as a part of the section on water supply. Sanitation in fact was never perceived as a priority especially in rural areas. Nor was it seen as a development programme- more often related to lower levels in the priority leader and left unmonitored. It was only in 1980, the UN declared the decade 1981-90 as the International Drinking Water Supply and Sanitation Decade and goals were set for programme for sanitation, the Central Rural sanitation Programme (CSP) in 1986 in the Ministry of Rural development. But during this decade also, the coverage with regard to urban sanitation (through sewerage and other excreta disposal methods) and for rural population was extremely low. However, the target set were 80 per cent for urban population and plan 25 per cent for rural population by the year 1990. The position of coverage for urban and rural sanitation was 25.04 per cent (40.03 million population) and 5 per cent (2.8 million) respectively. Since then, sanitation situation has been covered by variety of surveys like Census, National Sample Survey Organisation (NSSO), and National Family Health Survey (NFHS) etc. The figures continue to be alarmingly low. A temporal view in the availability of toilet facilities in rural and urban India has been presented in table-1.

Table 1: Per cent of Households with No Toilets facility in Rural and Urban India: 1988-98

Period	*Rural*	*Urban*
1988 (44th round)	89.0	31.8
1993(49th round)	85.8	30.6
1998(54th round)	82.5	25.5

Source: NSSO estimates of 44th, 49th and 54th rounds: NSSO (376, 429, 449)

The Central Rural sanitation Programme (CRSP) was restructured in 1999 and Total sanitation campaign (TSC) was introduced. The TSC was being initiated under the sector reform process to promote greater user involvement, lower subsidies, to facilitate NGOs role, and promotion of technologies. The 9th Five year Plan emphasised the need for undertaking all possible measures for rapid expansion and improvement of sanitation facilities in urban and rural areas. The sanitation coverage in terms of individual household toilets during the 9th Five Year Plan period (1997-2001) was 16 to 20 per cent of total rural households. Census 2001 data shows that about 22 per cent rural households use toilets.

Increasingly it is being realised that development is not only economic growth, rather it is the creation of enabling environment and enhancement of quality of life. It is this Millennium Development Goals (MDGs) and targets were set. India accepted the MDG targets and has since then evolved its policies to achieve them. India through its 10th Five Year Plan endorsed the ambitious growth target of providing rural sanitation to half of its population by 2015 with 8 per cent growth per year. In June 2003, GOI initiated an incentive based schemes for fully sanitised and open defecation-free Gram Panchayats, Blocks and Districts, called the Nirmal Gram Puruskar to encourage and improve sanitation conditions in rural areas through Total sanitation Campaign.

Sanitation and Policies Programmes for Urban Settings

At the union Government levels, there are some schemes and policies that focus specifically o water and sanitation in the urban setting. A major programme that provides facilities for water supply and sanitation in urban areas is Jawaharlal Nehru national Urban Renewal Mission (JNNURM), which aims at improving and augmenting economic and social infrastructure facilities of the cities, extending basic services to the urban poor including security of tenure at affordable prices and strengthening municipal governments and their functioning in accordance with the provisions of the 74th Constitutional Amendment. Services to the urban poor include access to water supply and sanitation which largely improves the sanitation facilities in the urban areas.

Urban Sanitation Policy of 2008 aims to transform urban India into community-led healthy and liveable cities and towns that will have universal sanitation coverage. It has an ambitious plan focusing on the urban poor and women that 'all Indian cities and towns become totally sanitised, healthy and liveable and ensure that sustain good public health and environmental outcomes for all their citizens with a special focus on hygienic and affordable sanitation facilities for the urban poor and women" (Ministry of Urban development: 2008). The main goals of the policy are awareness generation and behavioural change; open defection- free cities, integrated city-wide sanitation, sanitary and safe disposal, and proper operation and maintenance of all sanitary installations. Here, too the policy rests on the assumption that the states would draw up State Urban Sanitation Strategies and City Sanitation Plans. There is the constant threat of eviction and the areas lacks basic services such as safe water and sanitation facilities where the burden of collecting water and maintaining household hygiene falls on women who suffer the most from inadequate and inappropriate services in slums. The sanitation policy dwells on these issues but does not suggest ways to deal with the multiplicity of agencies and stakeholders involved in implementation of water and sanitation services.

State Sanitation Strategies

The Minister of State for Urban Development, Shri Saugata Roy informed the Lok Sabha today that under the National Urban Sanitation Policy (NUSP), all the States are encouraged to prepare State Sanitation Strategies taking into account their historic legacy with reference to sanitation, climate and physiographic factors, economic, social and political parameters and institutional variables, etc. It has been suggested therein that the State Government should monitor the performance of cities using instruments such as citizens' report cards, citizens monitoring committees, self-assessment systems, inter-city computations etc.

He further informed that at present, 9 States have formulated their State Sanitation Strategies viz. Andhra Pradesh, Madhya Pradesh, Karnataka, Kerala, Uttarakhand, Uttar Pradesh, Maharashtra, Orissa and Chhattisgarh. No financial support has been given to states including Haryana for formulation of State Sanitation Strategies. In a country ranked poorly on the health and environment front, Sikkim has done remarkably well to become India's first state with 100 per cent sanitation coverage, according to a report of the drinking water and sanitation ministry.

Sikkim, one of the eight north-eastern states nestled prettily in the eastern Himalayas, ranked first among the 28 states and seven union territories in terms of sanitation coverage for both urban and rural areas in households, schools, sanitary complexes and Aanganwadi centres. With 610,577 residents (2011 census), Sikkim is India's least populated and second smallest state in area after Goa.

According to a total evaluation study conducted by the Planning Commission in 2013, Sikkim emerged with the best performing gram panchayats and maintenance of sanitation facilities.

"The state has also sensitised people to adopt a holistic approach to improve sanitation and hygiene for a clean environment while accelerating overall development in the state," the Sikkim government said in a statement. The state has constructed 98,043 household latrines, surpassing the target of 87,014. Of these 61,493 latrines have been built for below poverty line (BPL) families. As many as 1,772 schools have been covered under the total sanitation programme. This was done under the central government's Nirmal Bharat Abhiyan sanitation drive. Sikkim Chief Minister PawanChamling launched a community-led total sanitation campaign in 1999 for achieving full sanitation in the 7,096 sq. km area of the state. And, to encourage sanitation activities, the state government has instituted a "Nirmal Gram Puraskar" (Clean village award). (IANS-Gangtok: 9th Feb. 2014; Indian Express: March 28, 2014). Now, Sikkim is first State in India with 100 Per Cent Sanitation Coverage.

3. Liberation and Rehabilitation of Scavengers

Founder of the Sulabh Movement and its executive wing, Sulabh International, Bindeshwar Pathak Obtained his Ph.D. from Patna University. For twenty years, Dr Pathak has been working for the liberation of scavengers through the Sulabh Movement – mixed package of technology, extensive training and social reforms – which is different from other social reform movements in that it combines technology with idealism. Much has changed in the status of scavengers in these years, The Sulabh concept and technology have been accepted as an alternative to high-cost city sewerage systems, and a large number of scavengers have been liberated and resettled in other professions. However according to Pathak, the struggle has just begun,

The book on *Road to Freedom* is the result of twenty years of study, research and field work by the Pathak who is a Gandhian which long years in social service. It is seminal piece of work on scavenging which extensively discusses its sources, history and geographical spread.

The social inequality of the system has always concerned Bindeshwar Pathak who joined Gandhi's movement for the liberation of scavengers soon after his education. He suggests solutions based on his experience of having redeemed and resettled more than 25,000 scavengers. The source material of the book is the author's work experience as well as a deep study of the available documents on scavenging.

Road to Freedom is a holistic approach to the problem of scavenging, aimed at a total liquidation of the system. The author seeks to give scavengers new life and hope by providing a technology which has been accepted by UN bodies – an effective low – cost and appropriate alternative to scavenging.

When former manual scavenger Usha Choumar was "liberated" a decade ago, her only mission was to ensure that her little daughter does not get into this "dirty business". Today she is an important functionary in Sulabh International, working in the field of sanitation, while her daughter goes to a public school with dreams of doing "something big". Now Usha Choumar, having walked the ramp in New York on the invitation of the United Nations, is on another mission — to see sanitation be made part of school curriculum.

Bill Prohibiting Manual Scavenging

Rural Development Minister Jairam Ramesh said that the Bill prohibiting manual scavenging can be passed in the Budget Session of Parliament as there is consensus on this issue among all political parties. Addressing a seminar on sanitation at Delhi on Jan 28, 2013 Sh Ramesh said, Parliament has to exhibit its resolve to eliminate this despicable practice and added that the 1993 Act has failed to achieve its desired goal. The Bill titled Prohibition of Employment as Manual Scavengers and their Rehabilitation is pending in Parliament.

The Minister said that as per the Census 2011, there are about 26 lakh dry latrines exist in India and after the passage of the bill; all such toilets will be closed. Sh. Ramesh also called upon women self-help groups to find out alternate employment for women who carry night soil and he underlined that this practice is still prevalent in states like Madhya Pradesh, Chhattisgarh, Uttar Pradesh and Bihar. He said,Nirmal Bharat Abhiyan should achieve the target of open-defecation free country in the next ten years. Sh. Ramesh said this should become a national obsession rather than remaining only a governmental programme. *(Source:* Press Information Bureau*)*.

Early passage of the bill prohibiting employment of manual scavengers and their rehabilitation is necessary, stressed union Rural Development Minister Jairam Ramesh. "I urge parliament to support the Prohibition of Employment as Manual Scavengers and their Rehabilitation Bill. If we resolve, we can pass this bill in two to three months. "Unless these liberated scavengers are given alternative jobs, the purpose of the exercise would be defeated. They have to be given proper employment after imparting them some vocational training," said Ramesh.

According to the bill, the district magistrate has to ensure that no person within his jurisdiction is engaged as a manual scavenger or constructs an insanitary latrine and manual scavengers are rehabilitated. It makes it mandatory for municipalities, cantonment boards and railway authorities to construct adequate number of sanitary community latrines within three years of the act coming into force. If anyone employs a manual scavenger or constructs an insanitary latrine, he shall be penalised with imprisonment up to one year or a fine of up to Rs. 50, 000 or both.

Critique

Jeffery (1988: 99) argued that public health in India has to be seen as a qualified failure. Even in the towns most directly amenable to British influence and action the conditions of life of most inhabitants remained appalling, with very high mortality and morbidity rates in the worst areas. Only European areas enjoyed the benefits of civic concern. This racial distinction and the much more pronounced role taken by the state in Indian towns, provide the main points of difference between the Indian and British experience. Despite having a more centralised, active, and interventionist government than in Britain and one which attempted to draw on British experience, India gained remarkably few benefits. Capitalist development and the rapid unplanned increase of the urban population led to slums, overcrowding, and urban squalor in India just as in Europe.

How can we Achieve Sanitation Targets?

To achieve the targets, action must start NOW. Now is the time to act. Households, communities, local and national governments, civil society, and private companies all need to work together. Media and public opinion around the world can influence political leaders to act now. For the principal target audience of politicians and government officials (particularly aid administrators), the strategy for this year's World Water Day is designed to increase substantive awareness, ideally leading to decisive actions in support of improved sanitation. Related communication also considers the media, in developed but especially in developing regions, since the media have excellent capacities to inform the population and guide their opinions.

Key areas of action that could create impact are as follows: making political commitments; creating legislation and regulations to support improvement in access and quality of sanitation and hygiene services; bringing together more resources, having stronger institutions and better trained people; culturally sensitive and appropriate hygiene education; right choice of technology that are cost-effective and environment-friendly; giving attention to gender and equity; supporting small-scale entrepreneurs; monitoring progress; and making information flow.

References

Ahmed, S.U. (1980), *"Urban Problems and Government Policies: A Case Study of the City of Dacca, 1819-30"*, in K. Ballhatchet and J.B. Harrison, (eds.), The City in South Asia.

Annual Report of the Sanitary Commissioner with the Government of India (1902).

Anstey, V. (1936), *The Economic Development of India*, 3rd edition, London: Longman.

Arnold, D. (1985), "Medical Priorities and Practice in Nineteenth Century British India", *South Asia Research* 5, 2: 167-186.

Ballhatchet, K. (1980), *Race, Sex and Class Under the Raj*, New Delhi: Vikas.

Cairncross, Sandy (2003), 'Sanitation in the Developing World: Current Status and future solutions', *International Journal of Environmental Health Research*, 13 June, S123-S131.

Census of 1921.

Census of India (2001), 'Tables on Houses, Household Amenities and Assets', Series, 7, Haryana, Directorate of Census Operations, Haryana.

Esrey, S.A. (1996), 'No Half Measures—Sustaining health from water and sanitation systems', *Waterlines*, 14 (3); 24-27, London.

Farrell, J.S. (1973), *The Siege of Kishnapur*, London: Penguin.

Feachem, R.G., Bradlt, D.J., Garlick, H. and Mara, D.D. (1983), *Sanitation and Disease: Health Aspects of Excreta and Wastewater Management*, John Wiley and Sons, Chichester.

Gillon, K.L.O. (1968), *Ahmadabad: A Study in Indian Urban History*, Berkeley: University of California Press.

Government of Haryana (2006), Economic Survey of Haryana 2005-06, Economic and Statistical Association, Planning department, Haryana.

Government of India (2002), *India Assessment, 2002—Water Supply and sanitation: (A WHO-UNICEF Sponsored Study), New Delhi: Planning Commission.*

Harrison, J.B. (1980), "*Allahabad: A Sanitary History*", in K.Ballhatchet and J.B.Harrison (eds.), The City in South Asia.

Harvey, W. (1895), "*Presidential Address*", in Proceedings of the First Indian Medical Congress, Calcutta: Indian Medical Gazette.

Health Information India (HII: 2000), Health Information Statistics in India, Annual reports, Central Bureau of Health Intelligence, MOHFW, and New Delhi.

Hume, J. (1984), "*Colonialism and Sanitary Medicine: The Development of Preventive Health Policy in the Punjab* 1860-1900", Mimeographed.

Jaggi, O.P. (1979), *Western medicine in India: Public Health and Administration*, Delhi: Atma Ram.

Jeffery, Roger (1988), *The Politics of Health in India*, London: University of California Press.

King, M. (ed.) (1966), *Medical Care in Developing Countries*, Nairobi: Oxford University Press.

Klein, I, (1973), "Death in India", *Journal of Asian Studies* 32, 4: 639-659.

Kundu, Amitabh ((1991). 'Microenvironment in Urban Planning: Access to Poor to Water Supply and sanitation', *Economic and Political Weekly*, XXVI (37): 2167-71.

Meller, H. (1979), *"Urbanisation and the Introduction of Modern Town Planning Ideas in India 1900-1925"*, in K.N.Chaudhuri and C.J.Dewey (eds.), Economy and Society, 330-350.

Pathak, Bindeshwar (2006), Road to Freedom: A Sociological study of the Abolition of Scavenging in India. Delhi: Extreme Office Aids Private Limited.

Rajeshwari (2008). 'Sanitation Situation and disease Pattern in Haryana: A Spatial Analysis', *Demography India,* Vol. 37, No. 1 (January – June).

Rajeshwari (2008), 'Sanitation situation and Disease Pattern in Haryana: A Spatial Analysis', *Demography India,* Vol. 37, No. 1, pp. 79-94.

Ramasubban, R. (1982), "Public Health and Medical Research in India: Their Origins under the Impact of British Colonial Policy", Stockholm: SAREC Report No. 4, Swedish Agency for Research Cooperation with Developing Countries.

Sanitary Report 1865.

Statistical Report 1870.

UNDP (2006), Human Development Report 2006, Beyond Scarcity: Poer, Poverty and the Global Water Crisis, New York: United Nations Development programme.

WHO (2002), The World Health Report 2002, Geneva: World Health Organisation.

WHO, (1998), Guidelines for safe recreational-water environments: coastal and fresh-waters, Draft for consultation, Geneva: World Health Organisation.

9

Sulabh Sanitation Movement in India

Context

Considering the role played by soil in the spread of infectious diseases, proper sanitary practices need to be evolved to protect it from pollution. There is an urgent need for sanitation facilities in our cities and towns in view of rapid urbanisation and increasing population. Sanitation, drainage and maintenance of these services are important functions of municipal bodies. In villages where people defecate in fields, the natural biological degradation processes take place. But here too, the soil can get overloaded with faecal microbes. Contaminated top soil can be rich in pathogenic bacteria (Salmonella and Shigella) known to cause of typhoid, dysentery and several other infectious diseases. People are also known to use the top soil to clean their hands and utensils. These practices need to be discouraged. Therefore, Sanitation should not be dismissed in a casual manner by any community. Disposal of excreta and household wastes, combined with aspects of personal hygiene, especially washing of hands, are directly related to an individual's health status

The Sulabh Movement launched in the country by Dr Bindeshwar Pathak in recent years needs special mention. A rough analogy can be drawn between it and the Great Sanitation

Movement in the 1860s in the West. History reveals that standards of public hygiene deteriorated considerably in the early nineteenth century, especially in England. This was the time when the Industrial Revolution was at its peak and increasing numbers of people were daily crowding into towns and cities for jobs. Entrances of houses and any odd corners were used as lavatories, garbage was found all around, and people rarely bathed. Diseases such as cholera, tuberculosis, and typhoid took many lives.

By the 1840s, the scene started to change as several public-spirited men who included writers, lawyers and other professionals examined the living conditions of the poor. Edwin Chadwick, a lawyer, studied this situation in a systematic manner, and ingeniously grasped the strong correlation between a dirty environment and the spread of infectious diseases. (This correlation was apparently known to Indians also and perhaps can account for many of our strict norms of personal hygiene). Chadwick became convinced that cities and towns needed to be cleaned up and in 1842 submitted a Report, 'Sanitary Conditions of the Labouring People of Great Britain' to the Council of London. Among other recommendations, he urged the public construction of simple family houses with a garden and a toilet block away from residential quarters. Public parks were also a prominent feature of his city-plans. But his most radical recommendation was his emphasis on an underground sewage system which would collect liquid household wastes and discharge it far from residential quarters onto an open municipal ground. This report ushered in the Great Sanitation Revolution in the western world. The Public Health Acts of 1845 and 1875 and The Royal Commission of 1989 initiated civic action in sewage collection and treatment.

Unwittingly, Chadwick's report led to the elimination or cleaning up of the many places - reservoirs - where disease-causing agents used to breed and thrive, which among other included mosquitoes, rats flies, animals and, of course, a whole world of microorganisms. Today we have come a long way from Chadwick's time in the treatment of sewage and other wastes, with these processes becoming highly automated and specialised.

The situation is quite dismal on the sanitation front in India. Flush-toilets and underground sewerage systems are taken for granted by many in urban areas. In cities too, sanitation and waste water disposal are often the last facilities to be laid out in the process of city planning. Even today, several suburbs of the city of Bombay do not have an underground sewerage system! Sewage treatment is often a tardy and incomplete process. In villages and small towns, the situation is worse. Recent attempts of the government to introduce *'shauchalaya'* in different districts is making rather slow progress where sanitation is viewed as a convenience, and not as a measure which promotes good health.

According to the UNICEF, 'sanitation should not be treated just as an annex to water supply, nor should it be considered only in relation to water supply programmes...the disposal of excreta and household wastes and aspects of personal hygiene such as hand washing, are even more directly related to health status than is water supply'.

Sulabh Movement - Towards a Social Revolution

In 1970, Dr Bindeshwar Pathak founded the *Sulabh Shauchalaya Sansthan*, later named Sulabh International. The primary objective of this organisation is to prevent environmental pollution by promoting low-cost sanitation facilities. Equally important, this movement has freed lakhs of people from the humiliating scavenging job imposed on them by a cruel societal order. *Sulabh* is a complete movement, radical in its approach. While trying to solve the problem of sanitation in the country, it also seeks to rehabilitate scavengers and their family members into the mainstream. This is done by providing them with education and training for several types of jobs. Dr Pathak has given a fresh impetus to the work initiated by Mahatma Gandhi and BabasahebAmbedkar.

Provision of clean drinking water and sanitation facilities are important for any society in India these are available to a very small fraction of our population (p. 30). Absence of sanitary facilities forces people to defecate and urinate in the open and thus pollute the soil and air with harmful microorganisms. However, to provide water-borne sewerage or even septic tanks, as is done in some cities, is an expensive and a difficult proposition. The untreated or partially treated sewage is often dumped in the seas and rivers making them highly polluted.

In 1970, Dr Pathak came up with his simple design of *Sulabh Shauchalaya* (latrines-pour-flush toilet with twin leach pit). The latrine consists of a squatting plate or a pan with a steep bottom and side slopes and a gas-trap with a 20 mm water-seal. The water-seal checks the escape of foul gases and microbes into the atmosphere from the leach pits. About 1.5 to 2 litres of water are sufficient to flush the excreta into the leach pits through pipes or covered drains. One pit is used at a time and both pits are covered by air-tight covers. The gases disperse and the liquid infiltrates into the soil through holes in the pit lining. When one pit is full, excreta are directed to the second pit. In about 18 months, the contents of the filled up pit get digested into manure and are safe for handling. Now, the pit is emptied and can be used again after the second pit is full. Thus the two pits are used alternatively and continuously.

The advantages of *Sulabh Shauchalaya* are many: they are hygienically and technologically appropriate, low cost and easy to construct with locally available materials; the design and specifications can be modified to suit the needs and the paying capacity of the users; there is no different physical, geological and hydrogeological conditions and do not pollute surface or ground water, if proper precautions are taken in construction; their maintenance is simple and does not require the services of a scavenger or large volumes of water; fertiliser is made available; there is high potential for upgradation as it can even be connected to sewers when sewerage is introduced in the area; a low-volume flushing cistern can also be attached and the whole set-up needs very little space.

Dr Pathak has an impressive list of achievements to his credit. Some of these are: evolving a system of rehabilitating, educating and training of scavengers and their adoption by elite members of the society; entry of scavengers into temples; and setting up of public toilets and baths, and biogas plants for generating energy from human excreta. Recognising his yeoman services, he has been awarded several national and international awards, including the Padma Bhushan, K.P. Goenka Award and the International Saint Francis Prize.

One of the many Sulabh Toilets spread across India. Aesthetically designed Sulabh structures reflect the personal philosophy of Dr Pathak: No place or job should be shabby or looked down upon (Pathak: 1995: 25-26).

There has recently been considerable concern in scientific discourse regarding the social determinants of hygiene and sanitation. The concern is further expressed in the need to influence the hygiene and sanitation related behavior through various policies and programmes interventions for the practicing of safe hygiene and sanitation in the day to day life. Sulabh International from last several years has been doing a commendable job in improving the sanitation facilities and also removing the burden of carrying night soil on the head by the untouchables. They not only rehabilitate them but also provided them the alternative livelihood. They have also introduced various technologies for latrines which are available according to different climatic conditions of the country. They have also introduced the technique which is successful in saving the use of water.

According to the census of India – 2001, 63 per cent of households do not have a lavatory (78 per cent in rural areas and 26 per cent in urban areas). In India, as many as 50 diseases are caused by lack of proper sanitation, affecting over 80 per cent of the population. These include intestinal, parasitic, infectious diarrhoea, typhoid and cholera. It is important for us to realise the significance of the initiatives taken by Sualbh International to overcome this crisis. Did you know? India has the world's most ancient sanitation systems. The first private bathrooms complete with inlet pipes and drains and flush toilets were found in Mohenjo-Daro. All these date from 3000 BCE. Such bathrooms were found even in humble hoes. It is a shame that 5,000 years later, so many homes do not have adequate sanitation, and so many people do not have access to good public sanitation. (Source: Sulabh International Museum).

Long Wait for New Dawn

"Sulabh is not event but an idea and hence, it was never born. It happened without plan, without driving ambition or greed for money. It succeeded because of hard work, faith and commitment to save scavengers, a symbol of cruelty, whose miseries cannot be matched by any before. Nor is there any historical inevitability about scavenging which is an artificial social construct conceived in a sin worth confession. And, what keeps us going is the conviction that there would be a new dawn after midnight" (New Princess of Alwar: 2009).

Sulabh International – a social movement provides healthy and hygienic sanitation facility to everybody. But Sulabh is not a about community toilets only – it's a social revolution, freedom from detestable social customs of discrimination based on caste and creed, end of shameful practice of defecation in open spaces, eradication of inhuman practice of scavenging and liberation of scavengers engaged in this occupation. Further, end of contagious diseases and epidemics, boos to non-conventional energy sources, enormous employment

Opportunities, educational institutions – including multiple schools and vocational training centers, a toilet museum in the heart of a National capital – New Delhi and Delhi airport. The area where Sulabh is located is densely populated. Well equipped with technological facilities like telephone booth, ATMs and so on.

"We are going to turn the pages of history". In 1968, Dr Bindeshwar Pathak said to his father-in-law. Thirty-nine years later, his initiative is creating history with 15 million users' every day, steady flow of revenues, ever increasing demand and expanding geographical reach, worldwide appreciation, awards and invitations, and ambitious plans for future (see www.sulabhinternational.org).

Sulabh Movement for Sanitation – Historical Emergence, Phases, actions

We would like to enumerate here the historical background first before we give the details regarding the SullabhShauchalayas as discussed by Janak Singh (2013).

(a) **Pauranic Period**: In the Pauranic period people were forbidden to defecate near human habitation. It was suggested to them to go at a distance for defecation, to dig a small pit, put some grass and leaves and then defecate there, after defecation put some grass and leaves and fill it with the soil.

(b) **Mauryan Period:** In the Mauryan period there was a law stating that a person could be fined up to 100 Pun if he defecated in the open and 10 Pun if he urinated in public. However, if a person was sick or taking medicines it was suggested that no punishment be awarded.

(c) **Mughal Period:** In the Mughal Period the practices of defecation in the open and manual cleaning of human excreta by human scavengers continued.

(d) **British Period:** During the British period there was the introduction of the sewerage system and the septic tank but these could not be adopted on a large scale because of the heavy cost of construction and maintenance as well as the need of enormous quantity of water flushing. Even during the British period both these practices of defecation in the open and cleaning of human excreta manually continued without let or hindrance.

Mahatma Gandhi's Concerns

Mahatma Gandhi was the first person who wanted to end the practice of defecation in the open and manual cleaning of human excreta by human scavengers. He appealed to the people to keep India clean and restore human rights and dignity of the untouchables. Gandhi advocated the use of trench latrine which he himself was using while he was in Phoenix Ashram in Durban, South Africa. He asked his followers and freedom fighters to use trench latrines in their homes as far as possible and also suggested the use of"*tattipemitti*" i.e. covering human excreta with soil so that flies could not sit on human faces.

The celebrated novelist, E. M. Forster, the author of "A Passage to India" wrote the preface to the book 'Untouchable' by Mulk Raj Anand in 1935. It is relevant to quote a passage from the said preface:

> *"No God is needed to rescue the Untouchables, no vows in self-sacrifice and abnegation on the part of more fortunate Indians but simply and solely – the flush system. Introduce water-closets and main-drainage throughout India, and all the wicked rubbish about untouchability will disappear".*

Sulabh Shauchalaya, Sulabh Tools

Sulabh Shauchalayas: The 'Latrines Made Easy', or a 'Pour Flush Latrine' with a slight variation, popularly called the Sulabh Shauchalayas are indeed a popular adjunct and an aide to hygienic development in most of the cities of India and abroad. It is also a befitting appliance for the semi-urban as well as the rural areas. A Sulabh type of latrine, the precursor of the now gigantic Sulabh movement, is a simple and cost-effective device which consists of an Indian type commode joined to a septic tank which serves as a soakage pit also. Latrines apart, the Sulabh Movement has grown and gone side by side with the social upgrading of the families of a large number of scavengers in regard to their schooling, sanitation and status in society. We are glad to say that Sulabh has experimented in that direction with proven results. There has also been praise worthy efforts aimed at development of sanitation and hygiene by the civil society including some international organisations like WHO and Sulabh. But still there is a long way forward to be covered.

SULABH INTERNATIONAL SOCIAL SERVICE ORGANISATION

The Genesis

Sulabh is the brain child of Dr Bindeshwar Pathak. Dr Pathak was born in 1942 in a Brahmin family of Bihar state of India. During 1968, he was drafted into a committee to design celebration of birth centenary of Mahatma Gandhi, which was due in 1969. Gandhi worked tirelessly to restore the human rights and dignity of scavengers and to eliminate the evil of untouchables from the society. This was a turning point in young Dr Pathak's life. He started 'Sulabh Svachchh Shauchalaya

Prashikshan Sansthan' (Sulabh Clean Toilet Training Institute) in 1970, which was later registered as 'Sulabh Shuachalaya Sansthan' (Sulabh Toilet Institute). It was renamed as 'Sulabh International in 1980 before adopting its present name – 'Sulabh International Social Service Organisation (SISSO).

Present Status

The Sulabh International location is well connected by bus, auto and taxi. It is around 12 to 15 kms (1 hrs.) from the New Delhi railway station and 6 to 8 kms (30 mins) from New Delhi Airport. Sulabh International – a non-governmental organisation (NGO), founded in 1970 to address the sanitation problems facing low-caste, low-income groups in India (See exhibit 1 for the organisational chart). Apart from its scale, what makes its delivery system of wider interest is its commercial viability. Sulabh addressed the most significant problem of open defecation in India. Much of the defecation in India still occurs in open spaces.

Sulabh International is an Indian based social service organisation which works to promote human rights, environmental sanitation, and non-conventional sources of energy, waste management and social reforms through education. The organisation counts 50,000 volunteers.(The Hindu: 2008) Sulabh International is the largest non-profit organisation in India (Rose: 2008)

Sulabh International works towards the improvement of the state of sanitation in India. Sulabhhas been recognised as one of the largest pan- India social service outfit with over 35,000 volunteers. It began by helping the scavengers – men and women who carry and dispose of human excreta. They developed a two-pit pour flush toilet (known as Sulabh Shauchalaya) which does not require scavenging to clean. Subsequently, Sulabh also started pay-and use public toilets popularly known as Sulabh Complexes, with bath, laundry and toilet facilities. These are used by about approx. ten million people every day. Sulabh has also pioneered the production of biogas and bio-fertiliser from excreta-based plants. Thus the pioneering work by Sulabh International, has shown that human waste can be disposed of affordably (productively) and in a socially acceptable way.

Sulabh's approach is based on partnerships with local

governments, backed by community participants, and has substantially improved environmental quality in rural and urban slums inhabited by poor people. This practice can be called as a best practice in governance. Governance, as we have come to understand is a social function whose performance is crucial to the viability of all human societies; it centers in the management of complex

Interdependencies among the actors (whether individuals, corporations, interest groups, or public agencies) who are engaged in interactive decision making and taking actions that affect each other welfare. Given this understanding of Governance, Sulabh International can be considered as Best practice in governance. As the main purpose of Sulabh International is to restore and promote human rights of the most disadvantaged community, called the bhangis (in Hindi) or scavengers, a low caste community in India. Scavengers' occupation is to collect, transport and dispose human excretory wastes. Due to the great deal of negative social stigma attached to their occupation, scavenger communities remain isolated and various upper class.

Communities in India are prejudiced against them. Many children of the scavengers follow in the footsteps of their parents. As a result, children of scavengers end up becoming scavengers. The Sulabh International movement led by Dr Bindeshwar Pathak (popularly known as the 'Founder') performs the most required social function for the wellbeing of the most isolated and downtrodden population of the country. This pro-poor approach in addition to hygiene is no doubt a success story which contributes to the overall governance of our country.

Vision, Mission and Objectives

Sulabh envisioned as an agent of social and cultural change. Inspired by Gandhian philosophy of truthfulness, non-violence, and altruism, more importantly Sulabh believes and practices Gandhian principle of Trusteeship. Sulabh seeks to develop an egalitarian society, based on equal opportunity for every human being irrespective of their caste, race, and natural endowments. Sulabh adopts a holistic development approach and promotes the concept of a happy home (see Exhibit – 1).

Exhibit–1: Sulabh Happy Home Concept: Sulabh Toilet

Complexes will turn into a Sulabh Happy Home which will not only provide toilet facilities, but also a Health care Centre for poor slum dwellers at a nominal price, covering the cost of medical examination, medicines, etc. it will also provide free immunisation service to children and pregnant women and "free family planning service" to eligible couples, who want to practise small family.

Some of the Key objectives of the Sulabh International are as follows:

- Social and economic liberation of scavenging community from their unhealthy and subhuman occupation of handling others' excreta through:
- Motivating people to have Sulabh Shauchalaya facility in houses where none exists;
- Conversion of bucket privies into Sulabh Shauchalayas;
- Rehabilitation by training and placement in other jobs;
- Opening English Medium School to offer modern school education to their children along with other
- Assistance in building their houses away from slums so that they can be taken out from the stinking environment;
- Prevention of environmental pollution and improvement of health, hygiene and ecology by
- Providing appropriate and low cost technologies for individual toilets pay & use community toilet complexes, community toilets with biogas energy, and effluent treatment
- Tree plantation around public Shauchalayas;
- Procuring manure from Sulabh Shauchalayas and Sulabh toilet complexes anduse it to raise farm productivity;
- Promoting consultancy, research and development in technical and social fields;
- Disseminating innovations and creating awareness particularly on sanitation and hygiene through mass communication and education.

Outcomes

So far, Sulabh has converted 1.3 million bucket toilets into flush toilets, and also has constructed more than 8,000 public toilets at important places all over the country which are being used by more than 15 million people everyday. *(Source: IANS.).* Government constructed 54 million toilets based on Sulabh design. 15 million people using daily toilets based on Sulabh design. 640 towns made scavengers free. Major Sulabh's Achievements are as follows:

- The Sulabh technology has liberated and rehabilitated 60,000 scavengers so far from the demeaning practice of physically cleaning and carrying human excreta.
- In the state of Bihar Sulabh has installed 30,000 units and had converted 10,000 more from old dry-pit latrines.
- Sulabh has provided two-pit pour flush, water seal toilet systems to more than six million households (about 12,00,000 individual toilets) and 5,500 community centres in 1100 towns in 26 states and 3 Union Territories of India.
- Over 10 million people in India use Sulabh toilets daily.
- This self-sustaining system has helped in ending the uncivilised practice of open-air defecation and keeping the urban life clean and liveable particularly in squatter colonies and places of congregation.
- Sulabh is already operating and maintaining about 100 Shauchalaya complexes at important railway stations.
- Sulabh is producing and using biogas from human excreta from its 100 plants.
- A combined Sulabh action plan on human waste disposal and social reforms has provided jobs directly to 35,000 people, and has created 10,000,000 man days of work, making 240 towns scavenging free. Over 4000 scavengers have been provided vocational training.
- It has set up an English-medium public school in New Delhi and also a network of centres all over the country to train boys and girls from poor families, specially Scavengers, so that they can compete in open job market

The Concept of Sulabh Movement

Target Groups: The target groups of this project are impoverished residents of Delhi's slums and Resettlement colonies, in particular those who have no access to sanitary latrines. Special attention is given to the needs of women in these groups, as well as the scavengers who must carry away the human excreta from dry latrines. Geographically the target sites include locations throughout Delhi. Only seven of the 44 resettlement colonies have civic amenities and running water lines provided. In most of them, especially in areas across the river Yamuna, no sewerage facility or proper drainage exist. Most of these colonies are located in low-lying areas about 10 to 12 feet lower than the Yamuna bed. These areas across the river are primary targets for the Sulabh. Given the state of affairs, the only solution to the problem lies in low-cost sanitation techniques or Sulabh Movement (see above) and people's readiness to accept and use them. Sulabh Initiatives - Social Wellbeing and Innovative Initiatives:

Sulabh Movement for Sanitation

Sulabh Shauchalayas: The 'Latrines Made Easy', or a 'Pour Flush Latrine' with a slight variation, popularly called the Sulabh Shauchalayas are indeed a popular adjunct and an aide to hygienic development in most of the cities of India and abroad. It is also a befitting appliance for the semi-urban as well as the rural areas. A Sulabh type of latrine, the precursor of the now gigantic Sulabh movement, is a simple and cost-effective device which consists of an Indian type commode joined to a septic tank which serves as a soakage pit also. Latrines apart, the Sulabh Movement has grown and gone side by side with the social upgrading of the families of a large number of scavengers in regard to their schooling, sanitation and status in society. We are glad to say that Sulabh has experimented in that direction with proven results. There has also been praise worthy efforts aimed at development of sanitation and hygiene by the civil society including some international organisations like WHO and Sulabh. But still there is a long way forward to be covered.

Different Designs of Sulabh two-pit pour-flush Compost Toilet

The Sulabh toilet has been designed in such a way that the poorest of the poor, middle class and even the rich people can have the facilities of Sulabh toilets because the cost of construction is affordable and can vary from Rs. 1500 to Rs 55, 000. The technology remain so the same, only the building materials differ and the period of cleaning of the pits. The minimum period of cleaning a pit is two years and maximum 40 years.

Sewerage System

When the British came to India to rule the country they also thought over the problems of sanitation in this country. The two technologies i.e. septic tank and the sewerage system which they developed and adopted in Britain were also introduced in India. The sewerage system was laid down in London in 1850, in New York in 1860 and Kolkata was the third city in the world to have the sewerage system in 1870.

Therefore, in India out of 6933 towns and cities only 160 have sewerage treatment plants and in 900 towns and cities drains have been laid down without any sewerage treatment plant. This technology could not be acceptable on large scale in India and the three continents of Africa, Asia and Latin America.

Septic Tank

Majority of the septic tank had openings into open drains, which carry the liquid effluents from the septic tanks. This also leads to a high probability of ground or surface water pollution. Septic tank requires more space. The construction needs regular technical assistance and supervision. This needs ventilation, which adds to cost. Desludging of septic tank is needed on regular basis. The sludge and effluent from a septic tank cannot be used as a fertiliser straight away without causing health hazards. Therefore, it was not an appropriate option.

Sulabh Shauchalaya

For Appropriate Technology Option overcome these constraints, Pathak invented, innovated and developed the two-pit pour-flush compost toilet and gave it the name 'Sulabh Shauchalaya'. In this SulabhShauchalaya, there are two pits, one is used at one time and the other is kept on standby. When the first pit is full, it is switched over to the other one and the first one after two years converts to inert state as manure to be used in the fields to raise the productivity of the field and also used in flower plants, and fruit trees etc. it becomes a bio-fertiliser which contains phosphorous, nitrogen and potassium.

The construction of Sulabh Shauchalaya is also very easy and the same can be constructed without any difficulty. If there is space then one should make two round pits separately. The benefit of this is that the lower layer is absolutely dry and there is not even a drop of water. If there is shortage of space then both the pits can be made together with a partition wall in between. The partition wall is one foot deeper than the other walls and is also jutting out one foot on both sides. To make the walls stones, bricks, woods or mud baked burnt clay rings, coal tar etc. can be used.

Moreover, Sulabh Shauchalya also helps to economise the use of water which is not only the need of the country but the entire world. It is said that if a third World War happens in future that would be on water. Sulabh toilets require only 1 litre of water for flushing while the conventional toilets require ten liters. Most importantly manual scavenging is not required in cleaning of such toilets. Anybody can clean the pits because when it is cleaned there is no human excreta as the same has already been converted into manure. Thus, Sulabh toilet has become a tool of social change.

The technology is helpful in both ending the practice of cleaning night-soil manually and restoring scavengers' human rights and dignity on one hand, and on the other it is helpful to stop defecation in the open.

A. Community Toilet Technology

Those households, which either can afford an individual TPPF or has no space for it, need a community toilet. Such a facility is also needed for commuters, pavement dwellers and other floating population mainly in urban settlements. Sulabh studied the behaviour and attitude of people who did not use available public toilets in towns and cities. The study revealed that people would use such toilets if

- Facilities for bathing and washing clothes are provided alongside;
- The toilet is kept clean all the 24 hours of the day. Sulabh technology is providing community toilet complexes (known as Sulabh Shauchalaya Complex) with bathing, laundry and urinal facilities on the pay-&-use basis in urban areas and places where people congregate. The main features of a community toilet complex are:
- There is no burden on the public exchequer.
- A nominal charge is collected from each user.
- Children, disabled and poor are exempted from payment.

- No charge is made for use of urinals.
- The earnings are used for operation and maintenance of the complex.
- Attendants man each complex round the clock.
- Lighting during nights and 24 hour water supply is maintained.
- Soap for washing hands is provided free for the users.
- Aesthetically pleasing architecture together with tree plantation around the complex are provided.

> Mammoth community toilet in Shirdi, Near Pune at an estimated cost of 2 crore. Largest Community Toilet Complex at Shirdi-148 toilets and 108 bathrooms; with space for dressing, babysitting and breast-feeding; 5,000 lockers to care of the belongings of the pilgrims; the electricity made available through biogasgeneration from human excreta lights the complex; Upto 50,000 visitors use these facilities every day.

B. Excreta-based Biogas and Biofertilizer Technology:

Dr Pathak is probably the first person in the world who has promoted on a massive scale, the idea of obtaining biogas from human excreta collected in large-sized public toilets used by 2,000 to 5,000 persons a day. The first such biogas plant was set up at Patna in 1982 after almost six years of research. The successful and satisfactory functioning of this plant encouraged him to replicate the project all over the country. Excreta contain 66% methane, a burnable gas that can be used for cooking and electricity generation. In the absence of sewerage facility, the best option for human waste disposal, to be used in conjunction with large public toilets, is the biogas plant. It has the added advantage of being a source of renewable energy, which is lacking in the septictank system. Biogas so produced is used for lighting, cooking, etc. and the effluent is a rich fertilizer. To the biogas plant is attached the Sulabh effluent plant, that lowers down BOD of sewage from 200 mg/L to 10 mg/l. The effluent is made colourless, odourless and pathogen-free, fit for discharge into any water body, promoting a better and healthier environment. The biogas plant consists of an inlet chamber, an anaerobic digester and an outlet chamber. The digester is cylindrical with arched bottom and domed top and is installed underground. Excreta from the toilet seats flow under gravity through covered drains into the inlet chamber and then into the digester. The digested slurry comes out of the digester through the outlet pipe, reaches the outlet chamber and then flows out through covered drains into soakage pits. A large round airtight manhole is provided at the top of the digester for facilitating cleaning (desludging), and other maintenance jobs. A gas outlet pipe and a safety pipe are attached to the manhole. It is estimated that the 4.56kg of nitrogen, 0.55kg of phosphorus and 1.28 kg of potassium that the average human releases each year could produce enough wheat and maize for one person annually.

If the number of users is less than 100, then the use of two-pit Sulabh toilet is preferable but in high-rise buildings, five star hotels and housing colonies, the Sulabh biogas digesters is an environment-friendly technology that should be used.

C. Wastewater Treatment through Duckweed

Only 20% of urban India has sewerage systems for treatment and disposal of wastewater. Wastewater pollutes the natural streams like rivers and the environment. It currently afflicts nearly all the 5000 odd towns and cities of India, posing a big challenge to ensure safe and healthy living environment for ever increasing number of city dwellers. One of the major problems with wastewater treatment methods is that none of the available technologies has direct economic return. The available technologies are unaffordable due to high capital and

Maintenance costs. Duckweed has natural properties, which can treat even the toxic waste discharged from cities except for oil. The oil should be separated before the water is discharged into duckweed ponds. The water is purified and treated to the extent that it reduces BOD and COD and the quality of water is good even for pisciculture. One can rear fish in such water and it has been found on the basis of analyses of the brains and livers of the fishes that they have no harmful bacteria and, are, thus, perfectly edible. This technology is suitable for towns with a population up to 50,000. Sulabh has taken up research-cum-demonstration projects on duckweed based low-cost waste water treatment in collaboration with concerned government agencies. The ambitious projects are underway in some rural as well as urban areas with direct economic return from pisciculture and use of duckweed as nutritious feed for poultry and animals.

D. Sulabh International Centre for Action Sociology (SICAS)

(i) Sulabh Public School: Sulabh Public School was established in Delhi in 1992 with an objective of imparting quality education to children of scavenger community. The school is from primary to Xth class and the present strength of the school is around 400, of which a deliberate 60 per cent belongs to the children from scavenger community and remaining 40 per cent from other social classes. This type of class ratio prevents the social seclusion of children and helps them in mixing up with other communities. The mode of education is English and the school is recognized by Directorate of Education, Government of Delhi.

(ii) Vocational Training Centre: With an objective of making individuals skilled and independent, the first Sulabh centre was started in Patna in 1985. Subsequently, another vocational training centre was started in Mumbai, with collaboration of state government of Maharashtra. In Delhi, the Sulabh Vocational Training Centre was started in 1992 in the Sulabh Public School campus, with separate facilities for the training centre. The training is completely free for scavenger community, whereas other willing participants pay a nominal sum for training.

E. Sulabh International Institute of Technical Research and Training (SIITRAT)

SIITRAT runs refreshers and training courses for interested persons for skill building for constructing, operating and maintenance of various low cost water supply and sanitation schemes, and human excreta-fed biogas plants. Special training modules are designed with expert advice and experts of different disciplines are invited for lectures and demonstrations of innovative and update techniques of technology.

SIITRAT has also developed new technology – SulabhThermophilic Aerobic Composter (STAC). This technology requires only 8 to 10 days for making compost from any biodegradable waste, without any manual handling during composting. This technology does not require recurring expenditure. This technology is able to convert organic waste in manure and soil conditioner, to prevent spread of weed and disease. Also, it drastically reduces the cartage costs of waste to disposal sites.

F. Sulabh International Institute of Health and Hygiene (SIIHH)

SIIHH was set up in 1994 with a purpose of providing total health care. SIIHH is an outcome of Sulabh's emphasis on development of integrated health care approach, with an added emphasis on yoga, use of medicinal plants, hygiene and health conscious attitude, and safe and clean food and dirking water. The focus of this integrated health planning is women, children and youth in rural areas and urban slums.

G. Sulabh International Museum of Toilets

The Sulabh International Museum of Toilets is said to be only of its kind in the entire world. The museum has artefacts and their replica from different civilizations existing at different times. In addition, it has a detailed history of evolution of toilets since earliest available instances from 2500 BC and also detailed linguistic evolution of terms related to toilets and sanitation. The purpose of this museum is to educate students and general public about the historical trends in the development of toilets; to provide information to researchers about the design, materials and technologies adopted in the past and those in use in the contemporary world, to help policy makers to understand the efforts made by our predecessors in this filed throughout.

Financing

Sulabh International as discussed above gets its financing from the following sources:

1. Charging 10 percent of the construction costs of its projects finances Sulabh.
2. Collecting payment from users covers the maintenance costs.
3. In state-funded sanitation projects, half the cost of a TPPF is subsidized by the state. SC/ST's are entitled for a higher subsidy.

Replication

- All the technologies under the project are simple and indigenous.
- Their operation and maintenance is easier than other technologies.

- The on -site waste disposal technology can be replicated in various geological conditions.
- The public toilet complexes are most suitable for slums, railway stations, bus stands, court compounds etc. There are various designs of public toilets to suit space constraint area and different income sections of people. Cultural heritage is also taken into view while designing a toilet complex.
- Local skilled person can be trained to implement the whole system, which enhances its replicability chance in any locality.
- Biogas technology is also very simple and replicable at any place. The design is suited even in low temperature as it can bear temperature variation due to its underground structure.
- None of the technologies developed by Sulabh is patented; it is accessible to everybody interested with sanitation. Therefore, the chance of replication is high. More than one million TPPFs have been constructed by the organization itself.

Legal Dimension

The practice of defecation in open spaces is very prevalent, especially in rural areas. In addition, there are dry toilets, which are cleaned by human scavengers and the human excreta is carried on the head by scavengers. They have been forced into this humiliating practice for generations and treated as untouchables. In the year 1993; the Indian parliament passed the "Adoption of the employment of manual scavengers and construction of dry latrines (prohibition) act. This law prohibits the practice of construction of dry latrines and human scavenging.

However, 10 states (Rajasthan, Jammu and Kashmir, Himachal Pradesh, Uttaranchal, Kerala, Meghalaya, Nagaland, Manipur, Arunachal Pradesh and Mizoram) have still not adopted the act. Sulabh International movement played an important role in passing this act by the parliament. The activities of Sulabh International are legally supported after the passing of this act in 1993.

Efficient Service Delivery

- The Sulabh sanitation technologies are easily marketable due to their comfort, cleanliness, dignity, privacy and aesthetics.
- The Sulabh toilet technology has been globally accepted as the most suitable, affordable and absolutely safe for developing countries by international agencies like the UNDP/World Bank, UNICEF and WHO.
- Sulabh's cost-effective and appropriate sanitation system has been recognized as a global 'Urban Best Practice' by the United Nations Centre for Human Settlements at the Habitat-II conference held at Istanbul (Turkey), in June, 1996.
- Sulabh has been granted Special Consultative Status by the Economic and Social Council of United Nations in recognition of its outstanding service to mankind.
- International St. Francis Prize for the Environment "Canticle of all Creatures" was conferred on Dr Pathak in 1992 in recognition of his services to the cause of environment and social upliftment of oppressed people.
- The national and international media like Press, BBC, Doordarshan, Zee TV, and All India Radio have widely acknowledged the achievements of Sulabh.
- New York Times, The Washington Post, Nation (Bangkok), The Times of India, The Hindustan times, The Statesman, Indian Express,
- India Today, Dinman, Water World, The Telegraph, Source (UNDP monthly magazine) have published articles lauding the achievements of Sulabh in the fields of low cost sanitation, liberation of scavengers, harnessing of energy from human excreta, environment improvement.

Sustainability - Future Plans:

Believing in Gandhian philosophy and willing to work till the last moment of life for holistic social development of deprived, Dr Bindeshwar Pathak is still very enthusiastic about the plans he has for further expanding the work of Sulabh. He terms Sulabh as a movement, not an organization, which has to keep on moving till the last human is served. However, he is worried about the lack of interest if fresh talent in this field providing healthy and hygienic sanitation. Commending Sulabh's good work, HRH Willem-Alexander, the prince of Orange of the Netherlands, and chairman of the United Nations' secretary-general's Advisory Board on Water and sanitation (UNSGAB) said in New York on November 21, 2007: "Sulabh International showed me a good example during my recent visit to New Delhi. This organization has proved how effective small scale solutions can be and how they can be extended all over India within a short time span. Thousands of 'Pay and Use' public toilet-cum-bath complexes and more than a million pour-flus latrines in private houses have been built (and are maintained) and they are used by more than ten million people every-day. By doing so, Sulabh has restored human dignity and given a new future to thousands of untouchables"

Sulabh Events

1968: Sulabh Technology: Dr Bindeshwar Pathak joined the liberation of scavengers' cell of the Bihar Gandhi Centenary Celebration Committee in 1968 when he was entrusted with the task of finding out an alternative to scavenging. Dr Pathak modified and developed a technology of two-pit pour flush toilet (popularly known as SulabhShauchalaya). He also succeeded in demonstrating the effectiveness of the two-pit pour flush toilet system. Today, engineers not only from India but even from the World Bank have accepted that the on-site excreta disposal toilet system is an alternative to scavenging, open air defecation and unhygienic, unsafe systems of human waste disposal like trench and borehole latrines, in the developing countries of the world.

1970 Sulabh Organisation Registered: By the time, Dr Pathak found the alternative to scavenging; the Bihar Gandhi Centenary Celebration Committee was dissolved by the Government. That year, Dr Pathak founded a non-profit making voluntary social organisation, SulabhShauchalayaSansthan, (now known as Sulabh International Social Service Organisation) to carry out the work of liberation of scavengers from the sub-human practice of manual excreta cleaning in India and other related jobs. Thus, the seeds of the Sulabh Sanitation Movement were sown in 1970.

1970: Expansion: The mass movement by Dr Pathak started spreading all over the country with a cadre of about 50,000 Sulabh volunteers, now working from right atop the mountain at Vaishnav Devi, to deep down in South and in the farthest corners in the east and the west of the country, in 25 States and 987 towns. An organisational set up like this has not been made to spread out so fast and be managed by any other social voluntary organisation so far. Sulabh does not receive any aid, or subsidy from internal or external agencies; it raises its own resources to run its pan- India system and its campaign against social evils, and helps the weaker sections of society.

1972: Catalytic Agent: After developing a technology, Dr Pathak evolved a methodology which also spelt out how a non-profit making social organisation could work as a catalytic agent between the Government, local bodies and the beneficiaries. It was felt that the Government alone could not liberate scavengers from the subhuman occupation. House-to-house contact and campaigns in local languages for their liberation was suggested as part of the methodology which was adopted by the Bihar Government. Now it has been adopted by many States Governments.

1973: Scavengers Liberation: During the past 30 years, Dr Pathak brought the scavengers' liberation programme from the micro level to the macro-level. In 1973, he had put up just two Sulabh Shauchalayas for demonstration in the compound of the Area municipality, a small town of Bihar. Since then Sulabh has converted about one million bucket latrines into Sulabh Shauchalayas throughout the country; and more than 60,000 scavengers have been liberated and more than 240 towns have been made scavenging-free. (Base year Dec. 2002).

1974: Pay-and-use System: In 1974, the Sulabh Founder gave another concept of maintaining the community toilets and bath on the pay-and-use basis. Before 1974, public latrines in India were regarded as hell holes. Nobody was able to find a solution to this problem. Dr Pathak found one and, on that basis, over 6,000 public toilet complexes are being maintained absolutely clean, spick and span in 25 States and four Union Territories, in 1,075 towns, including metropolitan cities of Delhi, Bombay, Calcutta and Madras. These Sulabh toilet complexes are used by over ten million people a day.

1978: Historical Seminar: Seeing the success of the scavengers liberation movement in Bihar, the Ministry of Works and Housing, Government of India, in collaboration with the WHO and UNICEF, organised a national seminar at Patna in 1978 on conversion of bucket latrines and liberation of scavengers. In this seminar, representatives from the Planning Commission, Ministry of Health, Ministry of Works and Housing, international agencies like WHO, UNICEF, World Bank, and the Secretaries and Chief Engineers of all the State Governments participated. They all approved the Sulabh technology and methodology for adoption by individuals as well as institutions. And, thus the work of liberating scavengers and the maintenance of public latrines and baths started from Bihar to spread throughout the country in due course.

1980-81: Legal Protection: Dr Pathak persuaded the Ministry of Home Affairs, Government of India, to include liberation of scavengers and their rehabilitation programme on the "whole-town approach" basis. Under the scheme, implementation of Protection of Civil Rights Act 1980-81, was taken up in two towns of Bihar; Biharsharif and Purnia. In 1981-82, three more towns of Bihar, Daltonganj, Chaibasa and- Madhubani now in Jharkhand, were taken up. Later, the programme was moved on to other States. The State Governments agreed to provide alternative employment to liberated scavengers and, hence, all of them got jobs. No one has become unemployed so far. The Ministry of Welfare, Government of India, later took charge of this programme.

1984: Biogas from Public Toilet: The first Sulabh public toilet linked biogas plant was set up at Adalatganj, Patna. It produced electricity from biogas which was supplied to the 3 kms long Bailey Road, Patna.

1985: Training and Rehabilitation: With the help of the Ministry of Welfare, Government of India, Welfare Department, Government of Bihar, and the Bihar State Scheduled Castes Development Corporation, Sulabh started a training and rehabilitation programmes for the wards of scavengers in different trades like shorthand, typing, motor driving, mechanics, masonry work, carpentry, cane work, etc. A large number of children of scavengers have already been trained. This programme is being extended to cover the entire country. The programme was later expanded to include regular education and technical training.

1985: Technology Evaluation: The UNDP and the World Bank after evaluation of the Sulabh technology of the pour flush toilet and the methodology of the maintenance of public toilets and baths on 'pay-and-use' basis passed it on to the countries of South-East Asia, Africa and Latin America for their adoption.

1986: Protection of Civil Rights (PCR) Act: Dr Bindeshwar Pathak persuaded the Ministry of Welfare to give stipends to the wards of Muslim and Christian scavengers also for training and rehabilitation. Earlier, these were available only to Hindu scavengers. Without this, the wards of Muslim and Christian scavengers would have been left out and the movement for their liberation and rehabilitation would have suffered a setback.

1988: Scavengers in Temple: Dr Pathak solved the problem of entry of Harijans into Nathdwara Temple in Udaipur, Rajasthan, for prayers in 1988. The controversy of entering the temple had taken a serious turn and so many attempts, made by others, had failed. The situation became so serious that the then President of India, Mr. R. Venkataraman, wanted himself to lead Harijans into the temple. Even the political leaders and the State Government officials had to go to the temple with police protection. This attracted Dr Pathak's attention who, with 100 scavengers and orthodox Vedic Maithili Brahmins, entered the Nathdwara Temple, offered prayers and recited bhajans and kirtans. The scavengers and the whole group took their meal together. This programme was performed without police protection. On return from Nathdwara Temple, Dr Pathak, along with the scavengers and the Vedic Brahmins was given audience by the then President, Mr. R. Venkataraman, the then Vice-President, Dr Shankar Dayal Sharma and the late Prime Minister Mr. Rajiv Gandhi. This act of Dr Pathak was quite in line with Dr Ambedkar's who had led a group of Harijans to draw water from a public tank, Chodor Talen, at Mahad in Kolaba district of Maharashtra in 1927 and led another satyagraha to establish the right of the untouchables to enter the famous temple of Kalaran in Nasik in 1930.

1989: Casteless Puja: On his return from Nathwara, Dr Pathak launched a campaign to help the Scheduled Castes offer prayers in temples and performing puja at their homes by Vedic Brahmins.

Also, he started common puja and dinning programmes where members of the Scheduled Castes do fasting, sit on the puja and prepare Prasad. They also prepare food for lunch or dinner. After the puja is over, the Prasad and food are distributed by Scheduled Castes to all, including to Vedic Brahmins, who also eat with them. This programme, which is continuing since then, has got a wide acceptance.

1990: Social Up gradation of Scavengers: To improve the social status of scavengers in India, Dr Bindeshwar Pathak has launched a movement to socially upgrade them. This is a novel concept. There was a question mark as to whether after liberation, training and education, scavengers and their children will have upgraded status in society to be on par with the so-called upper caste people. To socially upgrade the scavengers' status in society, Sulabh started a social upgradation campaign, one high status family in society has to "socially adopt" a scavenger family who will be treated like family members. The association with these high-status people will raise the status of the scavengers. This programme has taken off very well. So far, 5,000 scavenger families have been "adopted" by high status people, including judges, advocates, journalists, ministers and planners. Among them are the former Union Dy. Commerce Minister, Mr. Salman Khurshid; Planning Commission member Ms. ChitraNaik; Times of India Editor, Mr. DilipPadgaonkar; former Prime Minister, Mr. I.K. Gujral and many others.

1992: Awareness Campaign: In February 1992, Sulabh organised a "National Seminar on Liberation and Rehabilitation of Scavengers" in New Delhi in which vice-chancellors, professors, planners, and administrators passed a resolution to make it a people's movement. The seminar was inaugurated by the former President of India late GianiZail Singh. Dr Pathak regularly takes steps to create social awareness against unfounded beliefs and prejudices. He organises conferences, seminars, workshops, plays and folk dances on these themes. The attempt is to involve a large number of people from all walks of life in order to speed up the pace of the movement. 1992 "Educate, Organise, Agitate": On the "educate, organise and agitate" principle of Baba Ambedkar, Sulabh has set up an English medium school in Delhi for the sons and daughters of scavengers wherein education is given in three principal areas: general theoretical education, compulsory vocational education (knowledge of office management, shorthand, typing and computer training), and optional vocational education (intensive training in specific vocations) so that they may not have to wait in long queues for employment. This will also enable them to be self-employed or get jobs. Fifty percent of the school's enrolment is of scavengers children and the rest is from other families to visibly obliterate discrimination. This unique experiment is being extended to other states also. The idea is: Education alone can empower the weak and poor.

1992: Housing Facilities: The Sulabh has started its new endeavour to provide housing facilities to scavengers to take them out of their stinking and unhealthy living conditions. A survey of 1000 scavenger families has already been done as Patna and attempt is being made to get land from the Government at nominal price and loans from HUDCO in order to build houses for them. A similar attempt is to be made in other states.

1994: The Sulabh International Museum of Toilets: The first of its kind in the world, the Sulabh International Museum of Toilets was set up in Delhi. The Museum, through artefacts, pictures, posters and other available materials, tells the story of the development of toilets through the ages. This is the star attraction at the Sulabh service centre, Palam. 1996 Duckweed Project: Sulabh has demonstrated an eco-friendly low-cost technology for waste water treatment through duckweed. The technology besides having low operational and maintenance costs, gives economic return in terms of pisciculture.

1997: STAC: Developed a new technology for composting of biodegradable wastes. The technology known as Sulabh Thermophile Aerobic Composting (STAC) requires only 8-10 days to degrade any biodegradable materials without churning.

1998: People's Commission: Sulabh set up a People's Commission on the Abolition of Scavenging. Prime Minister Mr. Atal Bihari Vajpayee inaugurated the Commission at a function organised on November 26, 1998 to honour him with the Honest Man of the Year Award 1997. Justice M.N. Venkatachalliah, former Chief Justice of India, and Chairperson of the National Human Rights Commission, is the Chairman of the Advisory Board of the Commission.

2000: Sulabh towards Villages: Started the programme of Sulabh towards Villages, a national campaign to improve rural sanitation.

2001: Training of Women: Started a country wide programme for involvement of women in sanitation, health and hygiene.

2002: SET Technology: Developed a new and convenient technology to make biogas plant effluents free from colour, odour and pathogen free. The technology known as SET (Sulabh Effluent Treatment) lowers BOD (Biological Oxygen Demand) of effluent to less than 10 mg/l, making it suitable for agriculture, aquaculture or safe discharge into a river or any water body or cleaning of floors of public toilets.

2003: Steps taken to establish a Sulabh University of Sanitation.

- A compilation of Encyclopaedia on Sanitation started.
- WASH campaign launched in collaboration with Water Supply and Sanitation Collaborative Council, Switzerland.
- Started another Sulabh Vocational Training Centre for liberated scavengers (NaiDisha) at Alwar, Rajasthan.
- UNDP recognizes Sulabh technologies in its Human Development Report 2003.
- A Sulabh delegation visited Afghanistan to take up sanitation work.

2004: Members of the U.N. Millennium Project Task Force on Water and Sanitation visit Sulabh Campus.

2005: Sulabh International Academy of Environmental Sanitation registered under the Societies Registration Act 1860 by the Registrar, Registration, Government of Delhi.

• 23 professionals from 5 countries attended the "International Workshop on Sani tat ion Technologies" organized by Sulabh International Academy of Environmental Sanitation in collaboration with UN – Habitat.

• Sulabh activities find mention in President of India APJ Abdul Kalam's book "Mission India"- A Vision for Indian Youth"

2006: UNDP recognizes Sulabh technologies in its Human Development Report.

- 24 professionals including representatives of UN–HABITAT covering 10 African countries attended the International Capacity Building Workshop organized by Sulabh International Academy of Environmental Sanitation in collaboration with UN – HABITAT.
- Stanford University includes article on Sulabh – "That Gandhi may not be born again" in its Curriculum.
- Five Public toilets with biogas plants were set up in Kabul, Afghanistan with the financial support of the Govt of India.

2007: Sulabh organized the World Toilet Summit 2007 in collaboration with WTO.

2014: In the 8th International conference of Sulabh International on January, 22, 2014, it was discussed to introduce the course on sociology of sanitation in the colleges and universities.

Other Activities

HT woman 2014 2nd runner up Manorani Devi gave her land to build a toilet in her village (Monday, April 7, 2014).

Man arrested for offering vote in exchange for public toilet (Wednesday, April 2, 2014). In Allahabad an AAP worker who rode a donkey in this Uttar Pradesh city to demand a public toilet in lieu of his vote was arrested for disturbing the peace. NGO has now stepped in to fulfil his wish (Wednesday, April 2, 2014-17:15). On April 2 (PTI) taking note of an AAP volunteer's protest against lack of sanitation facilities in the city, Sulabh International said it would do its bit by building low-cost pubic toilets.

Vrindavan widows revel in Holi colours, break social stigma. In a first of its kind, nearly 1,000 long-ostracized widows of Vrindavan gathered at an ashram to play Holi (Monday, march 17, 2014-01:00).

India's manual scavengers' keep working despite ban (Thursday, February 6, 2014- 10:45).

Saroj clears human waste from toilets in her village, but the government wants her to stop (Wednesday, January 22, 2014-11:30).

References

Singh, Janak (2013). 'Parliamentary Forum Applauds SulabhTechnoloy', *Sulabh India,* March, pp. 3-11.

The Hindu (2008). "Sulabh International gets U. N. recognition", Chennai (India): *The Hindu,* September, 2008-10-05

The Hindu (2008). "Sulabh know-how to go international" *The Hindu*: Chennai (India), 2008-11-11

Lonely Planet India - 10th edition

Pathak B. (1995). 'Low-cost on-site sanitation' presented by Pathak at the Third International Conf. on Appropriate Waste Management Technologies for Developing Countries, Nagpur, 25-26, February.

Rose, George (2008). *The Big necessity: The Unmentionable World of Human Waste and Why it Matters.* Metropolitan Books.

Times of India (2009). "Sulabh founder wins Swedish prize", New Delhi: *Times of India,* 2009-03-25. Retrieved 2009-03-25.

http://www.travelblog.org/Asia/India/National-Capital-Territory/New-Delhi/blog-404343.html

http://www.sulabhinternational.org/downloads/sulabh_ case_studies_iim.pdf

10

Globalisation and Sanitation

Idea of Globalisation

The origin of the concept of 'globalisation' is usually traced to Marshal McLuhan (1960), who first introduced the idea of what is today called 'global village' – a notion that implied a sort of compression of the world and intensification of consciousness of the world as a single entity. Therefore, many individuals, organisation and countries consider the world in this new millennium as the 'Global village'.

Globalisation refers to various multidimensional socio-economic and political processes by which the people of the world are incorporated into a single world society, a global village. It tends to homogenise the cultures as well as popularise even unknown cultures of the world. It acts as hetrogeniser with a possibility of pluralism. Globalisation strives to make the world as its market where all the people are being brought as buyer and seller on unequal terms.

Globalisation refers to the multiplicity of linkages and interconnectedness that transcend the nation-state and by implications the societies which make up the modern world system. It reflects a process through which events, decisions and activities in one part of the world would have significant consequences for individuals and communities of quite distant parts of the globe. However, for Giddens, globalisation embraces much more than a notion of simple interconnectedness. For him, "globalisation concerns the intersection of the presence and absence, the interlocking of social events and social relations at a distance with local contextualities (Giddens: 1991).

It may be understood as a dialectical phenomenon in which events at one pole having distance relation often produce divergent or even contrary occurrence at another. While communication and information are increasingly diffused on a global scale, the individuals locally appropriate these, inherently in contextual and hermeneutic way. Thus globalisation becomes glocalisation.

In order to talk about globalisation and its impact on essential services of water, health and sanitation of developing countries, we need to understand the driving forces of globalisation. These forces are as follows (Dissanayake: 1988):

1. Science and Technology
2. Communication and media
3. Market, trade and finance,
4. Migration and inter-cultural transactions.

All the above forces have a great role in the development of sanitation and health. In process of transition from the agrarian-industrial, post-industrial and finally the stage of the information society influence the idea of health and sanitation. In this chapter, the whole discussion moves around water, sanitation and hygiene in context to globalisation and sanitation

The Millennium Villages Project (MVP) seeks to increase sustainable access to safe drinking water and sanitation, and to improve hygiene practices in an effort to improve health outcomes and empower girls and women to be effective agents in their communities. A WASH program must be comprehensive and holistic in order to successfully address the many barriers related to the uptake of safe water, sanitation and hygiene related behaviors.

Water

To improve the quality and accessibility of drinking water, the MVP supports the construction and rehabilitation of improved water sources; builds capacity of water committees to operate, maintain and financially manage water sources; and promotes point of use water treatment and safe storage. Water Safety Plans are also designed in close collaboration with the community, and are key tools to empower communities and local authorities to take the lead on these efforts.

Sanitation

Generating demand for improved sanitation through community-led approaches and sanitation marketing is complemented by building the capacity of private sector actors to manufacture and supply sanitation commodities. For schools, health facilities and the most vulnerable households, the MVP also subsidises construction of improved latrines.

Hygiene

Promotion and demonstration of safe hygiene practices – i.e., hand washing with soap, food hygiene, menstrual hygiene management, safe stool disposal, and solid waste management – at the household, community and institutional level is carried out collaboratively with the health, education, community development and business development sectors working in the MVP. These practices include hand washing with soap, food hygiene, menstrual hygiene management, safe stool disposal, and solid waste management. The success of these programs involves ensuring that schools and health facilities enable the practice of safe hygiene behaviors (e.g., hand washing stations, waste disposal facilities) and those health workers and educators are trained on appropriate behavior change communication. Developing educational and communication materials for WASH, and strengthening school health club programs, are also instrumental to reinforcing hygiene promotion in schools. The efforts have been done through public-private partnerships (PPP) to the WASH agenda.

Public-Private Partnerships (PPP) for Water, Sanitation and Hygiene in the Millennium Villages

In recent years, public-private partnerships (PPP) have played an increasingly prominent role in the field of international development. PPPs are essential to the WASH agenda as these relationships offer not only capital for resource-intensive infrastructural projects, but also marketing and communication expertise that is instrumental for changing hygiene behaviors. Since 2008, the MVP has worked with GlaxoSmithKline to pilot the Personal Hygiene and sanitation education (PHASE) program in two village clusters: Mwandama, Malawi and Potou, Senegal. Dozens of schools and thousands of children have benefited from newly constructed gender-segregated latrines and hand washing stations, as well as engaging teaching materials on topics such as personal hygiene, water safety, safe sanitation and food hygiene.

Millennium Development Goals

In 2000, the UN Millennium Declaration was signed by 189 countries, and translated into eight Millennium Development Goals (MFDGs) for development of poverty eradication. Three of the eight MDGs are directly related to health (reducing child mortality, improving maternal health and combating HIV/AIDS, malaria and other diseases). The ambitious nature of these goals – which are supposed to be achieved by 2015-coupled with concern about the massive health challenges being faced by the world's poorest countries, has led to a growing momentum within the field of global health (Mahapatra2011): We would like to discuss here the millennium development goals on sanitation in the context of India.

Indian Situation

According to joint finding of the WHO and the UNICEF in 2919, about 683 million of the 1.1 billion people worldwide who defecate in the open are Indians. Meaning, every second person in the country defecates in the open. Going by the present pace of progress, India will achieve the millennium development goals on sanitation only by 2054. While some States has already achieved the target and some are close to it, other populous states such as Madhya Pradesh and Orissa will reach the target only in the next century, according to WHO and UNICEF's Joint Monitoring Programme for water Supply and sanitation (JMPWSS).

According to JMPWSS's report, which tracks the progress on drinking water and sanitation, 17 states, including Kerala, Haryana, Meghalaya, Himachal Pradesh, Punjab and most Union Territories, had already achieved the MDG target while Assam, Andhra Pradesh and Arunachal Pradesh will achieve it in the next 10 years. Karnataka, Maharashtra, Tamilnadu, Chhattisgarh are some states that will meet the MDG target I the coming 25 years, while Madhya Pradesh is expected to achieve the goals in 2105 and Orissa in 2160 unless special strategies are adopted to speed up the progress, the report has said.

The world has pledged to reduce by half the proportion of people without sustainable access to safe drinking water and basic sanitation by 2015 from 1990 figures. Though India has already achieved impressive results on water supply, with 85 per cent of its people having access to safe drinking water, 51 per cent or 626 million in the country defecate in the open, accounting to 60 per cent of the world's total open defecations.

India has seen an improvement in the sanitation figures from 1990, when 75 per cent people defecated in the open as against 51 per cent in 2010. But this improvement is seen only in the urban settings, where 28 per cent has no access to sanitation in 1990 as against 67 per cent in 2010, indicating that it was the rich who has more access to sanitation.

Four out of every 10 people who have gained access to improved sanitation since 1990 live in China or India, and more than half of the 2.5 billion people without improved sanitation too live in these two countries. In India, 251 million people gained access to sanitation between 1990 and 2010 but the percentage continues to be low because of the annual increase in the population. Over 1.7 million (22 per cent of the world total) children under five who died in 2010 were Indians, diarrhoea being one among the largest killer diseases and accounting for 13 per cent of the deaths. World-wide, over 80 per cent of diarrhoeal deaths are due to unsafe water, inadequate sanitation and poor hygiene.

Critique

South Asian Conference on sanitation (SACOSAN) held in April 2010 in Colombo pointed out that India needs to make sure that every citizen has access to a toilet within a year. Else the world will fail to meet the millennium development goals by 2015. Worried about India's slow progress in sanitation coverage- it is the least among the SAARC (South Asian Association for regional Cooperation) countries- experts and policy makers unofficially admit it is not possible to achieve the millennium development goals on sanitation. A mid-term assessment of India's progress towards the goals by the Union Ministry of Statistics and Programme Implementation in May 2010 shows that 63 per cent of rural India is likely to have no access to sanitation by 2015; the target was to reduce the no sanitation areas to 47 per cent. In urban India, 15 per cent of the areas would have no sanitation facilities against a target of 12 per cent. Given the assessment, India's own deadline seems unattainable.

India has completed 25 years of the Central Rural sanitation Programme in 2011, the country's first structured programme to ensure sanitation facilities. However, we are unable to achieve the success of the same. India has been constructing 1.5 million toilets a year under its Total Sanitation Campaign. But 50 per cent of the them remain unused, going by Prime Minister Man Mohan Singh's admission in SACOSAN in Delhi in 2008.

Sticking to toilet-using habit depends on several factors:

- good structured that protects privacy,
- availability of water and
- awareness of the economic benefits of good sanitation
- How the sanitation programme is approached

How achievable is this target? Even to meet India's own commitment of "toilets for all" by March 2012 it has to construct a toilet every second for a year.

A Success Story of Achieving the Target

In Odisha, some 700 villages have stopped defecating in the open in the past 20 years and one of them reverted to the old practice. Rather, they have put together Rs. 7 crore as corpus to ensure fund for needy people to build toilets. Using toilet has become a habit for them. Sanitation campaign in these villages was started by a non-profit, Gram Vikas. It adopts a diametrically opposite strategy than that of the government's Total sanitation Campaign. A village first works on assured water supply and then build toilets. These toilets cost almost double of what the government provides under its programme, but they are of usable quality. The cost difference is shared by the community: every household deposit Rs. 1,000 to a corpus that takes care of future needs of toilets. At times it takes six to 14 months for

Gram Vikas to mobilise a community before people commit to take up water and sanitation works. The village elects a vigilance group, with power to impose penalty, which monitors the use of toilets and drinking water facilities. Assessments of this now-famed Gam Vikas model show that the economic benefits of sanitation coverage, such as drastically reduced medical expenses, have ensured that communities stick to sanitation habits.

The message is clear: sanitation is not just about toilets. It is an issue that also concerns drinking water and health departments as everyday people defecating in the open leave behind an estimated 100,000 tonnes of excreta. This pollutes water sources leading to diseases. But they do not work hand in hand. The information and communication needed to make using toilets a habit is also highly inadequate in Total sanitation Campaign and least expenses are allocated towards this. Without any community mobilisation, the sanitation campaign has been reduced to a toilet construction drive.

Globalisation and Sanitation

The United Nations Special Rapporteur on Adequate Housing UN Commission on Human Rights, Kothari, Miloon (2002:49-65) prepared a Repot of the Special Rapporteur on an adequate housing as a component of the right to an adequate standard of living. This report reviews some of these recent developments as well as the preliminary results of research undertaken for my work as UN Special Rapporteur on Adequate Housing. In the ensuing section of this chapter, we have adapted the excerpts inferred from the report of Kothari (2002).

It is estimated that 600 million urban dwellers and over a billion rural persons now live in overcrowded and poor quality housing without adequate water, sanitation, and drainage or garbage collection. More than 1.2 billion people still have no access to safe drinking water, and 2.4 billion do not have adequate sanitation services. This grave situation puts lives and health continually at risk. It also threatens a range of human rights, including the right to adequate housing. Globalisation policies have accelerated the trends towards privatising human rights, such as water, often leading to the violation of the rights of the poor.

While the debate continues at the international level on whether or not globalisation can bring benefits to the world's poor, the fact remains that the deepening inequalities of income and opportunity between and within nations has led to an increase in the number of people without adequate and secure housing. The human rights of people and communities to housing, water and sanitation—guaranteed under international law and commitments of development targets made at global summits including the Millennium Summit and the World Summit on Sustainable Development—continue to erode as the process of privatisation deepens and accelerate. It is time to rethink the current global economic and social policies and to recommit ourselves to the human rights principles and standards that offer the only real paradigm for improving the lives of millions of the poor.

Globalisation and the process of increasing economic integration have limited the capacity of States to provide adequate resources for fulfilling the economic, social and cultural rights of their citizens, including housing and essential social services. Notwithstanding the constraints and difficulties placed upon them, central governments still have an important role to play in reconciling macroeconomic policies with social objectives, keeping in mind the primacy of their human rights obligations. Governments have the responsibility to make targeted interventions in order to ensure universal access to public services, including water and sanitation, on a fair and equitable basis; this is fundamental for the fulfilment of the right to adequate housing. However, government is leaving their welfare responsibility for essential services like water, sanitation and making it private venture.

Water is essential to human life and to all life on Earth. The freshwater resources are part of the global commons, a collective resource, not a private commodity to be bought, sold or traded for profit. In General Comment NO. 15, the CESCR categorically states that: "The human right to water is indispensable for leading a life in human dignity. It is a prerequisite for the realisation of other human rights... Water should be treated as a social and cultural good and not primarily an economic good". Access to drinking water is one of the key aims of the UN's Millennium Development Goals (MDGs) to be achieved by 2015, and is directly linked to the achievement of other MDGs related to poverty, food, health and housing.

Sanitation has been historically accorded less attention, despite even lower rates of access and the great need for more support to this area. Some 2.4 billion people worldwide are estimated to lack adequate access to sanitation, more than twice the number of persons who lack access to safe drinking water. Sanitation is an important component of adequate housing, and is related to other rights including the right to life, health, food, and even to security and education. A welcome development is the recent establishment of a new target, agreed at the World Summit on Sustainable Development, to halve the number of people without access to sanitation services by 2015.

Privatisation of water and sanitation services warrants close attention when assessing the impact of globalisation on the right to adequate housing. Without access to potable water the right to adequate housing loses its meaning. In fact, corporate globalisation, and its clear expression of privatisation of services, is one of the greatest threats to universal access to clean drinking water and sanitation.

Privatisation often leads to rate increases. Cash-strapped and indebted governments are pressured through IMF and World Bank policies to raise consumer fees for water in order to attract private sector investment in the water services. In many cases, companies get profit guarantees written into their contracts. For example, if residents use less water than predicted, companies do not fall below a predetermined level. Another concern is that the World Bank and regional development banks often advocate for «unbundling» of services, which separates the profitable and unprofitable areas of water and sanitation services. The unprofitable sectors such as infrastructure, sewage treatment, providing water to slum settlements and rural water service, remain in the public sector. Unbundling the water services sector and making subsidies explicit is considered part of the groundwork necessary to provide private water companies with attractive investment packages (Gruski : 2002).

Privatisation often leads to job losses. Massive layoffs are common as companies try to minimise costs and maximise profits. Often, services and water quality are put at risk due to understaffing; thus lay-offs have a double negative impact as they hurt consumers as well as the workers involved. Services to vulnerable groups are inadequate and of poor quality.

Privatisation often results in reduced access by the poor to basic social services. In developing countries, finding safe and affordable water is a daily struggle for the majority poor population. In many cities and towns in developing countries, between 50 per cent and 70 per cent of the population live in slums and squatter settlements without adequate housing or basic services. Many of the poor end up paying up to twenty times more than the rich for water (WSSCC and UN:2002).

Higher prices for water mean the poor have to use less or go without. Risks to service delivery stemming from privatisation—interruptions in service or deterioration in the quality of water—pose serious health hazards. These can occur in any number of scenarios related to privatisation, for example in cases of projects failing (Tucuman, Argentina), of contracts becoming unworkable (Dolphin Coast, South Africa), of the company failing (Azurix, Buenos Aires province, Argentina), of socially unsustainable price increases (Cochabamba, Bolivia), and of corruption and distorted accounting (Grenoble, France). The increase in water prices has a particularly adverse impact on the poor due to their inability to access clean water and can pose serious health risks. For example, in South Africa, water charges imposed in 1999 forced some poor people in Kwagulu-Natal to rely on polluted river supplies for their water. Public health officials trace a 2001 cholera outbreak, which killed dozens, to the water pricing policy. General Comment No. 15 states that "violation of the obligation to respect follow from the State Party's interference with the right to water. This includes...discriminatory or unaffordable increases in the price of water."

Private operators are not accountable to the public. Privatisation can reduce accountability and local control. In many cases governments make long-term deals with the water companies, granting them exclusive distribution rights, thus sanctioning monopolies. Multinational corporations are accountable to their shareholders, not to the citizens in the countries where they operate. There have been cases of corruption in the privatisation process, where the system of checks and balances is weak (David Hall: PSIRU). Contract workings and details are usually done behind closed doors and this encourages bribery, while the common citizens, who are directly affected, are kept in the dark

There is a need to strengthen the participatory monitoring mechanism, as it is extremely difficult to reverse privatisation once implemented. Multilateral trade agreements provide corporations with powerful legal recourse. Legal claims for compensation by private water companies make terminating contracts prohibitively expensive. Ensuring that local needs are addressed through wider community participation is an essential factor in promoting broader accountability. In the Philippines, where cost recovery is well above the Asian average, water districts have an organisational structure that provides representation for users. In the state of Rajasthan, India, a civil society organisation, Tarun Bharat Sangh, has shown remarkable results by working with villagers to regenerate groundwater through environmental restoration (12 E/CN.4/2002/59).

Privatisation also undermines water quality and ecological sustainability. Water companies work to weaken water quality regulations and environmental standards when they are perceived as increasing the costs of doing business. Also, encouraging consumption is a typical strategy of any private corporation driven by the profit motive. In 1996, a World Bank team led by John Briscoe—now in charge of water policy—criticised leakage levels of between 1 per cent and 5 per cent in Germany's public sector system for being too low. According to the report, water should be allowed to leak away if the cost of stopping the leak is greater than the price for which the water could be sold at a profit. Briscoe's team not only thought that the private water companies would waste more water—they encouraged it (David Hall, op. cit.).

Aware of the bleak water predictions, corporations are in a rush to obtain access to water, which they can sell at huge profits. Mass extraction of water from its natural sources can result in ecological imbalances such as aquifer depletion and groundwater contamination (Adam Otis: 2002). Once aquifers are depleted or contaminated, they are almost impossible to restore. In light of these concerns, it is important to note that some of the best practices found in water and sanitation provision in developed and developing countries are publicly operated. The vast majority of people in North America, Europe and Japan receive water and sanitation services from publicly owned and operated facilities. These often compare favourably in terms of efficiency with privately operated facilities. Some examples of reforms of public sector water undertakings can be found in São Paulo, Brazil; Debrecen, Hungary; Lilongwe, Malawi and Tegucigalpa, Honduras (For further examples and evidence, see David Hall:2001). Indeed, a multi-country comparison of public service delivery in developing countries found that «purely public water supply systems were among the best performing services overall» (quoted in Martin, Brendan :2001:28)

Women and Inadequate Housing Water and Sanitation

The consequences of having inadequate or no access to water are devastating—especially for women and children [An estimated 2.2 million people in developing countries, most of them children, die every year from diseases associated with lack of access to safe drinking water, inadequate sanitation and poor hygiene. (See www.unicef.org]. When water is not readily available, it is particularly the women and children who have to spend a large amount of time fetching water back to their houses. This has detrimental impact on their health, security and education. It has been found that where there are no latrines, girls commonly avoid school.

Women and girls carry the bulk of the burden in providing water for households in rural areas and often have to walk great distances in search of water to meet minimal household needs[According to the water Supply and Sanitation Collaborative Council, the average distance that women in Africa and Asia walk to collect water is 6 km. The weight of water that women in Africa and Asia carry on their heads is about 20 kg. (From "WASH facts and Figures", Information sheet).

In the poorer countries, one in five children die before the age of five, mainly from infectious diseases related to inadequate or impure water (OHCHR (2002). Water stress contributes too many other hardships for women. As an example, in India, because of the low availability of water, vegetation growth is low, which means there is less green fodder, which decreases production of both milk and cow dung, which is used for fuel and manure. Lower production of cow dung means reduction in agricultural yields. Low agricultural yields affect food quality and the nutrition of women. There is thus a vicious cycle of water and ecological destruction affecting the health of women and causing «eco-stress» (Parsuram: 1998). Also, with increasing opportunities for women to engage in productive employment activities, their time increasingly carries monetary value. In many instances, if this cost is included in the decision making about the choice of technology and strategies for household water security, it will be found that in rural areas women and girls are paying far more for water than they do in urban areas. Also, equity issues need to be kept in mind not only as between men and women but also between rich and poor women from different socio-economic situations have different needs, which affect their level of interest and participation in various activities (Pangare:2002)

Lack of sanitation facilities affects both men and women, but sanitation needs and demands differ with gender. Women have particular needs and concerns of privacy, dignity and personal safety. The lack of sanitation facilities in the homes can force women and girls to use secluded places, which are often away from home, exposing them to the risk of sexual abuse; in other circumstances, girls are forced to defecate only at home and help their mothers to dispose of human and solid waste. Because of this extra work girls might have to stop attending school. The lack of access to clean and sufficient water and sanitation facilities contribute to diseases, which result in more expenses, and thus perpetuate the vicious cycle of poverty and disease. This cycle is further aggravated by other impacts of the lack of hygiene and sanitation facilities: for example, it is primarily girls (and women) who are more likely to be kept at home to look after ailing family members. This leads to reduced school attendance and poorer educational performance. Studies have also found that the access to sewage disposal often depends on the sex of the head of household; for example in Nairobi, Kenya, about 9.2 per cent of female-headed households used the bush for faecal disposal, whereas in the male-headed households the rate dropped to 2.2 per cent (Kothari: 2003) . In many countries, women and men do not enjoy equal access to basic resources and services. Female-headed households have less access than males, and if the services are privatised then the problem increases. Greater attention needs to be paid to the discrimination women face and to policies and measures adopted to alleviate it. There is also a need for laws and policies that regulate or define the habitability of housing to take into consideration the special needs of women (www.unhchr.ch/housing).

International Cooperation

The Millennium Declaration adopted by the General Assembly recognised «solidarity» and «shared responsibilities» as fundamental values essential to international relations in the twenty-first century(General Assembly resolution 55/2, paragraph 6). Such recognition is necessary for the essential task of evolving strategies for distributive justice, including land reform and increases in social spending on areas critical to the realisation of the right to adequate housing, such as access to potable water and sanitation. Such a reallocation or redistribution needs to be balanced with targeted support from international cooperation, including «joint» and «separate» action by States, as called for by the general obligations to international human rights instruments.

The Way Forward

This brief review has shown the urgency of undertaking systematic research across the world to assess the impact of privatisation of housing, water and sanitation on the human rights of low-income and marginalised communities. It is essential that we develop human rights-based indicators and benchmarks to assist in the implementation of human rights (and MDG's) relevant to these issues (Kothari:2003) The primary role for States and civil society is to ensure the rigorous implementation of human rights principles and instruments. This will ensure that national and international trade, investment and debt policies and agreements are designed with respect to the rights of individuals and communities. It will also ensure that the principles that guide neo-liberal approaches on the privatisation and commodification of housing, water and sanitation, such as «cost recovery» and «unbundling, » can be challenged by the human rights principles of «non-discrimination and equality», «progressive realisation» and «accountability». Failure to grasp the enormous potential that human rights have for sustaining environment and development and ensuring social justice will only lead to a world where we will witness dispossession and homelessness on an even larger scale. Miloon Kothari is United Nations Special Rapporteur on Adequate Housing UN Commission on Human Rights.

References

Adam Otis, Ginger (2002). "World without Water" August.

Commission on Human Rights (2002). "Report of the Special Rapporteur on a adequate housing as a Component of the right to an adequate standard of living", by Miloon Kothari: E/CN.4/ 2002/59, March 2002, paragraph 49-65. See also papers prepared by David Westendorff, Deepika Naruka andLiana Cisneros, Research currently underway in the MERCOSUR countries: Uruguay, Argentina, Paraguay and Brazil, www.cooper.net/ direitoshumanosrmc/index htm. See alos the "Global Survey on the Right to Adequate Housing and Social Services" prepared by Social Alert, as a contribution to the work of the Special Rapporteur, at www.socialalert.org/e-camp.html

David, Hall, PSIRU. "World Bank – Politburo of water privatisation", www.bicusa.org/ptoc/htm/psriu_water.htm

David, Hall (2001). "Water in Public Hands", June, available at www.psiru.org

Dissanayake, Ellen (1988). What is Art For? Seattle: University of Washington.

Human Rights, Poverty reduction and Sustainable Development: Health, Food and water, OHCHR Backgroung paper, WSSD Johannesburg, 26 August- 4 September, 2002

Kothari, Miloon (2002:49-65)."Report of the Special Rapporteur on a adequate housing as a Component of the right to an adequate standard of living", Commission on Human Rights.

Kothari, Miloon (2003). Report of the UN Commission on Human Rights, (E/CN.4/2003/5)

Kothari, Miloon (2003). Women and Housing, Report for the Commission on Human Rights, Nairobi, Kenya: Mazinira Institute

Mahapatra, Richard (2011). *Down to Earth*, 15 April.

Martin, Brendan (2001). "Privatisation of Municipal Services: potential, limitations and challenges for the social partners", ILO Workin Paer No. 175, Geneva, ILO, p. 28.

OHCHR (2002). Background paper, "Human Rights, Poverty Reduction and Sustainable development: Health, Food and Water", WSSD Johannesburg, 26 August – 4 September.

Pangare, Vasudha (2002). *Gender Issues in Watershed Management*, Oikos.

Parsuram, Ray (1998). "Its Grave, Not Watery", Grassroots, 4 February.

Gruski, Sara (2002). Profit Streams: The World Bank and Greedy Global Water Companies, Public Citizen Report, September, (www.citizen.org/documents/Profit Streams-World per cent 20Bank.pdf)

Giddens, Anthony (1991). *The Consequences of Moderning:* Cambridge:, Polity Press, p. 64.

WSSCC and UN (2002)

Website www.unhchr.ch/housing

www.unhchr.ch/housing/i2echou.htm.

11

Epilogue

Sanitation is a basic, as well as a long-standing, public health issue. When early peoples settled in communities and started to cultivate crops and raise animals, sanitation became a primary concern for society. The Book of Leviticus, in the Torah, includes specific guidelines regarding the disposal of wastes, the placement and disinfection of wells, and related issues. Today, as urban areas grow, more pressure has been put on local water supplies, for the quality of the water that is available to a community greatly impacts all aspects of health. Worldwide, 40 per cent of the population does not have ready access to clean, safe drinking water, and approximately 60 per cent does not have satisfactory facilities for the safe disposal of human waste. Infectious agents in drinking water and food cause the diarrheal deaths of several million children annually. Sanitation includes the appropriate disposal of human and industrial wastes and the protection of the water sources. Mark Jenner and Mark G. Robson highlight such issues in the Gale Encyclopaedia of the early Modern World.

The book consists of ten chapters excluding preface, biographical note, epilogue, case studies, glossary and appendices (includes safeguarding humanity, historical development of toilets and glimpses of Sulabh.

The first chapter starts with an Introduction which deals three things: I. Sociology of Sanitation: Concept and Genesis; II. Sanitation and its Relationship with other Disciplines and associated Dimensions: (i) Environmental, (ii) Public Health, (iii) Women and (iv) Sustainable development; III. Sanitation and its relationship with other social institutions.

The second chapter analyses three things: (i) Perspectives and Orientations, (ii) Approaches to Public Health, and (iii) Social Perspective on the sanitation challenges.

The third chapter traces the relationship of sanitation, health and society explaining the conceptual clarification of the terms: (i) Sanitation (ii) Hygiene (iii) Scavenging (iv) Purity and pollution, (v) Environment (vi) Wastage: public and private space.

The fourth chapter explores the cultural context of sanitation discussing the social components of scavenging and cleanliness – culture and dirt, attitudes, beliefs and values associated with dirt problems of scavenging, purity and impurity, development and sanitation.

The fifth chapter examines three things to understand the social structure and sanitation: (i) Caste and class of scavengers – Origin, nature and functions, socio-economic conditions, historical deprivation, social and religious disabilities, contemporary Scenario, (ii) Gender and sanitation – Health, hygiene, education and employment, gender equality, and (iii) Children and sanitation – Health and Hygiene.

The sixth chapter highlights toilet as a tool of social change on the bases of two things, namely, first the origin of toilet and its benefits, and second, toilet and social change.

The seventh chapter emphasises on the problem of environmental sanitation which includes: (i) Problems of Environmental Sanitation in India (ii) Concept of Environmental Sanitation (iii) Environmental and Social Sanitation (iv) The Environmental Burden of Disease (v) The Scope and Subjects of environmental Hygiene and sanitation (vi) Promoting Sanitation, and (vii) Water and Sanitation.

The eighth chapter delineates the role of state in context to sanitation indicating three things related to the State and sanitation In India: (i) Sanitation in the policies and programmes in India and its critique (ii) Implementation and utilisation of sanitary programmes in rural and urban communities, and (iii) Liberation and Rehabilitation of scavengers.

The ninth chapter describes Sulabh Movement for Sanitation – Historical Emergence, Phases, and actions. This reflects social revolution towards sanitation in India highlighting the features of Sulabh International social Service Organisation.

In order to talk about globalisation and its impact on essential services of water, health and sanitation of developing countries, the tenth chapter tries to understand the four driving forces of globalisation (i) Science and Technology, (ii) Communication and media, (iii) Market, trade and finance, and (iv) Migration and inter-cultural transactions.

The last chapter indicates challenges of sanitation. There are two basic challenges: The **first** challenge to solve the problem of access to sanitation. The **second** challenge is to decide what aspects are the most important in context to sanitation.

Regarding these two challenges, ***WHO*** prepared a draft *in cooperation with* ***UNICEF*** **and** ***WSSCC*** related to the issue of Sanitation. They deal things we need to know about Sanitation.We would like to describe here the ideas given by WHO to deal the challenges to solve the problem of sanitation.

Size of the Problem

In 2004, only 59 per cent of the world population had access to any type of improved sanitation facility. In otherwords, 4 out of 10 people around the world have no access to improved sanitation. They are obliged to defecate in the open or use unsanitary facilities, with a serious risk of exposure to sanitation-related diseases. While sanitation coverage has increased from 49 per cent in 1990, a huge effort needs to be made quickly to expand coverage to the MDG target level of 75 per cent . Investing in sanitation infrastructure involves a long project cycle. If the MDG sanitation target is to be achieved, innovative approaches need to be developed to reduce the time span from policymaking to services delivery. The global statistics on sanitation hide the dire situation in some developing regions. With an average coverage in developing regions of 50 per cent, only one out of two people has access to some sort of improved sanitation facility. The regions presenting the lowest coverage are sub-Saharan Africa (37 per cent), Southern Asia (38 per cent) and Eastern Asia (45 per cent). Western Asia (84 per cent) has the highest coverage among developing regions. Out of every three persons unserved, two live in Southern Asia or Eastern Asia. Looking to the gravity of the problem there is a need to focus on sanitation.

Wherever humans gather, their waste also accumulates. Progress in sanitation and improved hygiene has greatly improved health, but many people still have no adequate means of disposing of their waste. This is a growing nuisance for heavily populated areas, carrying the risk of infectious disease, particularly to vulnerable groups such as the very young, the elderly and people suffering from diseases that lower their resistance. Poorly controlled waste also means daily exposure to an unpleasant environment. The build-up of faecal contamination in rivers and other waters is not just a human risk: other species are affected, threatening the ecological balance of the environment. The discharge of untreated wastewater and excreta into the environment affects human health by several routes:

- By polluting drinking water;
- Entry into the food chain, for example via fruits, vegetables or fish and shellfish;
- Bathing, recreational and other contact with contaminated waters;
- By providing breeding sites for flies and insects that spread diseases;

Challenges of Sanitation

The **first** challenge for countries seeking to solve the problem of access to sanitation is to define what "sanitation" really means. The **second** challenge is to decide what aspects are the most important. In other words, what aspect of the problem is going to be dealt with as a priority? This problem is not simple one and many professionals confuse the two steps. With respect to defining sanitation most professionals would agree that "sanitation" as a whole is a "big idea" which covers inter alia:

- Safe collection, storage, treatment and disposal/re-use/recycling of human excreta (faeces and urine);
- Management/re-use/recycling of solid wastes (trash or rubbish);

- Drainage and disposal/re-use/recycling of household wastewater (often referred to as sullage or grey water);
- Drainage of storm water;
- treatment and disposal/re-use/recycling of sewage effluents;
- Collection and management of industrial waste products; and
- Management of hazardous wastes (including hospital wastes, and chemical/ radioactive and other dangerous substances).

For countries with very low access to basic sanitation, increasing the effectiveness of management of excreta at the household level may have the biggest health implications and it may be the biggest challenge. For this reason some countries may legitimately decide to focus their efforts at this level in the short term. In other cases, specific inter-linkages between elements of sanitation mean that a more complete solution may be better – for example in a particularly congested urban community some form of off-site (sewered) sanitation may be the only viable technical choice – in which case there will probably need to be some interventions to improve management of solid wastes and storm water drainage–otherwise the sewers won't work. Yet other countries or communities may try for a more complete solution which includes a focus on protecting the environment from contamination (as is the case in countries which already have universal access). In some cases, it will be possible to start with an "ecological" approach to sanitation which seeks to contain, treat and reuse excreta where possible – thus minimising contamination and making optimum use of resources.

The key issue here is that each community, region or country needs to work out what is the most sensible and cost effective way of thinking about sanitation in the short and long term and then act accordingly. Flexibility and pragmatism should be the key words – and both professionals and politicians need to try and see past "experience" and ideas which are developed elsewhere – a pragmatic local approach with an eye to wider environmental issues is likely to result in more progress than blind adherence to a rigid global definition.

In this direction, Dr Bindeshwar Pathak envisaged Sustainable Technology for better environment healthier society and human dignity through the tool of Sulabh technologies. We are referring here as reported by the Sulabh Organisation: "The use of various technologies developed by us for human excreta disposal in the last three and a half decades are described below:-

For individual houses-the Sulabh two-pit, pour-flush, on-site technology which is appropriate, affordable and eco-friendly, to help in construction of two-pit, pour-flush, eco-friendly toilets and conversion of dry toilets to pour-flush, toilets in individual houses, to prevent defecation in the open and eliminate manual cleaning of human excreta by a class of people known as scavengers.

For public places, high-rise buildings, places of congregation and in non-sewered areas, to construct and maintain public toilets on a long term?pay and use? basis to provide a sustainable sanitation solution. Biogas digesters attached to public toilets recycle human excreta to biogas for further use. This promotes environmental improvement as well as provides human dignity. Other technologies are for waste-water treatment through duckweed with direct economic returns from pisciculture and composting of solid wastes through Sulabh Thermophilic Composting Treatment (STAC).

Our methodology is that we propagate and implement the above technologies. This is done by education and motivation of beneficiaries when we go house to house, give information to them, motivate, educate and train them. We help them to construct toilets themselves, or design it and construct it for them. Implementation, maintenance and follow-up are done by members of our organisation.

Regarding construction and maintenance of public toilets, the land and funds for construction are provided by the local bodies and then leased to Sulabh for monitoring them on a pay and use basis. But, recently, the Govt. gives land and construction is done under Build-Operate-Transfer (BOT) system. We follow a whole-town approach and cross-subsidise the funds.

The technique is that we have developed a model on how NGOs should work in partnership with Government agencies and local bodies on the one hand and people on the other; using appropriate and more useful technologies for effecting sanitation coverage. Sulabh has developed various strategies towards meeting the Millennium Development Goal on sanitation with involvement of all stakeholders and in partnership with Government, local bodies and communities.

United Nations ECOSOC and Sulabh International Social Service Organisation plan to work together in joint collaboration to help in empowering people throughout the world to achieve the Millennium Development Goal on Sanitation.

Our project is innovative and unconventional as in the sustainable technologies developed by us, complete recycling of human waste takes place and it provides an alternative to the old technologies of sewerage and septic tank systems which are costly to construct, difficult to maintain and further pollute the environment.(*Source:* Sulabh International Social service Organisation)".

The development of these technologies have shown how to eliminate defecation in the open and remove the practice of manual cleaning of human excreta by the people and enabled women to use toilets with dignity and safety and girls to secure benefits of toilets in schools. There is reduction in mortality rate of children because of diarrhoeal diseases. Untouchability and social discrimination have been removed from society by liberating and rehabilitating scavengers.

The cost associated with the development and implementation of Sulabh activities is much lower than that involved in conventional styles of human waste disposal, which are expensive and unaffordable. Sulabh technologies based human waste disposal systems lead to decentralised, on-site human waste disposal system, besides being appropriate and affordable, even to the poorest of the poor, enabling them to easily adopt them and find a sustainable solution as compared to defecation in the open. (*Source:* Sulabh International Social service Organisation).

We may infer from the above discussion that there is a need to motivate, educate and train people explaining the benefit of sanitation for better environment healthier society and human dignity. For example, in the draft of the WHO mention that how does sanitation prevent disease.

Human excreta have been implicated in the transmission of many infectious diseases including cholera, typhoid, infectious hepatitis, polio, cryptosporidiosis, and ascariasis. For a sanitation system to provide the greatest health protection to the individual, the community, and society at large it must:

- Isolate the user from their own excreta;
- Prevent nuisance organisms (e.g. flies) from contacting the excreta and subsequently transmitting disease to humans; and
- Inactivate the pathogens before they enter the environment or prevent the excreta from entering the environment.

It is important to understand that sanitation can act at different levels, protecting the household, the community and 'society'. In the case of latrines it is easy to see that this sanitation system acts at a household level. However, poor design or inappropriate location may lead to migration of waste matter and contamination of local water supplies putting the community at risk. In terms of waterborne sewage the containment may be effective for the individual and possibly also the community, but health effects and environmental damage may be seen far downstream of the original source, hence affecting 'society' (WHO).

Furthermore, the health impact of inadequate sanitation leads to a number of financial and economic costs including direct medical costs associated with treating sanitation-related illnesses and lost income through reduced or lost productivity and the government costs of providing health services. Additionally, sanitation also leads to time and effort losses due to distant or inadequate sanitation facilities, lower product quality resulting from poor water quality, reduced income from tourism (due to high risk of contamination and disease) and clean-up costs. Increases in female literacy (due to increased school attendance where proper sanitation facilities exist) contribute to economic growth.

Many people do not realise the health and economic benefits to the individual, the community and to society from improving sanitation. The high cost of improving sanitation is often cited as a barrier to implementing sanitation projects. Improving sanitation is often low on the list of priorities. There are so many other pressing needs for the attention of governments: food supply, education, medical treatment and dealing with war and conflict. Most people are aware that poor sanitation has a health impact, but there is a lack of awareness of the extent of ill-health that it causes.

On the other hand, human society has developed very different sociocultural responses to the use of untreated excreta. This ranges from deep disgust to practical preference. While determined partly by survival economics, these cultural differences apply to many water poor countries, as well as to water rich areas of the north. For example, in Africa, the Americas and Europe, excreta use is generally regarded as culturally unacceptable, or at best with indifference. This result from the strongly held view that human excreta, especially faeces, are repugnant substances best kept away from the senses of sight and smell. Products fertilised with raw excreta are regarded as tainted or defiled in some way. These views are less rigid in the case of using excreta in compost and sludge for agriculture, but still pose a barrier to use of waste.

We may view that efforts should be made for the progress on sanitation. Now, our government is determined to move ahead in this direction.

Early in his election campaign, Narendra Modi caused a stir when he expressed a preference for building toilets over temples. It was not an off-the-cuff remark. BJP's election manifesto pointed out poor hygiene and sanitation has a "far reaching, cascading impact". It added malnutrition will be treated as a national priority. The manifesto got it right. Sanitation has been a neglected aspect of Indian public policy and society is worse for it. It is not a silver bullet, but sanitation is the thread that connects some of our pressing social and health issues. Prime Minister Modi and his colleagues should articulate a plan and timeline to deal with this neglected challenge.

Numbers do not always tell the story, but in the case of sanitation they put things in perspective. More Indian homes have a telephone than a toilet within their premises. Women in more than half of India's homes have to step outside, often in unsafe circumstances, to attend to basic needs. The proximate cause of the horrific rapes in Badaun, Uttar Pradesh, was because victims had to step outside their homes. Women's safety has other dimensions and UP falls desperately short on most of them, particularly provision of law and order. However, tardy progress on sanitation just adds to challenges women face.

India's poor record in sanitation has adverse consequences in other areas too. Research on high malnutrition rates among Indian children shows open defecation plays a significant role in their stunting. Almost 50 million urban Indians defecate in the open, a number that exceeds Spain's population. If the Modi government creates an environment which throws up effective ideas to quickly end this practice, it will be a giant step forward in India's war against malnutrition.

Indian governments have largely ignored the positive spin-offs of investing in improvement of public health facilities such as provision of clean drinking water and sanitation. These areas need a sharper focus as they are people-friendly dimensions of social infrastructure investments. The resources generated by governments on account of economic growth should be utilised to improve public health facilities as they link economic progress to a tangible improvement in lives of ordinary IndiansHowever, we would have made an excellent start on tackling the most pressing ones (see The Times of India| The Economic Times: 9th June 2104).

The new NDA government under Narendra Modi set to embark on an ambitious multi-million dollar sanitation project that seeks to clean up around 1,000 Indian towns besides eliminating manual scavenging as a tribute to Mahatma Gandhi whose 150th birth anniversary will be celebrated in 2019.

Tentatively named the 'Mahatma Gandhi Clean India Programme', the project will start from three cities in Uttar Pradesh, including Modi's Lok Sabha constituency Varanasi, according to people working on the project.

This will be the first among six mega projects lined up by the so-called Team Modi, an eclectic bunch consisting of technocrats, young professionals employed in the West now on a sabbatical to assist Modi, and his own set of bureaucrats from Gujarat.

In his interactions with the team working on the project, Modi reportedly said, "our mothers and sisters have no access to closed toilets while we talk about 'nari-sanman' and 'nari-gaurav'. We must make a commitment that nobody will defecate in the open.""Modi believes that Kachde se bhikanchanban sakta hai-...Waste is wealth for him and he will rope in professional companies with machinery and technology," says one of his close confidantes, adding that the project will not be left to politicians or bureaucrats and that the involvement of private companies and professional management will ensure that it is different from mega projects like MNREGA launched by the previous UPA regime.A special part of the project is about building 2 lakh toilets for women in 5,000 villages.

The project envisages providing sanitation and sewerage facilities to over 36 million households in the country in the first phase. Modi had asked his team of over 100 qualified professionals to find out the financial implications of providing urban infrastructure like drinking water, gutter, solid waste management, storm water drainage, roads, transport and street light in 500 cities first, as phase one of the project.

Modi, said one official, has clearly told people that the first phase of the project encompassing 500 cities need to get over by by 2019."By 2022, the 75th year of independence, he wishes to make them model cities in terms of cleanliness, green cover and infrastructure," the official said.

The focus will be on water supply, drainage system and roads as Modi believes every city should be a 'nirman nagar' with excellent drains and roads. Experts have suggested a unique model of people owned public toilets in the cities as part of the project, said some of the people associated with the project.

The funding could be divided between the government and private investors, say his team members. The project will have tenders given out to companies abroad for recycling solid wastes generated into organic fertilisers for horticulturists to grow fruits and vegetables.

The role models for the project are cities like Amsterdam, Singapore, Freiburg (Germany) and Kobe (Japan). The project will be implemented on a P4 (people-public sector-private sector-partnership) model (Venugopal: 2014). In his Speech in the parliament on June 9, 2014, Pranab Mukherjee said: "We must not tolerate the indignity of homes without toilets and public spaces littered with garbage. For ensuring hygiene, waste management and sanitation across the nation a "Swachh Bharat Mission" will be launched. This will be our tribute to Mahatma Gandhi on his 150th birth anniversary to be celebrated in the year 2019."

References and Further Readings

Corbin, Alain. *The Foul and the Fragrant: Odor and the French Social Imagination.* Cambridge, Mass., 1986.

For a website devoted to the history of the water supply of the city of Rome: http://www.iath.virginia.edu/waters/.

Gale Encyclopaedia of Public Health:

Gale Encyclopaedia of the Early Modern World:

http://timesofindia.indiatimes.com/followceleb.cms?alias=sanitation problems in India, sanitation problems, crimes against women

Jenner, Mark S. R. "From Conduit Community to Commercial Network? Water in London 1500–1725." In *Londinopolis: Essays in the Cultural and Social History of Early Modern London.* Edited by Paul Griffiths and Mark S. R. Jenner. Manchester, U.K., and New York, 2000.

McKenzie, J., and Pinger, R. (1997). *An Introduction to Community Health.* Sudbury, MA: Jones and Bartlett.

Merson, M.; Black, R.; and Mills, A., eds. (2001). *International Public Health: Diseases, Programs, Systems, and Policies.* Gaithersburg, MD: Aspen Publishers.

Morgan, M. T. (1997). *Environmental Health.* Madison, WI: Brown and Benchmark.

Riley, J.C. *The Eighteenth-Century Campaign against Disease.*Basingstoke, U.K., and London, 1987.

Roche, D. "Le temps de l'eaurare: Du Moyen Age à époque Moderne." *Annals: Economies, sociétés, civilisations* 39 (1984): 383–399.

Rosen, George. *A History of Public Health.* Reprint. New York, 1993. Chaps. 3–5.

Stuart, Kathy. *Defiled Trades and Social Outcasts: Honor and Ritual Pollution in Early Modern Germany.* Cambridge, U.K., and New York, 1999.

Sulabh International Social service Organisation

TOI Tech directly at www.toitech.com

Venugopal, Vasudev (2014),Modi plans multi-million dollar sanitation project to clean up 1,000 Indian towns, *ET Bureau,* May 24.

12

Case Studies

In the social sciences and life sciences, a case study (or case report) is a descriptive, exploratory or explanatory analysis of a person, group or event. In this context, we would like to describe the five case studies of different situation which reflect the sanitation problem. These are as follows:

1. An Admirer of Sulabh Movement: Ram Updesh Singh, IAS (Retd.) has considered all aspects of sanitation and hygiene in the villages of India.
2. Improving Women's Status, One Bathroom at a Time: NILANJANA S. ROY
3. Indian garbage garbed in grand theories: Paras Nath Chaudhary
4. Sociology of Sanitation: A Memory Ethnography: Vinay Kumar Srivastava
5. Social Construction of Hygiene and Sanitation in Haryana: MadhuNagla

1. An Admirer of Sulabh Movement: Ram Updesh Singh, IAS (Retd.)

Singh (2013) narrates his own experiences about sanitation and hygiene. Way Forward: Having been born and brought up in a very backward rural area of eastern UP, I have considered all aspects of sanitation and hygiene in the villages of India where over 80 per cent of the people dwell. From my childhood, I have heard of and taken recourse to a Pit-Latrine which entails making a small ditch on the earthy surface and covering it with the soil after defecation. In course of time, the excreta would melt into the earth, as it were, and at the same time add to the fertility of the soil. Pit Latrine is in fact a latrine with a small pit for collection and decomposition of excreta. It costs little but delivers a lot. I feel that the adoption of the age-old concept and practice of pit-latrines could substantially add to the other popular interventions in vogue and thereby change the scenario of sanitation and hygiene at the grass-root level in rural India. Making a speech, amidst the galaxy of intellectuals assembled here for this thematic workshop, has been to me a tall order.

2. Improving Women's Status, One Bathroom at a Time

Count the number of public toilets for women in India, or the availability of something as basic as low-cost sanitary napkins, and the invisibility of women's needs becomes apparent. But as campaigns like the "No Toilet, No Bride" effort in the northern state of Haryana make an impact, India's women are beginning to demand basic rights.

This isn't often easy. Just a few kilometers away from showrooms that advertise gold faucets and offer ways of turning bathrooms into glamour rooms, the women of Kusumpur, a slum area in Delhi, are lining up to use public toilets in distinctly unglamorous conditions. Kusumpur has almost no private toilets and only one public toilet for every 500 women. As Usha Kumari, a longtime resident, says, the impact on these women's lives is stark.

"If you have to go to school or a job, you have to be up early to line up for water from the common tap to wash, then for the toilet," she said. "Some days I have to use the flying toilet and freshen up in the Metro bathroom."

The "flying toilet" is a common solution in Indian slums to the lack of bathrooms. Women with no access to clean public toilets often use a plastic bag, then deposit the bag and its contents in the trash later.

In a 2009 study, the Center for Civil Society, a non-profit organisation, estimated that the capital had only 132 public toilets for women, many of them barely functioning, compared with 1,534 for men. The effect of this, in Delhi and across urban India, is to severely limit the mobility of women and their ability to work efficiently.

Marie Rodriguez, a market stall owner in Margao, in the south-eastern state of Goa, described the difference toilets can make. "Once the municipality installed a toilet for women here, I could take over the shop from my son," she said. "Before that, I could come in and help, but staying the entire day was impossible."

For thousands of women across India, the existence of a toilet near their workplace is no small thing. It affects women's ability to work, their safety (many rapes in slums and rural India happen in areas where women have to walk a long way to reach the toilet) and their mobility.

The impact on women's lives, as a study by the nonprofit organisation ASER shows, begins early. Its Annual Status of Education Report for 2010 confirms the link between providing separate toilets for girls in schools and girls' dropout rates. Only 4 in 10 government schools, according to the group's data, have functioning toilets for girls, and this strongly influences the girls' ability to attend school. In Jharkhand, Bihar and Chhattisgarh — three states with the lowest percentage of toilets for girls — the numbers for girls' school attendance are correspondingly low.

There are signs of change, though, and one of the most surprising may be in the matrimonial market. Four years ago, the Haryana government started its "No Toilet, No Bride" campaign, painting walls across the state with the slogan: "I won't allow my daughter to marry into a home without toilets."

Today, as 23-year-old Nimmi Singh, who is now engaged to be married, insists, a groom with a loo is essential. Her family in the city of Rohtak rejected two bathroom-less grooms before locating a family willing to install one in time for the wedding. "It's a matter of pride," she said. "Why should I have to go to the fields?"

And in Delhi, marriage brokers — who provide a popular service in a country where arranged marriages are still the norm — confirm that many families will now ask whether the groom's family has a bathroom of its own before going ahead with nuptial negotiations.

A recent survey by the nongovernmental organisation Plan India indicated how great the need for innovations of this kind are here. It found that 68 per cent of rural women in India could not afford something as basic as a sanitary napkin. It also found that reproductive tract infections were 70 per cent more prevalent among women who lacked access to such hygienic supplies for that time of the month.

Women like Asha Bibi, 46, who lives in the village of Baharpur in Uttar Pradesh, consider commercial brands of sanitary napkins unaffordable. "I've seen the ads on television," said Ms. Bibi, who uses cloth napkins even though she finds them uncomfortable and restricting. "But two packets cost as much as my food budget for a week. They're for rich women, not for women like me."

Meanwhile, in the southern state of Tamil Nadu, an inventor is hoping to usher in a separate but equally important revolution. A few years ago, A. Muruganantham made news with his campaign to create a low-cost sanitary napkin that could be used by poor women in both urban and rural India. He pursued a "Gandhian operation" to make cheap sanitary napkins: women would use his company's technology to set up their own manufacturing units at home, much as the charkha was used to spin homespun cloth two generations ago. He isn't alone — Procter & Gamble has entered a partnership with the Ministry of Health & Family Welfare's National Rural Health Mission to produce inexpensive sanitary napkins for rural women in the north-western state of Rajasthan.

That, says Mr Muruganantham, is what he is trying to change. "I wanted to make cheap napkins affordable for women like my wife and my sister," he said in an interview. "With the 'small is beautiful' model, we want to give dignity back to women." (Roy : 2011)

3. Indian Garbage Garbed in Grand Theories

Chaudhary(2013) explores Indian garbage garbed in grand theories through presenting his own experiences as follows: Living healthy and long: this has been one of the primal urges of man. Initially, all his efforts to fight teeming infections and diseases surrounding him had been to no avail. But man did not give up and kept struggling for a solution. Finally, the French invented the word and concept 'hygiene" and with it developed the idea of keeping oneself and the ambience clean. It bears special mention that this meant the beginning of organised systematic sanitary practices. The latter transformed the world. That is to say, man began living longer and healthier. Attainment of basic hygienic standards turned out to be one of the hallmarks of the advancement of a modern human society. In contrast, the lack or absence of it is acknowledged as being a mark of a failed society. Against this background, sanitation became a goal of deeper sociological enquiry. It is a pity that India has yet to imbibe the idea of general hygiene and sanitation. However, our refusal to access even the most elementary civilisational gains has only reduced us to the status of a sick society in the literal sense of the term.

India has been ranked as a notoriously unclean society. The management of human feces in particular has been abysmal. This can easily be put down to the lack of toilet facilities. All of us know, the public crapping is a common thing in this country. We betray the total ignorance of social hygiene. There has been a surfeit of studies conducted on this aspect of our society and all of them have yielded the conclusion that dirt management barely figures in Indian scheme of things so the country reeks of dirt. Noble laureate V.S.Naipaul when he visited India in the early 50s was 26 appalled by the squalor he saw lying all round. He wrote a book " an area of darkness' in which he says Indians defecate everywhere and one sees human excreta on road-side, home side and in sum every side. He has described India as a defecating society. I wish, the book had been translated into Hindi. One can draw a whole list of international dignitaries who have equally barbecued " incredible " India's image by their caustic comments on its lack of sanitation.

Last year I was in Patna with a group of film makers from Europe. I was assisting them as a local consultant. It was a pleasure working with these wonderful Europeans and hearing them sing praise for our beautiful Bihar. But soon it was in for a shock when I had the unenviable task of answering their persistent question why Indiansare adept at the preservation of dirt and loving it. They had become worn out throughout their stay inspecting stubborn, decayed and voluminous dirt all over the city. They were unhappy also because it was something that had compromised the experiences they wanted to take back home. One of them said, this simply meant Indians had a very low self-esteem. I kept mum as I had no answer.

I had an American student who lived in an upscale neighbourhood in south Delhi –not too far from the ring road. One day she looked depressed and overcome with a deep hatred of this country. She had to daily negotiate a mass of human excreta lying on the road when going to her workplace. The dirt was forbidding and all over. That the dirt existed in the country's capital passed her comprehension. She called India the dirtiest country in the world.

Another student of mine from Manchester was riled by the sheer lack of basic civic sense on the part of the residents in the colony he lived in. It was difficult for him to understand why the residents themselves keep littering the park with foul smelling dirt where they and their ladies sit and gossip. He was flummoxed by such behaviour. I am sorry to say; hardly a day passes without my students sharing with me their stories on Indians' passionate attachment to dirt.

I had a mail from a young man from Stuttgart, Germany who recently visited India as a tourist. He spent about twenty days in Tamil Nadu and Kerala. He had nice experiences wherever he went. He met scores of interesting people especially in Kerala. He was, however, shocked about the huge problem of waste that weighed down this country. He had not expected it to be so bad and he was appalled. According to this young German, India faces an enormous challenge in this regard. In Nizamuddin in Delhi a girl was shot dead when she objected to a man urinating in front of her house. The man simply could not abide the girl's audacity to tell him off. Instead of making amends for the dirty act and indecent exposure he had indulged in, he went away but immediately came back with a gun to kill the girl who had asserted her right to cleanliness. The incident was instant copy for the media including the international portion of it.

One theory that is often advanced is that while Indians exhibit very high standards of personal hygiene, they are only a little wanting in public cleanliness. This is a theory that does not seem to stand scrutiny. There is a close relationship between the two and sanitation happens only when the two meet. The Euro-American belt is an example. This part of the world enjoys both public cleanliness and personal health. It is entirely thanks to their efficient and quick dirt management. Apart from very few civilisational diseases, most of the common diseases that seriously challenge our health are wholly absent there. The state is always willing to invest resources in keeping the environment clean. The west is antiseptically clean and it is said one can eat from a road without being exposed to any infection. Maintenance of this kind of cleanliness is no mean achievement considering the world's highest per capita waste output obtains there.

The less said about us the better. There are millions of men and women still working as manual scavengers and their continuing to engage in this abominable profession is an annoying commentary on our sense of priority as a nation. No wonder there are hardly any countries in the world that could dare surpass us in dirt. It is the ubiquitous stinking dirt that prompted one of our union ministers recently to say India could easily annex noble laurels in being the dirtiest country on the planet.

There is another of repeated theory that puts forward poverty as the explanation for India's dirt. The theory has no legs to stand on in that there are a number of countries poorer than us that have much better sanitary conditions. To our embarrassment, some of these countries exist in our close neighbourhood. One can mention impoverished Burma and Bangladesh, for example. That Pakistan happens to be still cleaner only compounds our sense of humiliation.

There is yet another theory that on occasions gets deployed to defend India's dirt. This is the transcendental theory that argues Indians strive for an elevated spiritual cleanliness and do not give a fig about the mundane cleanliness. According to the theory, Indians consider this world as a relative truth and thus as an illusion. Their preoccupation with the absolute truth and a different kind of purity is barely appreciated creating incomprehension about them. However, the theory is dismissed outright as nonsense unlimited and a defence of the indefensible. A saying that bears recall in this context is - cleanliness is next to godliness.

All these theories are groundless and merely a smorgasbord of illogic, non-sequiters and hogwash. They do not help us understand and fix the problem at all. But India is not bare of ingenuity and genius. Dr Bindeshwar Pathak the founder of Sulabh International has shown it. When appalled by his country's squalor, he did not weave theories nor did he withdraw into the academia's cocoons. Instead, he had a resolution to make a difference. The rest of the story is too well known to merit repetition. I would close by saying the good work he began on a modest scale has expanded over the years acquiring the status of a social revolution.

4. Sociology of Sanitation: A Memory Ethnography[1]: Vinay Kumar Srivastava

1.

Srivastava does not attempt to delineate the subject matter of the 'sociology of sanitation.' Instead it renders a sociological understanding of his observations, collected from his childhood, of dealing with toilets in Old Delhi. Srivastava narrates: When I stepped into my teenage, I was deeply ashamed of the fact that the street in Old Delhi – known as Gali G.D. Joshi (Peepal Mahadev, HauzQazi) – where I lived with my parents and maternal grandparents did not have flush latrines. Each morn, the night soil that had collected over past twenty-four hours was manually collected for disposal by a family of scavengers, locally regarded as belonging to the caste-community of the *jamâdar, mehtâr* or *bhângi*.[2] Since I was a student of one of the best schools of those days, Anglo Sanskrit Victoria Jubilee Higher Secondary School, located in Darya Ganj (Delhi), boys from the elite colonies and upper-class families of Delhi and New Delhi were my class mates; and being a good student, I was quite friendly with them. Often I used to accompany them to their houses in posh areas, some of them being government colonies, beautifully built, open, green, clean, uncrowded, and peaceful.

Toilets in these houses impressed me – the shining pots were installed with flush and a regular supply of water with pulling the chain attached to the overhead cistern, and were clean, 'unsmelly', to use a local expression, where one could stay for longer time than was usually required. In one of the corners of these toilets lay a couple of brushes and a bottle of acid. Each night some acid was poured in the pot to disintegrate the yellow crust of urine and faecal material that had deposited inside the pot, which was later wiped away with the brush. The task of cleaning the toilet was of the members of the household. The toilets were located right inside the house and because of the observance of the norms of purity and pollution in the household, the professional toilet cleaners (the erstwhile manual scavengers) were not permitted in the house. Thus the task of cleaning the toilet – which in any case did not present the ungainly sight of its Old Delhi counterpart – was of the household members. Cleaning the toilet was no more a dirty job, for it did not bring one in contact with human manure. I think the dirtiness of Old Delhi was because of its unclean lavatories, which for a considerable part of the day were heaps of body waste.

2.

The thought of inviting my friends to my house left me bloodless, for my neighbourhood was crowded, dirty, with litter scattered all around, and lacked privacy. A common sight was of people carrying out many of their activities outside their houses in the street (such as women grooming, cleaning, and picking nit and lice from their hair; cutting vegetables; men playing cards, *chaupar*, chess in the open; children defecating in open drains in the street; boys sitting outside their houses and chatting, what was derogatorily called *addâbâzî*). More than that the cause of embarrassment was the type of latrines – the 'dry latrines' (*pâkhânâ*) – we had, which even after being cleaned and washed, which happened only once, in the morning, around eight or so, emitted a foul (or rather, 'faecal') smell, always unbearable, a type of malodour that stayed permanently in the ground floor where these latrines were located.

Latrines in Old Delhi houses were invariably built on the ground floor, away from the rooms in which family members lived. Generally, rooms on the ground floor, if there were any, were reserved for receiving and entertaining guests, and none of the family members ordinarily stayed there permanently. The smaller of these rooms were called *baithak* (the 'place where people sit [*baithnâ*]'), and the larger, *dâlân*; the latter were used for the stay of the outstation guests or for feeding people on festal occasions or at the time of the life-cycle rituals. However, the important, respectful guests, in terms of kinship, were accommodated in the rooms built on the upper floors of the house, and it was then that the family members moved to the ground floor temporarily. A symbolic expression of the respect accorded to a guest was when a family offered its own room for his stay whilst moving to a zone of less comfort – it meant that 'one forsook one's comforts for the sake of others'. If the family was large, and the members felt greatly inconvenienced, some more latrines were built on the subsequent floors of the house, but the norm of just one latrine a house, and that too situated on the ground floor, was largely followed, and I think it was primarily because of the impurity that was associated with it. And, obviously, the question of the attached bath, which included the toilet as well, was ruled out.

The latrine used to be extremely small, just enough to accommodate one person, dingy, almost like a dungeon, and poorly-lit and -ventilated, without any facility of water inside. Hurriedly white-washed annually just before the 'festival of lights' (Diwâlî) with material of cheap quality, it was the most unaesthetic place, where one spent the least amount of one's time. Just outside the latrine was a small tank (called *haudâ*), built of cement, filled with water, and this water was used for filling the small-sized bucket that one carried to the toilet for filling the mug (*tâmlot*) kept in the toilet for anal cleaning (*dhonâ, dhoîdhoî*). We shall call the former 'latrine-bucket' and the latter 'latrine-mug'. The former was carried to the latrine to fill its mug, but was never kept on its floor. After filling, it was kept near the tank, its usual place. The latrine-mug might be brought outside to be filled by someone else. Once the latrine-mug had been touched, one would not touch any other thing, the bucket, or the tank.

When one returned from the latrine, he requested a family member to pour water on his hands that were washed with ash (*râkh*) from the hearth or soap, in case the family could afford it. In other words, the water tank remained 'unpolluted'; when one poured water (with the help of a bucket that was kept in the tank or on one of its walls) in the 'latrine-bucket', one was 'alright' and one did not touch it, but on picking it up, one was rendered 'unclean'. After coming out of the latrine, one was more 'unclean', for one's fingers and palm (of the left hand) had come in touch with the faecal material and anal opening, and if one touched the tank or the vessels kept near it, they would all be consigned to 'uncleanliness', and thus the help of an 'assistant' was needed for washing one's hands. The 'assistant' was usually a younger member of the family, a boy in most cases, and in affluent families, one of the domestic servants. Anal cleaning was always done with left hand. One of the reasons of why the left hand was regarded as impure was its association with faecal impurity; so left hand should not be used for eating, writing, or for any ritual performance. Interestingly, although it had been washed, sometimes repeatedly, it harboured a kind of 'permanent impurity', therefore to be avoided forever for certain activities regarded as 'pure' (like ritual) or bearing semblance to purity (like eating).

Of all the body orifices, the 'dirtiest', the 'impurest', was the anus. Right from beginning, children were taught not to thrust their fingers in any of the orifices of their bodies. They were told that besides being an example of bad manners, it was also dangerous and might cause damage to the internal organs and layers of cells. One of the verses commonly recited in this connection was: *'nâkmeinunglīkânmeintinkâ mat kar mat kar mat kar; ankh meinanjandântmeinmanjan nit kar nit kar nit kar'* ("Don't put finger in [your] nose, don't poke a straw in [your] ears; apply kohl in [your] eyes everyday, brush [your] teeth everyday"). This indicates that personal hygiene was given the utmost importance. One was expected to wash one's hands even if one inadvertently put one's fingers in his mouth, ears, nostrils, or eyes.

3.

The water from this tank (situated near the latrine) was used for none of the other activities – such as bathing, washing of clothes – except for cleaning the latrine, the floor, and the area outside the house. Situated at the entrance of the house, with its rear opening facing outside, the toilet was the most defiled space. The latrine was used exclusively for defecation; for urination, men and male children went out to the street, relieving them in the open drains, whereas women used the bathrooms (or the 'bathing corners') in their houses, sluicing the urine away with mugs full of water. At night, these bathing places inside the house were used by men as well. In many traditional houses, latrines were used only once, in the morning, before a bath, and if one was constrained to use it again during the day, one was expected to bathe and change one's clothes. My grandmothers – both paternal and maternal – had sets of different clothes that they wore on their visits to the latrine; these clothes were washed every day and kept separated from the other clothes. Similarly, there were separate pairs of shoes (or rubber slippers called *chappal*). Called *pâkhânekekapre* ('clothes for the latrine') or *pâkhânekîchappal*('slippers for the latrine'), these objects carried enormous impurity even after being washed with soap. They were touched only when one was preparing to visit the latrine. If by chance, anyone touched these clothes or the slippers, or the door of the latrine, or the latrine-mug, one was expected to wash his or her hands immediately. This impurity was 'physical' and 'hygienic', and was supposed to be crucial for maintaining good health. Women, particularly elderly, observed these norms of impurity far more punctiliously than did men, and men were often castigated for being lax about these.

Children were often asked if they washed their hands after defecation. In case of small children who could not wash their hands properly, their mothers (or some other relatives) applied ash or soap on their hands and washed these. Children who could not wash them were helped by their mothers, sometimes fathers or any other member of the family. The process of learning to clean oneself passed though three stages: the first was of the parents (or any other member of the family) cleaning their children; the second was that whilst the child squatted, water was poured from above and the child cleaned itself; and the third was that the child learned to clean its bottom and then wash its hands. In the first case, the child did not wash its hands, but in the other two cases, toilet training involved washing the hands well. Infants might be free from the norms of purity and pollution, but as they grew up, they were expected to internalise these practices. The maintenance of hygiene was an essential component of the process of socialisation. Another common practice was that people washed their face and rinsed their mouth after they had cleaned their 'dirty' and 'soiled' hands.

Rather than being dichotomised into purity and impurity, or 'clean' and 'unclean', the ethnography of lavatorial practices in Old Delhi adds to our knowledge a couple of new ideas. Whilst referring to the tank-water, the people said that it was *thîk*, rather than *sâf* (clean) or *pavitra* (pure), an idea that could be conveyed in English word 'alright'; the water in the bucket, before it was taken to the latrine, was also 'alright', but 'not-so-alright' as was the water in the tank. The water in the latrine-mug was 'not-so-alright' as was the water in the latrine-bucket; and the water left in the latrine-mug after it had been used for cleaning was the 'worst', and it must be thrown there. If the toilet-mug was emptied in the tank, the latter would be defiled, for what defined the 'alrightness' of the water was the container, the context of its use, and where it was placed. Once the mug had been placed on the floor of the toilet, its water was 'less alright' than what it was earlier. The latrine-mug was to be emptied there because its water was at the bottom of the 'degrees of alrightness'.

The point I wish to put forth is that the Hindu of Old Delhi think in terms of several binary oppositions and one of them is of 'what is alright' and 'what is not'; although this opposition has been understood here with the example of the lavatorial behaviour, it comes up in other behavioural contexts as well, overlapping with the other oppositions, such as 'auspicious' (*shubh*) and 'inauspicious' (*ashubh*), 'pure' (*pavitra*) and 'impure' (*apavitra*), 'clean' (*sâf*) and 'unclean' (*gandâ*), and good (*acchâ*) and bad (*burâ*). As we noted earlier, for 'what is alright', the word used is *thîk*, but no single word exists for 'what is not alright'; for this the expression used is '*thîknahinhai*' ('[It is] not alright'). So, what is 'auspicious', 'pure', 'clean', and 'good' is also 'alright', and what is 'inauspicious', 'impure', unclean', and 'bad' is also 'not alright'. But, the idea to be noted is that 'what is alright' may not be 'auspicious', 'pure', 'clean', and 'good'; in other words, each opposition should be understood in the context of its usage. Water in the tank is 'alright' but it will not be used for cooking or washing kitchen utensils, although the same water pipe line that fills the tank is also attached to the kitchen. The water tank, though a cleansing agent, is associated with a type of body emission that is regarded as 'most defiled', 'most obnoxious'. Defilement is contagious; therefore, the things should not come in contact, lest they pollute the others. The latrine-mug and the hand used for cleaning are the most defiled, and therefore, they must not come in contact with 'alright' things. The social universe defines the status of the things in a system of relationship – one is 'more alright' than the other or one is 'not-so-alright' in comparison to the other. Both 'alrightness' and 'not-so-alrightness' are graded on a continuum, and one is understood in relation to the other. What pervades the Hindu universe is the gradation of objects, ideas, events, and thoughts on the continua of several oppositions. At the centre of the universe is the human body, interacting with the other systems of the world.

4.

Latrine was busily engaged in the morning. Family members adjusted their toilet habits according to the needs of the others. For instance, the old people visited the latrine either before dawn or waited for the school- and office-goers to finish their work. Children, from beginning, were trained to clear their bowels in the shortest possible time. Constipation (*kabz*) was the biggest ailment and social embarrassment; and so was the flatus (*pâd*). If old people broke wind in public, it was more a matter of amusement, and also, not unexpected considering their age and the slackness of their digestive system (*maidâ*); the old were often heard telling their friends and physicians that they were not able 'to open their bowels (*pet sâfhonâ*) satisfactorily' and were feeling gassy (*hawâbharnâ*). However, the young were expected to be free from flatulence (*bharîpan, afârâ*). They were expected to have evacuated their bowels in the morning. Being colicky meant 'being dirty'. Foods were classified in terms of those which produced wind and which did not; and those expected to produce wind were avoided especially at night, for they would fill the belly with gas and make one extremely uncomfortable, thus hampering one's sleep. That gastric (particularly wind and constipation) and dermatological (eczema [*dâd*], itching [*khujlî*]) ailments were quite common in India may be inferred from the fact that a number of posters pasted on the walls of the street and inside the inter-state buses provided information about the specialists that promised complete cure of these problems. A large numbers of preparations, ointments, and medicinal condiments were (and are) available in the market for these ailments, and their efficacy used to spread through the word of mouth.

The family entrusted with the task of cleaning latrines and the lanes used to arrive around seven in the morning. It comprised four of them – the mother (known as Anaro), her sons (Dhammo and 'Dhammo'sbrother'), and Dhammo's wife. We could never come to know the names of Dhammo's brother and wife, for they were never called by their actual names but in teknonymic terms ("so-and-so's brother or wife"). Anaro was a widow; she wore cotton clothes, while his daughter-in-law, being married, was dressed brightly and gaudily. She also wore metal jewellery and almost half-a-dozen glass bangles in each wrist. Both these women were dressed in *kurtâ* (shirt) and *salwâr* (pyjama), and not in *dhotî* or *sârî*, the usual dress that women in the neighbourhood wore. Both these women covered their faces with translucent wraps, which while allowing them to see clearly and do their work, kept them concealed from the gaze of the men and women of the neighbourhood. Only when these women were in the company of the other women of the neighbourhood, they did not hesitate in uncovering their faces, but the moment they saw a man, they veiled them. The relation of these women with the other women in the neighbourhood, notwithstanding their caste statuses, was friendly; observing the norms of keeping distance and not entering the houses beyond a certain limit, they had in the afternoons when their stipulated work was over rounds of conversation with upper caste women, sharing the gossip of the neighbourhood and the facts and truths of their life. Such a relation did not exist between the men of the scavenging caste and those from upper castes. This would explain why upper caste women seemed to know more about scavenging castes than their men, regardless of the fact that they were stringent custodians of the norms of purity and pollution. It is interesting to note that while maintaining the ritual boundaries between communities, the women were also able to develop close interactive relations with women of lower castes.

5.

I often wondered why Dhammo or Anaro had just one name, whereas we had two or three names. Why we had 'surnames' (caste/sub-caste names) attached to our names? Why we had titles (like Babu, Raizada, Raibahadur, Lala, Kunwar, etc.) placed before our names? My maternal grandfather was named 'BabuBrijLal Srivastava', my father 'Bharat Bhushan Srivastava', my mother 'Shanti Devi Srivastava', and I was also given three names, and so were my other siblings. Then why just one name for some people? I could not find a satisfactory answer to this question till I read the literature on the sociology of caste system and spoke to people about the place of caste in their lives. I learned that the members of upper castes have three or more names; higher the caste more the names. Middle castes have two names, whereas lowest castes have to be content with just one name. Names of higher castes generate 'surnames' – for instance, the caste of the Brahmin in North India has several surnames (such as Bhardwaj, Gaur, Mishra, Pandey, etc.) and its 'umbrella surname' is Sharma. The same applies to the other 'twice-born' (*dwija*) castes. This, however, has not been the case with the castes at the lower rung of the hierarchy. And when members of these castes started looking for surnames, which traditionally they did not have, they either used their caste name as surname (for instance, the Meghwal), or adopted the name of Valmiki (the author of Ramayana whom they revere) as their surname, or one of the general surnames, used across castes, such as Verma, was taken. In some cases, the surnames were improvised after the name of the village of their origin, or some local god; but even today, a large number of them use two names and do not have surnames.

After their arrival to the neighbourhood, the first task the men of the scavenging caste did was to collect garbage from each house, which they did in a couple of baskets they carried from one house to the other. One of the men would go to a house, call out to the people in the household to bring their 'waste' (*kûr*â) and deposit it in the basket he carried. All this garbage would be emptied in a hand-driven wooden cart or wheelbarrow, which would be carried to the 'garbage house' (*kûr*â*ghar*), a huge vacant space under the local office of the electricity department, contiguous with the stand where the *tong*â(horse-driven carts) were parked. The 'garbage house' was always full to the brim; although the waste disposal department of the local municipality was supposed to empty it every alternate day, it was rarely done so. It was always a loathsome sight, and one could see people spitting as they walked on the road opposite it. A typical Indian reaction to a disgusting and repellent smell is clearing the throat to collect sputum and then spitting it. One could also see dogs, stray cows, cats, pigs, and crows eating away from the mountains of garbage the pieces of food they fancied the most; somewhere from its bottom also emerged moles, mongooses, rats, and cockroaches of various shapes and sizes. Anyone who saw this was impressed by the peaceful living of scavengers of different species, sharing the same habitat, and each picking up those morsels of food that suited it the most and leaving the rest for the others.

The process of removing the garbage from each of these houses continued for an hour and a half; in some cases the men had to visit a particular house again since on an earlier visit the family just ignored the call for bringing their garbage out for disposal. Once over, then began the task of removing the night-soil from each house and cleaning the slab with water on which it laid. With a scraper, both men and women collected the excreta in metal buckets and big pans, kept it out, and called out to family people to throw water in the latrine from the front so that they could broom and clean it from the opening from where they removed the excreta. It was an important duty, generally assigned to an elderly woman of the house, for she had to supervise that the latrine is cleaned well otherwise it would stink the whole day. While she would empty buckets after buckets of water in the latrine, she would, in a reprimanding tone, tell the cleaner that since the latrine was not properly cleaned the earlier day, it was full of fetid (*badbû*) and the entire house was stinking. The cleaner would say that he or she had always taken care to clean the latrines well and that they did not derelict their duty, but in future they would be extra careful. They knew that what they could register the maximum was mild disagreement but not an outright rebuttal of what they were being told, and that was regarded as the proper response in the structure of dominance of which they were a part, although they also knew that irrespective of the degree of the dereliction of their duty, they would not be removed. The knew the power of negotiation that came with their occupation, but the best in any situation was to accept what they were being told and promise to be vigilant in future.

Once I asked my maternal grandmother as to why she said the same thing to Dhammo and his family every day, her answer was that it kept them on their toes and that their work would improve day by day. She, however, never praised the family for their good work. Perhaps, in this sub-culture, workers – whosoever they were – were not complimented for their jobs and duties; their faults were found and explicitly stated, for it was thought that it would not make them proud, as appreciation would, keep check on their work, and would resist their attempts to confront their employers or patrons. And, similar was the natural expectation of the workers that they would be taken to task, yelled at, threatened with wage cuts, looked at angrily, and ordered to work more and more, and improve upon its quality. It may be noted here that the nature of interaction between different communities reinforced inequality.

6.

The faecal material collected in the buckets and pans was to be taken away to the 'garbage house' for disposal; so it was emptied in the cart, covered with other garbage, leaves and ash, but then the buckets and pans had to be washed. Moreover, the latrine slabs were also washed. The water coming out of latrines – foul-smelling – ran in open drains, and here also were washed the buckets and pans in which night-soil was carried to be emptied in the cart or wheelbarrow. Sometimes when all the members of the scavenging family had not come, or were too tired to drive the cart or wheelbarrow, they would also sluice the excreta away in the open drain and clean it up with the broom. The open drain was shallow and its cleaning was possible, and the dirty water could be guided to the manhole. The neighbours seriously objected to any act of throwing the excreta in the open drain. They barely tolerated the cleaning of soiled buckets and pans in it. Dhammo was scolded for this and he tendered profuse apology, often in turn he rebuked his family members, promising to the neighbourhood that such acts would never be repeated. On one occasion, he slapped his younger brother in full view of the neighbours, who also kept telling him not to beat him up, but instructed all his family members not to ever repeat this in future, for when faeces were washed in open drain the stench was overwhelming, intolerable, and lasted for longer time in the street. The neighbours said that they only tolerated the water that came out of the latrine when it was washed, but all acts of throwing excreta in the drain should be stopped. This perhaps did not include the children's open defecation, with the faeces lying in the shallow drain, hindering the smooth flow of water that came out of the houses, and so the water ran sideways, creating mess in the street. The street dwellers did not make an effort to discourage open defecation, but on the contrary, they encouraged their children to use the open drains as lavatories as in mornings the queue outside the latrine was formidable. Once permitted, the children developed the habit of using the drains as lavatories. Not only that, they also saw adult men urinating in drains. All this developed different notions of shame, exhibiting genitalia, hygiene, and lavatorial practices. After defecation, children ran inside their houses to get cleaned, when someone would pour water and they would wash their anuses. Men would squat to relieve them; it was rarely that in public a man would urinate standing. The sacred thread, in case worn, was pulled up to encircle the right ear, so that it was not sullied by the drops of urine. Hands, sometimes the face also, were washed after urination.

When the latrines were washed and the water gushed out in the drain, and the buckets and pans used for carrying night-soil were cleaned, the entire street was stenchy. People closed windows and doors to keep the foul-smell out. "It's hell", my grandmother would always respond in these words to the washing of latrines in the street, since one followed the other, and the process continued for quite some time. On one day, when this was going on in the street, one of my schoolmates, who lived in Lodi Road (New Delhi), arrived. I hurried took him to the roof of my house, since the evil-smell was expected to be less there. He quickly responded to this saying: "Doesn't this smell sail in your mind for the whole day, perhaps forever?" He seemed to be so awfully perturbed with this that he did not want to stay in my house for long. After that I decided not to invite any of my friends home, although I visited them, admiring their ways of living and houses, particularly their toilets.

After all the latrines had been washed, the scavenging family cleaned the entire lane, with houses supplying water for this purpose. In the mean time, the malodorous air seemed to subside.

The lane looked clean and we all wished it to remain as it was 'forever'. When the work had finished, the male members of the scavenging family left for home, not less than two kilometres from the street where they worked. Although I never visited, I knew they lived outside the Walled City, the other name of Old Delhi, in a settlement of their caste persons. They walked to their respective places of work. Once, by then I had joined Hans Raj College for graduation, I asked Dhammo's brother why they did not hire a cycle-rickshaw to reach the street, his answer was that it was an expensive proposition; but when I asked the same question to my grandfather, he said they feared that the rickshaw-puller might be unwilling to take them as his passengers for their caste status was known to everyone, and one who did not know them personally would be able to infer it from their dresses and demeanours. My grandfather was referring to what I later learned from the work of McKim Marriott (1959) as the 'attributional theory of caste ranking'.

7.

Whilst the men went away, the women stayed in the neighbourhood for some more time. Around the lunch time, they went from one house to another, seeking a couple of 'leavened breads' (*rotī*) from each one of them. Like the round of collecting the garbage, here also the women called for the households to give them *rotīs* – the call used to be '*rotī do*' ('give bread'). With *rotī*, however, curry or any vegetable preparation was generally not given. The number of *rotīs* given by the lady of the house varied, but in any case, they were not less than two. Whilst some gave freshly baked, others those that were made the night before; whilst some *rotīs* were smeared with clarified butter (*ghī*), the others were rather dry. Whatever be the quality of the *rotis*, Dhammo's mother and wife accepted these with gratitude; when the lady of the house came with *rotīs*, one of them, whosoever was there at that time, would spread her wrap, giving it the shape of a well, to collect them. The *rotīs* would be tossed in the wrap – no physical contact between the parties. I was told that the scavenging families would simply cook vegetables and lentil, or some non-vegetarian dish, and eat *rotīs* with this. The women would leave for home around early afternoon. They would either stay till the evening or come again when a feast took place in the neighbourhood, where their job was to collect the left-over food, which they would take home, and the leaf-plates to be disposed at the 'garbage house'. For this job, they also came with their young children, who would help their mothers in various ways; otherwise they did not come in the morning hours when cleaning of the human waste took place.

I think that communities are intellectually bounded units, in the sense that they have scant understanding of the others – the way they live, the kind of thoughts they hold and cultivate, how they meet their needs, the goals they set for future. In fact, they know the others in terms of a set of stereotypes, which are transmitted to posterity. The same applied to the community of scavengers – we learnt that they were non-vegetarian and addicted to spirit, had their own gods and goddesses, were knowledgeable about supernatural cures, had considerably lax sexual mores, etc.[3] At the same time, one was supposed to be kind towards them and extend them help whenever they needed.

My grandfather told me what he said was a true happening. His spiritual preceptor was popularly known as Borewaley Baba, for he always wore clothes (a loin-cloth and a shawl) made up of jute. Sporting matted hair, he was famous for his idiosyncrasies all over the street and also in the adjoining ones. In the morning hours he sat in the larger room of our house on the ground floor, known as *dâlân*, receiving guests, rendering spiritual advice. Although generally he did not want money from any of his visitors, he accepted it from some of them, to be eventually spent on his travel to different pilgrim centres. On one occasion, he told his visitors that he was planning to go to Rameshwaram (in Tamilnadu); and instantly a businessperson from another street offered him several silver coins – they were in circulation at that time – to take care of the expenses. He smelled these coins and refused to accept, saying that they were earned by advancing loans on interest to lower castes (particularly the scavenging) and since it was an immoral way of earning money, he would not accept these. The man who had offered these coins left the room enraged, hurling abuses at the mendicants in general. And, then the Borewaley Baba gave a short lecture to his visitors exhorting them not to ever charge interest from the scavenging families, since they were already extremely poor, and if they had to pay interest they would be further impoverished. Any loans to them should be, he said, like 'do good deeds and forget about them' (*nekīkarkuen may dāl*). In relationships with one's serving castes, one should never forget the values of goodness and humanity. My grandfather later learnt that the man who was earning money from usury fell ill – 'his body turned black, appetite waned, in course of time festers grew on his body, and he died soon'. All this was supposed to have resulted from the bad words he spoke against the Baba.

8.

In addition to receiving the daily round of bread, the scavenging family was paid five rupees every month by each of the households it served. There was no separate payment for removing litter from houses. I was told that monetary payment did not exist in past and came up with the general monetisation of the economy; so from then onwards, payment in cash and kind went hand in hand. As a child, I often wondered if they were not paid in cash, how would they buy vegetables and lentils, salt and sugar, clothes, and medicines? Since I had not seen the non-monetised economy, I could not conceptualise people living without money. Perhaps, they lived without these things; or their patrons provided these – not just bread but other things as well. Clothes were also given, but I learned that people were rather reluctant to part with their clothes, since they believed that these could always be used for casting black magic on the individuals who wore them. I had seen people keeping an eye on the clothes hanging on drying poles, for they feared that their jealous relatives and neighbours might cut a little thread from the clothes (or a tassel from the *sārī*) and use it for magical purposes. Later, as an anthropology student, I learned that this was an example of contagious magic, based on the principle of 'once in contact, always in contact.'

The truism is that things have not changed much and millions of people are even today engaged in cleaning latrines and carrying loads of human waste on their heads. The Census of India, 2011, recorded that not less than 750,000 families were still working as manual workers. The *Live Mint and the Wall Street Journal* (19th November, 2013) reported the case of a woman named Saraswati, one of the manual scavengers, who along with fifty other women, leaves early morning for a village in Ghaziabad (Uttar Pradesh) called Farrukhnagar, to 'physically remove human excrement from dry toilets of high caste families', for which she gets fifty to sixty rupees a month, and she receives an extra amount of ten rupees for cleaning the litter. Not only that what she gets paid for the work she does is a mere pittance, but also she suffers from many illnesses the cause of which can be traced to the kind of work she does, where she is exposed to all sorts of germs. What is particularly touching in this case is Saraswati's image of the self: She thinks that even after multiple baths, each part of her body stinks. "Give me any job, but please take me out of the hell," is her plea to the interviewer.

The World Toilet Day, designated by the United Nations General Assembly, observed on 19 November every year, is expected to draw the attention of the states and governments to the fact that 2.5 billion people do not have access to a clean and safe toilet. In India, the estimate of the World Health Organisation and the United Nations Children's Fund is that over fifty per cent people (620 million) practice open defecation (*The Times of India*, 19 November 2013; *The Hindu*, 20 November 2013). It is well known, as has been reported by the Census, that the number of the houses with television and telephones far exceeds that with toilet facilities. Cases of newly-married women who returned from their husbands' houses, since they did not have toilets, have garnered media attention, with some of these women receiving awards for boldly walking out of the toilet-less houses, notwithstanding the damage they might have caused to their reputation as well as to the prospect of a happy matrimony; but in this way, they have drawn attention to the importance of toilet in matters of hygiene and also the fact that because of the norms of modesty, toilets are far more central to women than to men. To put differently, men can relieve them publicly, rather unabashedly, which is not the case with women. In one of the focus group discussions we conducted with women on the problems of living in a squatter in Delhi (known as Yamuna Pushta), the demand on which consensus existed was 'toilets exclusively for women', which should not be accessible to men, since as one woman said, 'men dirty the toilet'. Our androcentric ways of thinking and administration are such that while distributing public facilities, we generally forget women and their specific problems.

Many suggestions have been given. For instance, there is no disagreement on the issue that manual scavenging must come to an end. Construction of dry latrines must stop. The government should build flush toilets in those settlements where people are too poor to build these with their own resources. Railways should build modern toilets where human waste could be collected and disposed off mechanically, where human intervention is only in terms of operating the machines rather than handling the waste. Needless to say, this waste could be used as manure. The former scavengers could be rehabilitated in other occupations and jobs. The fight against untouchability should be intensified. Even when legally prohibited, the scourge and stigma of untouchability continues unabated, not only in villages but also in towns and metropolises, and often its perpetrators escape punishment. On record are cases of the children of manual scavengers, particularly vulnerable to discrimination in their schools, who drop out of schools because their teachers force them to perform cleaning and scavenging tasks (*The Tribune,* 6 September 2009).

9.

The Gandhian romanticism on scavenging is retrogressive. In one of his articles in *Harijan* (1934), Gandhi called scavenging 'one of the most honourable occupations'.[4] For him, it was not an 'unclean occupation'. The scavenger was like the Brahmin – the latter looked after 'sanitation of the soul', whereas the scavenger, the 'sanitation of the body'. A mother also handled 'dirt' (meaning faeces) – of her child – but then no one called her occupation 'unclean', Gandhi said. In his other article of 1936 (titled 'The Ideal Bhangi', published in *Harijan*), Gandhi thought that the manual scavenger was a sort of 'physician' and a 'warner'; he wrote:

> My ideal Bhangi [the manual scavenger] would know the quality of night-soil and urine. He would keep a close watch on these and give a timely warning to the individual concerned. Thus he will give a timely notice of the results of his examination of the excreta. That presupposes a scientific knowledge of the requirements of his profession.

When I read this, the sight of an early morning dry latrine, before it is cleaned, came to my mind, and I was reminded of its description in the article, mentioned earlier in the context of the life-history of a woman from the community of manual scavengers:

> Dry toilets are toilets that do not flush and have no running water. People shit, shit on it again, and the entire day's excreta from the entire family is heaped in a plane between two cemented elevations that they call latrines.

The stench emitting from the heap of human waste, lying on the slab of the latrine for hours is so overpowering that howsoever 'medically-oriented' (or rather 'pathologically-oriented') be the scavenger, he would neither have time nor patience to examine the excreta, which in any case is not of an individual, but of the members of the household and also the visitors. And, in any case, a pathological (or rather 'ethno-pathological') examination of human stool is no where in the objectives of the scavengers. What I remember from my childhood is that Dhammo and his family people hurriedly collected the human waste with the help of a scarper (or tin plate), dumped it in the bucket, kept the bucket out, called the members of the house to pour water on the slab of the toilet, wash it, and move to the next house. Where was the time to 'study' the excreta? And, who wanted the advice of the scavenger on the quality of the faecal material?

By equating the work of the 'manual scavenger' with that of the 'mother', one forgets that the cultural construction of the faeces of the child is different from that of an adult. The notions of dirt and filth (which are culturally defined, interpreted, and understood) are differentially associated – the faeces of a child may not be regarded as 'dirty' as that of the elders. The act of a child's urination on the clothes of an adult is taken sportingly, jokingly, and it does not incur the kind of pollution which is incurred when the drops of urine of an adult fall on one's clothes, or even when one's own urine drops fall.

Scavenging may be highlighted as 'honourable', for what the scavenger does, none would be able to do, or none would like to do. I would here like to refer to the case of Saraswati, who came from a family, which although belonging to the caste of manual scavengers did not engage itself in that occupation. The separation of caste from social function is well known – holding membership in a caste does not imply pursuing its occupation. After her marriage, Saraswati came to a house where her mother-in-law worked as a manual scavenger and wanted her to take up the caste occupation. Though reluctant, Saraswati was without option; one can imagine here what she would have passed through while handling human waste. It is not only that today she feels bodily dirty, but also stigmatised, discriminated, and polluted; and the 'honourable' occupation brings her a measly amount of money. The occupation consigns her to lowly social and economic position.

Designating scavenging 'honourable' is a reminder of how ruling classes justify the existing ideology and legitimise false consciousness so that the system continues as it is, because within its ambit, some are privileged and advantaged, whilst others are at the lower rungs.[5] Ruling communities, rich people, people with high status are conservative in their approach, desiring the society to remain as it, since their privileges flow from it. Just by telling people that they respect the scavengers, or following their occupation symbolically – such as picking up brooms and tin plates – to bring an end to the inequality between castes, is an example of utopian thinking. What is required is concerted effort to stop once and for ever manual scavenging and the construction of dry toilets and the conversion of the existing dry toilets to the ones in which the flush system is fitted. We have high expectations from the Prohibition of Employment as Manual Scavengers and their Rehabilitation Act, 2013.

5. Social Construction of Hygiene and Sanitation in Haryana: Madhu Nagla

Nagla delineates on the individual/communities in terms of understanding of hygiene and sanitation. Further, it also tries to understand their unhygienic behavior and what efforts are made to bring the proper scientific hygienic sanitation behavior. It results in a concern for understanding certain questions at two levels, viz, individual and community and in two ways, i.e. not merely what but the 'why' people do. For example, why people do not follow the scientifically guided hygiene and sanitation behavior? Why people do not want to change or what obstructs them to change?

The research questions might not necessarily be explanatory alone but exploratory as well to understand community's perception about the hygiene and sanitation and their behavior pattern. Such concern for research questions, which are beyond numbers, has resulted in an acknowledgment (among medical scientists) of the contributions of qualitative research through the work of social scientists. Thus, recently there have been studies that advocate for triangulation of research tools and methods (quantitative method typical or epidemiological surveys and qualitatively characteristics of social science more particularly sociology/anthropology). The study of hygiene and sanitation thus provides a platform for greater academic exchanges between these two streams, a fact increasingly acknowledged both by anthropologists and medical scientists, including public health specialists. This has resulted in a growing interests of studies exploring possibilities of combining research methods (qualitative and quantitative) and perspectives from these different streams in the larger interest of public health (Baum: 1995; Carey: 1998; Roberts et al.,: 2002; Goering and Streoner :1996; Nakaash et al.,:2002; Nichter et al., :2002).

Methodology

We conducted a study to explore community members' understanding of hygiene and sanitation and their practices, perceived risk factors and their views on possible improvement. This study is a part of another study on health and its various dimensions during period of 2006-2007. We conducted Focus Group Discussion (FGD) with people from different caste, class, and gender category between April to June 2006. People for group discussion were drawn on the basis of housing structure, occupation, education, income and gender. Profiling of people was done on the basis of consultation with Sarpanch and our own observation. In all five FGD were conducted in Dhandhlan village, in Jhajjar district in Haryana with a total of 30 respondents (13 males and 17 females). The age group ranged between from 25 to 62. Data were analysed concurrently with data collection. This helped us to identify issues emerging in one FGD to bring back for discussion in subsequent ones, thus each FGD enriched the process of data collection. The following section discusses the results.

Interpretation of Data

There are certain uncomfortable situations which we observed at the level of Sanitation Facilities at home and in turn they brings nightmare for disabled and old age people. We are citing them below:

Case Study 1

Sarita and her husband Ramphool both are disabled and struggle to make ends meet to support their three young children. They are disabled, therefore, they are unable to do any type of work and moreover they are not so efficient also. They are daily wage laborers. The physical effort required to get water from different water points is an exhausting and time consuming chore, limiting time available for other productive work and causing considerable hardship for the family. Local support is also not available particularly for the daily routine things like collecting water etc.

Case Study 2

25 year old Farzana suffers from severe mental and physical disabilities. She is unable to walk to move without the capacity to walk. Farzana cannot independently visit the nearby fields to practice open defecation as other community members do. She is forced to defecate where she lives in bed. Consequently her mother spends hours each day giving her bath and cleaning her bed. This is a source of distress for Farzana and her family.

Case Study 3

Ompati an elder women living in outskirts of the village, lost her eyesight in both eyes 20 years ago. Life is difficult for Ompati because water is not easily available in her community and she does not have a toilet at home. When she needs to collect water, she must tube well with the support of others. If she goes alone, she is often injured.

Case Study 4

Krishna middle aged women, suffering from knee pain. She lost her husband and does not have her son. She has three daughters and all are married and living in distant villages. When the winter approaches, she severely suffers from the severe pain in her knees and even unable to walk properly. All the more it is difficult for her to sit in the ordinary toilet and defecate. She wants something like chair system on which she can sit and defecate. Till now every winter she suffers from severe pain and wants some alternative. Like her there are many people in the village who are suffering from this type of problem.

Storing Drinking Water

Safe storage of drinking water means at least keeping it covered. There should be no visible particles in the water and there should be no contamination in the water. Although the study found reduced contamination at village water sources, household water quality did not improve. Except countable households, people in village do not likely to purchase and use household water purifier, filter, indicating that price is the barrier. Most of the household in the village strain water through a cloth.

Implication for Public Health

Modern health promotion programmes counsel hygiene, ostensibly for reasons of disease avoidance. But the multiple and confusing messages that are issues contain other values. Why do some programmes advise disinfecting vegetables and boiling drinking water, others concentrate on food storage and handling, and still others issue certificates of food vendors, advice cutting fingernails, disinfecting latrine labs, or cleaning nipples before breastfeeding? Perhaps concern with order, morality, or purification ritual to render safe that which crosses the body boundary can be discerned behind such counsel. Take, for example, hygiene education programmes that encourage the boiling of drinking water. However, this may be misleading and costly advice for mothers, whose children could be getting much higher doses of intestinal pathogens from their domestic environment, than for water they drink. But the fear of polluted substances crossing the body boundary, epitomised as microbes, is such a potent threat that it is easy to see why hygiene educators tend to keep prescribing purification rituals such as boiling or filtering. It may also explain how marketers contrive to sell vast quantities of bottled water (which may even be less bacteriologically pure than tap water) on images of purity.

Intervention

Non Governmental organisation should be invited to promote community led sanitation models that trigger demand for improved health and hygiene behavior. Hygiene awareness campaigns and inter-personal communication for behavior change by involving in communities, schools and Aganwadi centres are appreciated. NGOs should work with communities that already sanitation facilities and water points to make sure these are better used and maintained.

Conclusion

Rules about hygiene are to be found throughout every society. Hygiene is not only the private practice of individuals, but it is requirement of each society. Hygiene provides not only a barrier to the transmission of disease, but it also provides a barrier to disorder, chaos and social collapse. Sanitation is the hygienic means of promoting health through prevention of human contact with the hazards of wastes as well as the treatment and proper disposal of sewage wastewater.

Majority of the houses are having flush latrines, therefore, they need not to go outside except very poor people. The entire households had soap for washing hands however; washing of hands with soap was only observed after defecation not after urinating. Generally in the city houses are usually swept daily and the refuse is thrown out near some empty plot or some vacant place. Alternatively sweepers of the municipal corporation come and load in their carts and throw them outside the city. In the planned colonies the refuse is not thrown outside the house but house maids collect them in some polybags and dispose it off in the big bins collected in the corner of the colonies. The study found reduced contamination at village water sources, household water quality did not improve. Except countable households, people in village do not likely to purchase and use household water purifier, filter, indicating that price is the barrier. Most of the household in the village strain water through a cloth. Outside defecation and collecting water from distant place is a difficult task and it becomes more difficult in the case of physical, mental disabilities and in old age.

Notes

1. This article does not attempt to delineate the subject matter of the 'sociology of sanitation.' Instead it renders a sociological understanding of my observations, collected from my childhood, of dealing with toilets in Old Delhi. An intimate link exists, as was noted by Talbot (1896) more than hundred years ago, between sociology and hygiene, and it needs to be sufficiently appreciated.
2. For historical and sociological understanding of various communities that were regarded as 'untouchable', see Prashad (2000). The other term *chûrâ*, which observers (such as Kolenda, 2002) have noted in other parts of the country, was not used here.
3. Gandhi often advised manual scavengers to stop drinking liquor and eating up flesh of dead animals.
4. Gandhi wanted to bring about a change in the attitudes of upper castes towards manual scavengers. He used the euphemism Harijan, meaning 'children of god', for manual scavengers. He learnt scavenging in South Africa and was known among his friends as a 'great scavenger'.
5. It is important to note here that the scavengers were denied the right to protest, go on strike, for this would jeopardize the system of cleaning and taking the garbage away. Gandhi did not support the strike of the Harijans and did not want them to give up their work even for a day. Ramaswamy (2005) tells us that at the time of the Partition, the state of Pakistan did not allow the Hindu manual scavengers to migrate to India. The state regarded scavenging as one of the 'essential services.' Dr B.R. Ambedkar wrote to Shri Jawaharlal Nehru in 1947 in this connection (*Tehelka Magazine*, 22 December 2007, vol. 4, no. 49).

References

Chaudhary, Paras Nath (2013). [Formerly associated with the University of Heidelberg], 'Indian garbage garbed in grand theories', New Delhi: *National Conference on Sociology of Sanitation* - January 28-29.

Kolenda, Pauline (2002). Review of Prashad's Book. *Journal of Social History*, 35 (3): 744-6.

Marriott, McKim (1959). Interactional and Attributional Theories of Caste Ranking. *Man in India*, 39: 92-107.

Nagla, Madhu (2015), 'Social Construction of Hygiene and Sanitation in Haryana', in Bindeshwar Pathak (ed.) *Sociology of Sanitation*, Kalpaz Publications, Delhi.

Prashad, Vijay. 2000. *Untouchable Freedom: A Social History of a Dalit Community*. Oxford: Oxford University Press.

Ramaswamy, Gita. 2005. *India Stinking: Manual Scavengers in Andhra Pradesh and their Work*. Pondicherry: Navayana.

Roy, Nilanjana S.(2011) 'Improving Women's Status, One Bathroom at a Time' in *The International Herald Tribune,* March 16.

Singh, Ram Updesh IAS (Retd) (2013). 'An Admirer of Sulabh Movement', New Delhi: *National Conference on Sociology of Sanitation* - January 28-29.

Srivastava, Vinay Kumar. (2014) 'Sociology of Sanitation: A Memory Ethnography', socal change, June

Talbot, Marion. 1896. Sanitation and Sociology. *American Journal of Sociology,* 2 (1): 74-81.

13

Glossary

I
Introduction

Sociology of sanitation is a scientific study to solve the problems of society in relation to sanitation, social deprivation, water, public health, hygiene, ecology, environment, poverty, and gender equality, welfare of children and empowering people for sustainable development and attainment of philosophical and spiritual knowledge to lead a happy life and to make a difference in the lives of others.

Improved Sanitation - refers to the management of human faeces at the household level. This terminology is the indicator used to describe the target of the Millennium Development Goal on sanitation, by the WHO/UNICEF Joint Monitoring Programme for Water Supply and Sanitation.

On-site Sanitation - the collection and treatment of waste is done where it is deposited. Examples are the use of pit latrines, septic tanks, and Inhofe tanks.

Food Sanitation - refers to the hygienic measures for ensuring food safety.

Environmental Sanitation – It helps the control of environmental factors that form links in disease transmission. Subsets of this category are solid waste management, water and wastewater treatment, industrial waste treatment and noise and pollution control.

Ecological Sanitation – It is an approach that tries to emulate nature through the recycling of nutrients and water from human and animal wastes in a hygienically safe manner (see, for details, en.wikipedia.org/wiki/sanitation).

Sustainable Development refers to the policy of promoting growth consistent with protection of environment, e.g., via shift to renewable resources and local community participation in development projects.

II
Perspectives and orientation

A theory is a set of interrelated propositions or principles designed to answer a question or explain a particular phenomenon; it provides us with a perspective.

A perspective is simply a way of looking at the world. Sociologists analyse social phenomena at different levels and from different perspectives.

Orientation: Theoretical perspectives, or paradigms provide **with an orienting framework**—a philosophical position—for asking certain kinds of questions about society and its people.

Functionalism: According to the functionalist perspective, also called functionalism, each aspect of society is interdependent and contributes to society's functioning as a whole.

Manifest functions are consequences that are intended and commonly recognised.

Latent functions are consequences that are unintended and often hidden.

The conflict perspective explains various aspects of our social world by looking at which groups have power and benefit from a particular social arrangement.

The symbolic interactionist perspective, also known as symbolic interactionism, directs sociologists to consider the symbols and details of everyday life, what these symbols mean, and how people interact with each other.

III
Sanitation, health and society

Sanitation generally refers to principles, practices, provisions, or services related to cleanliness and hygiene in personal and public life for the protection and promotion of human health and well-being and breaking the cycle of disease or illness.

Hygiene refers to the set of practices perceived by a community to be associated with the preservation of health and healthy living.

Scavenging refers to the removal of human waste/excreta (night soil) from unsanitary, "dry" toilets, "dry toilets", i.e., toilets without the modern flush system. Manual scavenging involves the removal of human excreta using brooms and tin plates.

Sociology of Health is a specialisation within the field of sociology. Its main interest is in the study of health, health behaviour and health care institutions.

Solid waste is applied to unwanted or discarded waste material from houses, street sweepings, commercial, industrial and agricultural operations, arising from man's activities.

Public health is "the organised application of resources to achieve the greatest health for the greatest number. It would include not only prevention but also treatment and rehabilitation.

Purity and Pollution: Every human society subscribes to ideas of human purity and pollution in some form. Certain agents, activities, contracts, periods and substances are known to pollute, while others purify. Pollution, as opposed to purity, disturbs equilibrium, destroys or confuses desirable boundaries and states, and engenders destructive natural forces or conditions. Though also of much significance is given to modern temper (e.g. as in food, medicine and environment). All major religions (e.g. Hinduism, Judaism, Buddhism, Christianity and Islam) also variously elaborate on matters of sin, taboo, pollution and purity. Concept of purity and pollution is related to the pure (holiness, clean, sacred) and impure (magic, unclean, pollute) in the religious organisation.

IV
Culture and Sanitation

Culture is the accumulated store of symbols, ideas, and material products associated with a social system, whether it is an entire society or a family.

Dirt: Dirt is that it is matter out of its proper place. As physical objects which are in the wrong place, or hard to classify are labelled as "dirty", so the label "dirty" is given to marginal behaviours and social categories which provide a threat to the social order.

Sanitation Connection is an internet-based resource intended to facilitate access to information on sanitation.

Social Change is the alteration of mechanismswithin the social structure, characterised by changes in cultural symbols, rules of behaviour, social organisations, or values.

Empowerment: Sociological empowerment often addresses members of groups that social discrimination processes have excluded from decision-making processes through - for example - discrimination based on disability, race, ethnicity, religion, or gender.

V
Social Structure and Sanitation

Social Structure: Social structure is the organised pattern of social relationships and social institutions that together compose society.

Scavenger is one who is partially or wholly engaged in the obnoxious of manually removing night soil and filth.

Sex is biological category of human being

Gender refers to the culturally and socially constructed differences between males and females found in the meanings, beliefs, and practices associated with feminity and masculinity.

Family: In human context, a family is a group of people affiliated by consanguinity (by recognised birth), affinity (by marriage, or co-residence shared consumption.

Marriage (also called **matrimony** or **wedlock**) is a socially or ritually recognised union or legal contract between spouses that establishes rights and obligations between them, between them and their children, and between them and their in-laws. The definition of marriage varies according to different cultures, but it is principally an institution in which interpersonal relationships, usually intimate and sexual, are acknowledged. In some cultures, marriage is recommended or considered to be compulsory before pursuing any sexual activity. When defined broadly, marriage is considered a cultural universal.

Caste is a form of social stratification characterised by endogamy, hereditary transmission of a lifestyle which often includes an occupation, ritual status in a hierarchy and customary social interaction and exclusion based on cultural notions of purity and pollution.

Social Class also called class, a group of people within a society who possess the same socioeconomic status. Besides being important in social theory, the concept of class as a collection of individuals sharing similar economic circumstances has been widely used in censuses.

A custom is a cultural idea that describes a regular, patterned way of appearing or behaving that is considered characteristic of life in a social system.

A **ritual** "is a sequence of activities involving gestures, words, and objects, performed in a sequestered place, and performed according to set sequence." Rituals may be prescribed by the tradition of a community, including a religious community. Rituals are characterised by formalism, traditionalism, invariance, rule-governance, sacral symbolism and performance.

VI
Toilet as a Tool of Social Change

A toilet is a sanitation fixture used primarily for the disposal of human urine and feces.

Untouchables: India carries the shame of having manual labourers, mostly marginalised people who belong to a community formerly called "untouchables" or Dalits, to clean human excreta from open lavatories, even today in the 21st century.

Human capital, intangible collective resources possessed by individuals and groups within a given population. These resources include all the knowledge, talents, skills, abilities, experience, intelligence, training, judgment, and wisdom possessed individually and collectively, the cumulative total of which represents a form of wealth available to nations and organisations to accomplish their goals.

Human rights are commonly understood as inalienable fundamental rights to which a person is inherently entitled simply because she or he is a human being.

Dignity is a concept used in moral, ethical, legal, and political discussions to signify that a being has an innate right to be valued and receive ethical treatment. Human dignity is the idea that all humans should be treated with love and respect simply because they are humans and regardless of class, race, gender, nationality, culture, sex, education, religion or any other divisions. Human dignity should not have to be earned; it is inherent in the human.

Liberation is the highest goal of human life through which everything is accomplished.

Social transformation: One definition of social transformation is the process by which an individual *alters* the socially ascribed social status of their parents into a socially achieved status for themselves. However another definition refers to large scale social change as in cultural reforms or transformations. The first occurs with the individual, the second with the social system.

VII
Environmental Sanitation

Environmental sanitation means the control of all those factors in man's surroundings, which may or may not cause adverse effects on his health.

A public toilet (also called a bathroom, restroom, comfort room, powder room, toilet room, washroom, water closet, W.C., public lavatory) is a public toilet facility — in contrast to a private usually residential toilet room, which may be a standalone water closet, or part of a bathroom.

Soil sanitationEcological approach to sanitation which seeks to contain, treat and reuse excreta where possible - thus minimising contamination and making optimum use of resources. Is mostly limited to water supplies and disposal of human and animal wastes.

Ecological approach to sanitation which seeks to contain, treat and reuse excreta where possible - thus minimising contamination and making optimum use of resources.

VIII
State and Sanitation in India

Society: The simplest definition of society is a group of people who share a defined territory and a culture. In sociology, we take that definition a little further by arguing that society is also the social structure and interactions of that group of people. Social structure is the relatively enduring patterns of behavior and relationships within a society. Thus, a society is not only the group of people and their culture, but the relationships between the people and the institutions within that group. In sociology, a distinction is made between society and culture. Culture refers to the norms, values, beliefs, behaviors, and meanings given to symbols in a society. Culture is distinct from society in that it adds meanings to relationships.

State is a community of persons more or less numerous, permanently occupying a definite portion of territory, independent of external control, and possessing an organised government to which the great body of inhabitants render habitual obedience.

A **policy** is a principle or protocol to guide decisions and achieve rational outcomes.

Public policy is the action taken by government to address a particular public issue. Local, state, federal, and international government organisations all craft and implement public policy to protect and benefit their populations.

Social policy primarily refers to guidelines, principles, legislation and activities that affect the living conditions conducive to human welfare.

IX
Sulabh Sanitation Movement in India

Sulabh Movement – It is a great sanitation movement towards a Social Revolution:In 1970, Dr Bindeshwar Pathak founded the *Sulabh Shauchalaya Sansthan,* later named Sulabh International.

Sulabh Shauchalayas: The 'Latrines Made Easy', or a 'Pour Flush Latrine' with a slight variation, popularly called the Sulabh Shauchalayas are indeed a popular adjunct and an aide to hygienic development in most of the cities of India and abroad.

Sulabh Toilet Complexes turn into a Sulabh Happy Home which is not only provide toilet facilities, but also a Health care Centre for poor slum dwellers at a nominal price, covering the cost of medical examination, medicines, etc.

Sulabh International – a social movement provides healthy and hygienic sanitation facility to everybody.

Sociology of action is a science concerning itself with the interpretive understanding of social action thereby with a causal explanation of its course and consequences. Action is relates to how an actor attaches 'subjective meaning' to his behaviour (be it covert or overt) and it is 'social' to the extent that its subjective meaning takes account of the behaviour of others.

Action research is a research initiated to solve an immediate problem or a reflective process of progressive problem solving led by individuals working with others in teams or as part of a " community of practice" to improve the way they address issues and solve problems. There are two types of action research: participatory action research, and practical action research.

X
Globalisation and Sanitation

Global village: The origin of the concept of 'globalisation' is usually traced to Marshal McLuhan (1960), who first introduced the idea of what is today called 'global village' – a notion that implied a sort of compression of the world and intensification of consciousness of the world as a single entity.

Globalisation refers to various multidimensional socio-economic and political processes by which the people of the world are incorporated into a single world society, a global village. It tends to homogenise the cultures as well as popularise even unknown cultures of the world. It acts as hetrogeniser with a possibility of pluralism. Globalisation strives to make the world as its market where all the people are being brought as buyer and seller on unequal terms.

Water is a clear, pellucid, transparent fluid which forms the streams, lakes, oceans and rain, is the major constituent of the fluids of living things chemical compound, and the most widely used of all solvents.Water is essential to human life and to all life on Earth.

Migration: The term migration refers to the movement of people from one place to another. There are two types of migration: first, internal migration, i.e. migration within one country and secondly international migration, which means the movement from one country to another.

Science and Technology: The study of science and technology includes both processes and bodies of knowledge. Scientific processes are the ways scientists investigate and communicate about the natural world. The scientific body of knowledge includes concepts, principles, facts, laws, and theories about the way the world around us works. Technology includes the technological design process and the body of knowledge related to the study of tools and the effect of technology on society.

Technology

Media (singular **medium**) are the storage and transmission channels or tools used to store and deliver information or data. It is often referred to as synonymous with mass media or news media, but may refer to any means of information communication. In other words, it is a means ofcommunication, asradioandtelevision, newspapers, andmagazines thatr each or influence people widely. Theme diaare covering the speech tonight.

Communication (meaning "to share") is the activity of conveying information through the exchange of ideas, feelings, intentions, attitudes, expectations, perceptions or commands, as by speech, gestures, writings, behavior and possibly by other means such as electromagnetic, chemical or physical phenomena. It is the meaningful exchange of information between two or more participants (machines, organisms or their parts).

Mass communication is the study of how individuals and entities relay information through mass media to large segments of the population at the same time. It is usually understood to relate to newspaper, magazine, and book publishing, as well as radio, television and film,as these mediums are used for disseminating information, news and advertising. Mass communication differs from the studies of other forms of communication, such as interpersonal communication or organisational communication, in that it focuses on a single source transmitting information to a large group of receivers. The study of mass communication is chiefly concerned with how the content of mass communication persuades or otherwise affects thebehavior, attitude, opinion, or emotion of the person or people receiving the information.

Trade: A basic economic concept that involves multiple parties participating in the voluntary negotiation and then the exchange of one's goods and services for desired goods and services that someone else possesses. The advent of money as a medium of exchange has allowed trade to be conducted in a manner that is much simpler and effective compared to earlier forms of trade, such as bartering.

Commerce is the whole system of an economy that constitutes an environment for business. The system includes legal, economic, political, social, cultural and technological systems that are in operation in any country. Thus, commerce is a system or an environment that affects the business prospects of an economy or a nation-state. It can also be defined as a component of business which includes all activities, functions and institutions involved in transferring goods from producers to consumers.

Trade and commerce: The conduct of trade amongst economic agents. Generally, commerce refers to the exchange of goods, services or something of value, between businesses or entities. As a broad concern, nations are concerned with managing commerce in a way that enhances the well-being of citizens, by providing jobs and producing beneficial goods and services.

Appendices

APPENDIX-I

Safeguarding Humanity: Dr Bindeshwar Pathak

In this appendix, we have adapted Dr Bindeshwar Pathak as Safeguarding Humanity from Lifeboat Foundation and profile of a national crusedar: Dr Bindeshwar Pathak from Sulabh International Museum of Toilets

Dr Bindeshwar Pathak, Ph.D. is a great humanist and social reformer of contemporary India. To the weaker sections of society especially, he is the compassionate face of a paternal redeemer. He has the vision of a philosopher and the undying zeal of a missionary. He is the icon of a new culture which embraces the poor and extols the dignity of labor. His boundless love for the downtrodden finds expression in myriad and tangible ways. No wonder those who know him intimately swear that Dr Pathak is born to help the helpless.

He is the leader of a national crusade for restoration of human rights and dignity to millions of scavengers (cleaners and carriers of human excreta), traditionally known as untouchables; and for providing safe and hygienic human waste disposal systems to the 700 million Indians who go outside for open defecation even along roads and railway tracks described graphically by V.S. Naipaul and Ronal Segal. He has himself identified with the problems of the untouchables.

His Holiness Pope John Paul II gave audience to Dr Bindeshwar Pathak before awarding him with international St. Francis Prize for the Environment "Canticle of All Creatures" in 1992.

Dr Pathak's multi-pronged efforts in bringing scavengers, who are the worst victims of institutionalized caste discrimination and are engaged in a sub-human occupation, into the mainstream of national life has taken the shape of a movement for social justice. Moreover, he is an internationally acclaimed expert on sanitation and has developed and implemented on pan-Indian scale a low-cost and appropriate toilet technology recommended by UN bodies for about 2.6 billion people across the globe.

To him goes the credit of sensitizing Indians towards sanitation and those engaged in the sanitation work. Apart from low-cost sanitation, his contributions are widely known in the areas of bio-energy and bio-fertilizer, liquid and solid waste management, and poverty alleviation. In fact, he is a Renaissance Man and combines in himself the traits of a social scientist, an engineer, an administrator, and an institution-builder. What is remarkable is that he has ingeniously utilized all this expertise to enrich and empower the depressed classes.

The widespread phenomenon of defecation in the open remains grim even after 50 years of India's Independence. Women especially suffer a lot due to non-availability of toilets. Even today 110 million Indian houses have no toilets and 12 million houses have bucket toilets causing filth and diseases. The situation is so appalling that about a half million children die every year due to dehydration caused by open defecation.

Dr Pathak receiving National Citizen's Award from the then President, Dr Shanker Dayal Sharma.

Environmental cleanliness and sanitation was the dearest subject of Mahatma Gandhi who proclaimed that 'cleanliness is next only to godliness'. Gandhi had said, "There are many things to do. Let each one of us choose our task and stick to it through thick and thin. Let us pick up that position which we can handle best".

The Dubai International Award for best practices to improve the living Environment.

Gandhi had two ideas in mind while talking about sanitation: one, that no one should clean and carry human excreta of others just to earn one's livelihood. There must be some scientific method of human waste disposal system. Finding no other affordable alternative during his lifetime, Gandhi had suggested

'Tatti par mitti' (cover human excreta with soil) or use of the trench latrine which he himself used while living in Phoenix Ashram in South Africa. Secondly, Gandhi wanted that those who are engaged in sanitation work should not be treated as untouchables. They should get equal respect in the society, he took pains to emphasize, and in his typical style went on to declare that "the Bhangi (scavenger) is as important as the Viceroy".

After Gandhi, Dr Pathak is the man, more than any other in India, who has championed sanitation and upliftment of the untouchables as the mission of his life. For the last three decades he has been working relentlessly to keep the ecosystem clean and bring the marginalized sections of society in the mainstream.

The New York Times, in the article *Untouchables gain the help of a Brahmin,* hailed him as a "full-time crusader against the humiliations of untouchability". His contribution in abolishing the inhuman practice of scavenging is seminal and unparalleled in the sense that he not only studied the social evil but provided its categorical solution through a low-cost toilet-technology and developed a self-sustaining sanitation system across the country.

In the process of providing alternative to scavenging and rehabilitation and social upgradation of scavengers, Dr Pathak created a pan-Indian network with 50,000 volunteers and gave birth to what is popularly known as the Sulabh Sanitation Movement. "Nobody should go outside for defecation and every house in India should have a toilet" has become the passionate obsession of Dr Pathak.

In 1991, Dr Pathak was conferred Padma Bhushan by the President of India Mr R.Venkataraman for his "distinguished social service".

Dr Pathak's epic struggle has helped the world to understand that the technology of SulabhShauchalaya (two-pit pour-flush toilet) that he modified and developed and implemented on a large-scale could be a safe and hygienic human waste disposal system for about 2.6 billion people living on the planet Earth.

Expensive systems like sewerage and septic tanks are not cost-effective and affordable for the teeming millions in the Third World. When he came up with the Sulabh technology in 1970, it was first greeted with scepticism and derision; but in 1996 it was declared a global "Urban Best Practice" at the Habitat-II conference held at Istanbul and the Economic and Social Council of United Nations has granted Special Consultative Status to Sulabh in recognition of its outstanding service. Sulabh was also the recepient of the Dubai International Award for "Best Practice to Improve the Living Environment" in 2004.

"You are helping the poor", lauded Pope John Paul II when Dr Pathak received the International St. Francis Prize for the Environment in 1992. The President of India earlier conferred on him Padma Bhushan, a very distinctive national award like Knighthood in United Kingdom, for his distinguished services rendered to the nation. Honors and acclaims, both national and international, have come a dime a dozen for Dr Pathak but what inspires him is the deep love of his country and its people.

Radical beginning

Hon'ble Prime Minister of India Mr. Atal Behari Vajpayee, inaugurating Sulabh built community center in Lucknow.

Dr Pathak travelled all over the country, visited and lived

with scavengers in their villages, studied their habits and social mores (he did his Ph. D. on scavenging), their history and geographical spread to eventually declare that scavengers were a special class united in their miseries and social degradation. "Let us save them from squalid conditions and in doing so we'll be saving the national conscience", Dr Pathak said.

Significantly, it was not a mere emotional outburst by the young Dr Pathak, who by that time had fully equipped himself intellectually to construct an irrefutable thesis on the subject. He knew that slogans alone will not help and, hence, developed a technology which has become a credible alternative to scavenging in India.

He observed after studying scriptures that scavenging has no religious sanction and, hence, those who practice untouchability commit a sin; it is unproductive and revolting to manually clean excreta and we are wasting the waste which can be profitably used to raise farm production and produce biogas. He subsequently demonstrated this successfully. The union of theory and practice distinguishes Sulabh from other movements of similar nature.

Dr Pathak sought to abolish scavenging not only out of sympathy for scavengers but also out of the belief that it is a primitive, expensive, and unhygienic practice which may create an explosive situation in which case a highly dissatisfied group will become dispossessed and then work to destroy the social system. For that matter, the Sulabh Movement is different from other social movements: it is an indigenous concept based on experience and tested scientifically, combining in itself an appropriate technology and demand for social morality.

In simpler words, while other movements identified problems and injustices in society but failed to find solutions, Dr Pathak identified problems, developed a self-sustaining system, gave an appropriate technology and, finally, solved the problem.

A technological breakthrough

Technology has played a decisive role in the Sulabh Sanitation Movement. During Mahatma Gandhi's life and even thereafter, several attempts were made to develop a low-cost toilet technology but no tangible result emerged. Dr Pathak intervened successfully, gave the solution, applied the technology and showed to the engineers, administrators, planners, and masses how it functioned. It was a breakthrough in the Government of India's program for the eradication of scavenging as the Sulabh system is affordable, acceptable to the masses, and could be set up with the available local facilities. Thus, a low-cost technology was developed by Dr Pathak to make towns and villages scavenging-free.

The Sulabh technology is a very simple device. It consists of two pits and a sealed cover. While one is in use, the other pit, which has earlier been filled up, is left idle to convert the excreta to manure. By using this technology, there is no need to physically clean human excreta. This was named "SulabhShauchalaya", which could be adopted in different hydrogeological conditions with some precautions.

Dr Pathak convinced administrators, planners, and engineers that the two-pit pour-flush toilet in urban areas would be an affordable, safe, and hygienic system for the disposal of human waste in the absence of sewers and septic tanks. Before his arrival on the scene, nobody, including engineers, was ready to believe that this technology could work in urban areas.

Sanitation movement gathers momentum

Following rapid adoption of the Sulabh technology of pour-flush toilet system, more than 240 towns have been freed from

Dr Bindeshwar Pathak, Founder, Sulabh Sanitation Movement, explaining the Sulabh Model to Former Prime Minister Mr. H. D. DeveGowda at an exhibition organized to coincide with the national seminar on Housing "Adequate Shelter for All" Oct 7–11, 1996.

scavenging and 50,000 scavengers liberated and retraining into other professions. It was made possible by converting / constructing more than 1.1 million household latrines. Moreover, Sulabh has built 6,000 community toilets with bath, laundry, and urinal facilities operated on a "pay-and-use" basis.

Sulabh is now operating in 479 districts of 25 states and 4 Union Territories, with over 50,000 trained and experienced workers. Dr Pathak has achieved this stupendous success, working with a narrow resource base and almost single-handedly, leading a voluntary and non-profit agency. One cannot recall many names who have achieved so much for so many in such a short time. Dr Pathak did that quietly and without much fanfare.

Public-toilet-cum-bath-complexes

The year 1974 is a landmark in the history of sanitation when the system of operating and maintaining community toilets with bathing, laundry, and urinal facilities (popularly known as SulabhShauchalaya Complex) with attendants service round the clock was initiated on "pay-and-use" basis in Patna. Now Sulabh is operating and maintaining more than 6,000 community complexes in 1,296 towns across the country.

Sri Lankan Minister for Science and Technology, Dr Bernard Soyasa at Sulabh Toilet Museum, New Delhi.

One such complex is in Bhutan. Sulabh has constructed five community toilet complexes in Kabul (Afghanistan). The Ministry of External Affairs provided funds directly to Sulabh for this purpose. These complexes have electricity and 24-hour water supply. The complexes have separate enclosures for men and women. The users are charged a nominal sum for using the toilets and bath facilities. Some of the Sulabh complexes are also provided with bath with shower facility, cloak-rooms, telephones, and primary healthcare. These complexes have been widely welcomed, both by the people and the authorities, due to their cleanliness and good management. The pay-and-use system ensures self-sustainability without any burden on the public, government, or local bodies. The complexes have also improved the living environment considerably.

Social-commitment

After establishing neat and clean toilet complexes and liberating scavengers, Sulabh has set up a number of vocational training institutes. One such center is located in the Sulabh

Dr Pathak received the Indira Gandhi Priyadarshini Award at a colorful function in 1994 in New Delhi.

Complex at New Delhi. Here, liberated scavengers, their sons and daughters, and people from other weaker sections of society are given training in 10 trades including audio-visual repair, beauty care, computer applications, dress designing, electrical, embroidery, tailoring (cutting and stitching), shorthand, and typewriting. The purpose of imparting vocational training is to give them a new means of livelihood, alleviate poverty, and bring them into the mainstream of society.

Sulabh has set up an English medium school in Delhi for children of the scavengers, the first of its kind in India. Sixty per cent of the children are from scavanger families and the remaining are from other castes. This heterogeneous composition ensures that there is enough interaction between kids of scavengers and others. The school aims to prepare children from weaker sections of society for a better life. It brings quality education within the reach of boys and girls from scavenger families.

Dr Pathak continues his crusade for a better and egalitarian society, but the stigma of untouchability remains deep-rooted. A step-by-step program for the removal of this social curse has been initiated. In 1988, Dr Pathak led 100 scavengers along with Vedic Brahmins to the famous Nathdwara temple in Rajasthan with a view towards promoting social integration. In 1993, Sulabh embarked on a noble program of social upgradation and integration of thousands of scavenger families.

Under this program, he has made an open appeal to the elite of society to have social interaction with at least one such family to enable them to lead a dignified life as equals in the society. India's former Prime Minister Mr. I.K. Gujral was among the first few who responded warmly to this suggestion and adopted one scavenger's family. So far 10,000 scavenger families have been socially upgraded and brought into the mainstream of society. Similar programs are envisaged in a phased manner throughout the country for the removal of untouchability and restoration of human rights and dignity to those who have been deprived of basic civil rights for generations.

Technology mingles with humanitarianism

In 1970, Dr Pathak launched the Sulabh Sanitation Movement by setting up a social, voluntary, and non-profit organization, SulabhShauchalayaSansthan (which later became Sulabh International Social Service Organization) to carry forward the movement which combined in itself sanitation technology and Dr Pathak's humane ideology. This movement, like any other gradual revolution, seeks to change the social structure through reforms based on social consent and technology, judiciously combined in a package to subserve the ultimate goal for which Dr Pathak has worked all his life, braving the gauntlet of criticism and social scorn which only strengthened his determination to succeed where no one had before.

Sulabh is a protest movement, born out of concern for the liberation of scavengers from the demeaning practice of carrying human excreta on the head. Revolution is a sudden event while the movement indicates a slow gradual development. Sulabh is a movement because it developed step-by-step from technology to liberation to training to rehabilitation and, finally, to social upgradation when scavengers will be absorbed in the social system and scavenging will end forever.

Dr Pathak with Mr. I.K.Gujral, former Prime Minister of India.

Dr Pathak has raised a micro-level project on low-cost sanitation (starting in 1973 with a small town in Bihar where he put up two pour-flush toilets by way of demonstration) to the macro-level when the project was acclaimed by national and international agencies. No individual in India has raised the technology application from a small town to an international level. Now even UNDP and the World Bank recommend its adoption in other countries wherever feasible.

Biogas from human excreta

Dr Pathak is probably the first person in the world who has promoted on a massive scale the idea of obtaining biogas from human excreta collected in large-sized public toilets used by 2,000 to 5,000 people a day. Despite overwhelming odds, he got the first such biogas plant set up at Patna in 1982 after almost six years of research. The successful and satisfactory functioning of this plant encouraged him to replicate the project all over the country and today 176 biogas plants, connected with large-sized public toilets, are operating successfully in many States of the country.

It has been amply demonstrated by Dr Pathak that, in the absence of sewerage facility, the best option for human waste disposal to be used in conjunction with large public toilets, is the biogas plant. It has the added advantage of being a source of renewable energy which is lacking in a septic tank system.

Biogas from water hyacinth

Biogas from water hyacinth in dried and pulverized form is another achievement of Dr Pathak. While others had been using this waterweed in its green form by either chopping or pre-treating it with chemicals, Dr Pathak conducted experiments on dried and pulverized water hyacinth. Although the gas yield in the dried form is about 5–6% less, it is convenient in handling, storage, and transportation. This form also lends itself better for blending with cow-dung, human excreta, or other vegetable wastes used as feed material for biogas production. Yet another "first" Dr Pathak's credit is the granulated organic manure obtained from the dried sludge of biogas plants.

Sulabh International Institute of Technical Research and Training (SIITRAT) was founded by Dr Pathak in 1984 with a view towards providing technological support to the sanitation movement. SIITRAT, with a brilliant team of scientists and engineers, has come up with many new and sustainable technologies. It is now a part of the Sulabh International Academy of Environmental Sanitation.

Dr Pathak with sons and daughters of liberated scavengers in Patna.

Low-cost waste water treatment

Waste water syndrome and its concomitant river and environment pollution currently afflicts nearly all the 5,000 odd towns and cities of India, posing a big challenge to ensure safe and healthy living environment for ever-increasing numbers of city dwellers. One of the major problems with waste water treatment methods is that none of the available technologies has direct economic return. The available technologies are unaffordable due to high capital and maintenance costs.

Sulabh has taken up research-cum-demonstration projects on duckweed-based low-cost waste water treatment in collaboration with concerned government agencies. The ambitious projects are underway in some rural as well as urban areas with direct economic return from pisci-culture and use of duckweed as nutritious feed for poultry and animals.

Solid waste management

Solid waste management has been an increasing problem causing health hazards and environmental pollution. Composting is an important method of biodegradable solid waste management having direct / indirect economic return in the form of manure and soil conditioner. Sulabh has developed a new technology which requires only 5–6 days to make compost from any biodegradable waste without manual handling during composting. Besides quick conversion of wastes into compost, it also helps control diseases transmitted from wastes, as at high temperature pathogens are eliminated from the compost.

Poverty alleviation and rural development

Dr Pathak also developed the concept of "change agent" for poverty alleviation and rural development. Train a man in a skill and he will find a job for himself. With this conviction, he launched a massive program to expand the human resource base at the grassroots level. Human resource development includes creating ability and willingness to acquire skills and, thus, maximize utilization of available resources and raise productivity per unit of land and capital.

The increase in the level of skill, education, health, and experiences are the indices of human resource development of a society. Dr Pathak's approach has been to develop and expand the human resource base at the village level and train youths to work to become catalytic agents working between the suppliers of resources and the beneficiaries.

Sulabh is leading a well-orchestrated campaign for rural development. It is imparting participatory training to school teachers and students in the fields of environmental sanitation and community health. The trained students are playing the role of catalysts to bring about requisite changes in rural areas. Sulabh international Institute of Rural Development, Research and Training (SIIRD) is giving shape to several other projects.

Ensuring health and hygiene

Sulabh International Institute of Health and Hygiene (SIIHH) was started to develop a healthcare and sanitation model of urban slums and villages. Dr Pathak's initiative to involve teachers and students in sanitation education and training of women in urban-slums in sanitation and healthcare is radical in its outlook and humane in its approach. Under its medicare program, Sulabh has also opened healthcare centers in community toilet complexes. These centers being run in coordination with government health units, are providing yeoman's health service to the urban poor. It is training women volunteers in urban slums in collaboration with some national and international agencies. 12,099 of volunteers have been trained in 310 slums.

Sulabh is promoting women group formations after training, which will ensure self-sustainable development. SIIHH is working in collaboration with USAID, UNICEF, Delhi government, Family Health International, and AIDSCAP on many people-friendly projects. The Institute is also disseminating healthcare messages including AIDS awareness through handbooks and pamphlets in the public interest. Recently it has published a popular manual on "Women and Sanitation".

Museum of Toilets

Sulabh has also established this Museum of Toilets in New Delhi. The Museum has a rare collection of artifacts, pictures, and objects detailing the historic evolution of toilets since 2,500 BC. Moreover, the Museum wing under Dr Pathak's guidance, has undertaken the task of publishing an Encyclopedia of Sanitation, which perhaps will be the first of its kind in the world.

Mr I.K. Gujral, former Prime Minister of India, was among many eminent persons who adopted scavenger families on May 2, 1994 at a function in New Delhi.

Championing Action Sociology

An acknowledged pioneer of Action Sociology, Dr Pathak has been advocating the introduction of this novel discipline into the academic curriculum. Recently, Action Sociology was introduced in the syllabus at the university level by Rajasthan Vidyapeeth and some other universities. Its concept and vision was conceived and evolved by eminent sociologists under the aegis of the Indian Association of Action Sociologists and the Sulabh Centre for Action Sociology.

An action-oriented movement, Sulabh does not believe in mere armchair analysis of problems. Instead of studying ripples and indulging in sheer rhetoric, it strives to create its own waves. Waves symbolizing major initiatives for social changes. For instance, Sulabh loves to work for the removal of human rights violations through its constructive programs. Championing human rights through mere words has never been the Sulabh ideal. It has been a philosophy of action and a sociology in action.

World toilet summet

Recently, Sulabh was the cosponsor and organizer of World Toilet Summit-2007, held at New Delhi, wherein governmental and non-governmental organizations and individuals, working in the field of sanitation from all over the world, had gathered to exchange ideas, experiences, and technologies, so that they may be used in synergy for greater common good.

Prolific writing

A versatile personality, Dr Pathak has authored several well-received books including *Road to Freedom*. He has also frequently contributed thought-provoking write-ups on diverse topics for serious newspapers and magazines. He edits *Sulabh India*, a development monthly magazine published in English and Hindi.

He has participated and presented papers in a large number of national and international seminars. Dr Pathak is a widely-travelled person and has visited many countries to disseminate the Sulabh message and technology, and to exchange ideas on environmental sanitation and growth with international experts in the field. The press, both in India and abroad, has widely covered Sulabh's stupendous track record.

Distinguished visitors from more than 100 countries have visited Sulabh headquarters in Delhi and have appreciated Dr Pathak's spirited striving for sanitation and development with equity. Eminent journalists and writers have written extensively on Dr Pathak — sketching his multi-faceted personality and extraordinary achievements.

Innovative leadership

Sulabh is now diversifying into a number of innovative and environment-friendly development projects to uplift the lot of the poor. Under the dynamic and inspiring leadership of Dr Pathak, a dedicated team of sociologists, scientists, engineers, journalists, and public-spirited people, has built a large national network and Sulabh is all set to write a glorious chapter in the annals of post-independent India.

Dr Pathak has become synonymous with Sulabh (its toilets are being used by 10 million people every day) which, in turn, has become the byword for public toilets in India. Besides, being recipient of several awards, laurels, and distinctions, Dr Pathak is a member of numerous national and international agencies / committees on environmental sanitation, urban development, and related areas. He is also deeply associated with many social, cultural, and philanthropic organizations.

He has rendered yeoman's service to make our society and environment more healthy and harmonious. He did what no social reformer managed to achieve — he blended his humanitarian philosophy with an environment-friendly technology. It is for these remarkable achievements that he has become a household name in India and is held in high esteem by a grateful society. Mulk Raj Anand, India's leading writer, has correctly observed, "What Abraham Lincoln did for Blacks in America, Dr Pathak has done for scavengers in India. Both are great redeemers".

APPENDIX-2

Historical development of Toilets

This article is adapted from Wikipedia, the free encyclopedia. *This article is about a sanitation fixture used primarily for the disposal of human waste. For a room containing a toilet, see Toilet (room). For other uses, see Toilet (disambiguation).*

Flush toilet in a bathroom, with common accessories including a dispenser for toilet paper and a toilet brush in its holder

A **toilet** is a sanitation fixture used primarily for the disposal of human urine and feces. They are often found in a small room referred to as a toilet/bathroom/lavatory. Flush toilets, which are common in many parts of the world, may be connected to a nearby septic tank or more commonly in urban areas via "large" (3–6 in or 7.6–15.2 cm) sewer pipe connected to a sewerage pipe system. The water and waste from many different sources is piped in large pipes to a more distant sewage treatment plant. Chemical toilets are used in mobile and many temporary situations where there is no access to sewerage, dry toilets, including pit toilets and composting toilet require no or little water with excreta being removed manually or composted in situ.

Ancient civilisations used toilets attached to simple flowing water sewage systems included those of the Indus Valley Civilisation, e.g., Harappa and Mohenjo-daro which are located in present day India and Pakistan and also the Romans and Egyptians. Although a precursor to the modern flush toilet system was designed in 1596 by John Harington, such systems did not come into widespread use until the late nineteenth century. Thomas Crapper was one of the early makers of toilets in England.

Diseases, including cholera which still affects some 3 million people each year, can be largely prevented when effective sanitation and water treatment prevents fecal matter from contaminating waterways, groundwater and drinking water supplies. Infected water supplies can be treated to make the water safe for consumption and use. There have been five main cholera outbreaks and pandemics since 1825. In London alone, the second killed 14,137 people in 1849, and the third took 10,738 lives in 1853-54. In 1849 the English physician John Snow published a paper *On the Mode of Communication of Cholera,* in which he suggested that cholera might be water born. During the 1854 epidemic, he collected and analysed data establishing that people who drank water from contaminated sources such as the Broad Street pump died of cholera at much higher rates than those who got water elsewhere.

According to *The Global Water Supply and Sanitation Assessment 2000* by the World Health Organisation, 40 per cent of the global population does not have access to "good" "excreta disposal facilities"—they live mostly in Asia and Africa. There are efforts being made to design simple effective squat toilets for these people. Usually, they are made by digging a hole, then installing a premade plastic squat toilet seat atop this hole, covering the walls with canvas.

History

Further information: History of sanitation

Ancient civilisations

Model of toilet with pigsty (see Pig toilet, China, Eastern Han dynasty 25 - 220 AD)

Stone toilet found in 8th century BC house in the City of David, Jerusalem

Roman public toilets, Ostia Antica

According to Teresi et al. (2002):

The third millennium BC was the "Age of Cleanliness." Toilets and sewers were invented in several parts of the world, and Mohenjo-Daro circa 2800 BC had some of the most advanced, with lavatories built into the outer walls of houses. These were primitive "Western-style" toilets made from bricks with wooden seats on top. They had vertical chutes, through which waste fell into street drains or cesspits. Sir Mortimer Wheeler, the director general of archaeology in India from 1944 to 1948, wrote, "The high quality of the sanitary arrangements could well be envied in many parts of the world today."

The toilets at Mohenjo-Daro, built about 2600 BC and described above, were only used by the affluent classes. Most people would have squatted over old pots set into the ground or used open pits. The people of the Harappan civilisation in Pakistan and north-western India had primitive water-cleaning toilets that used flowing water in each house that were linked with drains covered with burnt clay bricks. The flowing water removed the human wastes.

Early toilets that used flowing water to remove the waste are also found at Skara Brae in Orkney, Scotland, which was occupied from about 3100 BC until 2500 BC. Some of the houses there have a drain running directly beneath them, and some of these had a cubicle over the drain. Around the 18th century BC, toilets started to appear in Minoan Crete; Egypt in the time of the Pharaohs and ancient Persia. In Roman civilisation, toilets using flowing water were sometimes part of public bath houses.

In 2012, archaeologists founded what is believed to be Southeast Asia's earliest latrine during the excavation of a neolithic village in the RachNúi archaeological site, Southern Viet Nam. The toilet, dating back 1500 BC, yielded important clues about early Southeast Asian society. More than 30 preserved feces from humans and dogs containing fish and shattered animal bones from the site provided a wealth of information on both the diet of humans and dogs at R□chNúi, but also on the types of parasites each had to contend with.

Roman toilets, like the ones pictured here, are commonly thought to have been used in the sitting position. But sitting toilets only came into general use in the mid-19th century in the Western world. The Roman toilets were probably elevated to raise them above open sewers which were periodically "flushed" with flowing water, rather than elevated for sitting. The Romans weren't the first civilisation to adopt a sewer system - The Indus Valley civilisation had a rudimentary network of sewers built under grid pattern streets and it was the most advanced seen so far. Squat toilets (also known as an Arabic, French, Chinese, Japanese, Korean, Iranian, Indian, Turkish or Natural-Position toilet) are toilets used by squatting rather than sitting, and are still used by the majority of the world's population. There are several types of squat toilets, but they all consist essentially of a hole in the ground or floor with various provisions for human waste.

Early Modern Europe

***Bourdaloue* chamber pots from the Austrian Imperial household**

Chamber pots were in common use in Europe from ancient times, even being taken to the Middle East by Christian pilgrims during the Middle Ages. By the Early Modern era, chamber pots were frequently made of china or copper and could include elaborate decoration. They were emptied into the gutter of the street nearest to the home. During the Victorian era, British housemaids emptied household chamber pots into a "slop sink" that was inside a housemaid's cupboard on the upper floor of the house. The housemaids' cupboard also contained a separate sink, made of wood with a lead lining to prevent chipping china chamber pots, for washing the "bedroom ware". Once indoor running water was built into British houses, servants were sometimes given their own lavatory downstairs, separate from the family lavatory.

By the 16th century, cesspits and cesspools were increasingly dug into the ground near houses in Europe as a means of collecting waste, as urban populations grew and street gutters became blocked with the larger volume of human waste. Rain was no longer sufficient to wash away waste from the gutters. A pipe connected the latrine to the cesspool, and sometimes a small amount of water washed waste through the pipe into the cesspool. Cesspools would be cleaned out by tradesmen, who pumped out liquid waste, then shovelled out the solid waste and collected it in horse-drawn carts during the night. This solid waste would be used as fertiliser. The perception that human waste had value as fertiliser, and in ammonia production, delayed the construction of a modern sewer system in Paris as a replacement for the city's cesspool system. In the early 19th century, public officials and public hygiene experts studied and debated the matter at length, for several decades. The construction of an underground network of pipes to carry away solid and liquid waste was only begun in the 1880s, gradually replacing the cesspool system, although cesspools were still in use in some parts of Paris into the 20th century. The growth of indoor plumbing, toilets and bathtubs with running water came at the same time.

America

American lavatories followed the pattern of constructing cesspools in urban areas, using the practise already established in Europe, although the use of the outhouse near the family home was also common where more land was available, and keeping the waste well away from the well water was not a challenge. A textbook of architecture from 1903 indicates that cesspool construction was ideally done with 20-inch thick quarried stone, with cement mortar, and 6 feet deep. The chain-pull

Outhouse near Hidden Lake and Round Valley hike, Palm Springs

indoor toilet, invented in England in the 1880s, was soon introduced to America, in the homes of the wealthy and in hotels. Flush toilets were introduced in the 1890s. Public awareness of germ theories about disease, as well as inexpensive manufacturing methods, helped the flushing toilet to spread to middle class and even working class households. Important American inventors who contributed to the development of the toilet during the early 1900s included William Elvis Sloan (1867-1961), of Chicago, Illinois, and Philip Haas (1875-1927), of Dayton, Ohio. Sloan introduced the 'Flushometer' and was responsible for several flush valve designs. Haas obtained numerous patents for flush valves, flushing systems, and water closet designs. Indoor plumbing, including flushing toilets, was common in American households by the 1920s. Edward and Clarence Scott began selling white perforated toilet tissue during this era, bringing additional convenience to the American public, who had until then relied on rough paper for toilet use.

Flush Toilets

Operation

Flush toilet bowl

Sound of flush toilet in operation

A typical flush toilet is a vitreous, ceramic bowl containing water plus special plumbing made to be rapidly filled with more water. The water in the toilet bowl is connected to a hollow drain pipe shaped like an upside down U connecting the drain. One side of the U channel is arranged as a hollow siphon tube longer than the water in the bowl is high. The siphon tube connects to the drain. The bottom of the upside down U-shaped drain pipe limits the height of the water in the bowl before it flows down the drain. If water is poured slowly into the toilet bowl it simply flows over the bottom of the upside down U and pours slowly down the drain—the toilet does not flush. The water in the bowl both acts as a barrier to sewer gas entering and as a receptacle for waste. Sewer gas is vented through a vent pipe attached to the sewer line.

When a user flushes a toilet, a valve opens, and allows the toilet tank's water to quickly enter the toilet bowl. This rapid influx of water into the toilet bowl from the tank causes the swirling water in the bowl to rapidly rise and fill the upside down U-shaped drain and the siphon tube mounted in the back of the toilet. This full siphon tube starts the toilet's siphon action. The siphon action rapidly (4–7 seconds) "pulls" nearly all of the water and waste in the bowl and the on-rushing tank water down the drain—it **flushes**. When most of the water has drained out of the bowl, the continuous column of water up and over the bottom of the upside-down U-shaped drain pipe (the siphon) is broken when air enters the siphon tube. The toilet then gives its characteristic gurgle as the siphon action ceases and no more water flows out of the toilet. After flushing, the flapper valve in the water tank closes, and various water lines and valves connected to the household water supply refill the toilet tank and bowl. The toilet is again ready for use.

At the top of the toilet bowl is a rim built into the toilet with many slanted drain holes connected to the toilet tank to fill, rinse and induce swirling in the toilet bowl when it is flushed. Mounted above the toilet is a large holding tank with about (now) 1.6 to 1.2 US gallons (6.1 to 4.5 L) of water. This tank is built with a large drain 2.0 to 3.0 inches (5.08 to 7.62 cm) diameter hole at its bottom covered by a flapper valve that allows the water to rapidly leave the holding tank. The toilet's plumbing is built to allow entry of the toilet tank's water into the toilet in a very short period of time. This water pours through the holes in the rim and a siphon jet hole about 1.0 inch (2.54 cm) diameter in the bottom of the toilet. Other toilets use a large hole in the front of the rim to allow rapid filling of the toilet bowl.

Manufacture

A two-piece attaching seat and toilet bowl lid are typically mounted over the toilet bowl, to allow covering the toilet when it is not in use, and to provide seating comfort while using the toilet. A toilet's body is made from vitreous china, which starts out as a thin clay mixture called a slip. It takes about 20 kilograms (44 lb) of slip per toilet.

Toilet with an elevated cistern of water and a chain attached to the tank to release water and flush the waste away

This slip is poured into the space between plaster of Paris molds. Toilet bowl, toilet rim, toilet tank and toilet tank lid all require separate molds. The molds are assembled and set up for filling and the slip-filled molds sit for about an hour after filling while the plaster of Paris molds absorb moisture from the slip making it semisolid next to the mold but staying liquid further from the surface of the molds. Then, the workers remove plugs that allow any excess liquid slip from the centers of the mold to pour from the mold—this excess slip is recycled for later use. This drained-out slip leaves voids inside the fixture using less material, keeping it both lighter and easier to fire in a kiln, and it allows the formation of intricate waste lines in the fixture—the drain's centers are poured out as slip.

At this point, the toilet parts without their molds look like and are about as strong as soft clay. After about one hour the top core mold (interior of toilet) is removed. The rim mold bottom, which includes a place to mount the holding tank is removed, and it has the appropriate slanted holes for the rinsing jets cut and the mounting holes for tank and seat are punched into the rim piece. Large flapper valve holes for rapid water entry into the toilet are cut into the rim pieces. The exposed top of the bowl piece is then covered with a thick slip and the still uncured rim piece is attached on top of the bowl piece. The bowl and hollow rim are now a single piece. The bowl plus rim is then inverted and the toilet bowl is set upside down on the top rim mold to hold the pieces together as they dry. Later all the rest of the mold pieces are removed. As the clay dries further it hardens more and continues to shrink. After a few hours the casting is self-supporting, and is called greenware.

After the molds are removed' workers use hand tools and sponges to smooth the edges and surface of the greenware and remove the mold joints or roughness: this is called *fettling*. For large scale production pieces these steps may be automated. The parts are then left outside or put in a warm dry room to dry before going through a dryer at about 93°C (200°F), for about 20–36 hours.

After finishing the surfaces, the bowls and tanks are sprayed with glaze of various kinds to get different colors. This glaze is designed to shrink and contract at the same rate as the greenware while undergoing firing. After being sprayed with glaze the toilet bowls, tanks, and lids are placed in stacks on a conveyor belt or "car" that slowly goes through a large kiln to be fired. The belt slowly moves the glaze covered greenware into a tunnel kiln, which has different temperature zones inside it starting at about 200°C (400°F) at the front, increasing towards the middle to over 1,200°C (2,200°F) degrees and exiting around out 90°C (200°F). During the firing in the kiln, the greenware and glaze are vitrified as one solid finished unit. Transiting the kiln takes glaze covered greenware around 23–40 hours.

When the pieces are removed from the kiln and fully cooled, they are ready for inspection for cracks. After inspection, the flushing mechanism may be installed on a one piece toilet. On a two piece toilet with a separate tank the flushing mechanism may only be put on the tank with final assembly waiting installation. The seat too may be installed at this time, or the parts may be sold separately and assembled by a plumbing distributor.

Water usage

Various forms of flush toilets have become widely used in modern times The amount of water used by modern toilets is a significant portion of personal water usage, totaling as much as about 90 liters (24 US gal) of water per capita per day.

The bowl drain is visible at the rear of the bowl, connected to the waste pipe

When a toilet is flushed, the water flows into a sewage system and eventually ends in a water treatment plant. Here the water is cleaned, sanitised and possibly re-used.

Modern low flush toilet designs allow the use of much less water per flush—1.6 to 1.2 US gallons (6.1 to 4.5 L) per flush—but may require the sewage treatment system be modified for the more concentrated waste. Dual flush toilet allow the use to select between a flush for urine or feces saving a significant amount of water over conventional units. You push the flush handle up for one kind of flush and down for the other. In some places users are encouraged not to flush after urination. Flush toilets, if plumbed for it, may also use greywater (water previously used for washing dishes, laundry and bathing) for flushing rather than potable water (drinking water). Some modern toilets pressurise the water in the tank which initiates flushing action with less water usage. Heads (on ships) are typically flushed with seawater.

Other toilet types

Pit toilets

A **pit toilet** is a dry toilet system which collects human excrement and urine in a large container or trench and ranges from a simple slit trench dug in the ground to more elaborate systems with seating and ventilation systems. They are more often used in emergency, rural and wilderness areas as well as in much of the developing world. The waste pit or trench, in some cases, will be large enough that the reduction in mass of the contained waste products by the ongoing process of decomposition allows the pit to be used more or less permanently. In other cases, when the pit becomes too full, it may be emptied or the hole covered with dirt. Pit toilets have to be located away from drinking water sources (wells, streams, etc.) to minimise the possibility of disease spread. Army units typically use a form of pit toilet when they are in the field and away from functional sewerage systems. The use of correctly located pit toilets were found to prevent much of the spread of various diseases which used to kill many more soldiers than the bullets and artillery used in pre-1940 warfare.

Pit toilets

Dry toilets

Outhouses are still in use to a limited extent in rural areas (Herøy, Norway)

Dry toilets, which use very limited or no water for flushing include the pit toilet (a simple hole in the ground, or one with ventilation, fly guards and other improvements), the composting toilet (which mixes excrement with carbon rich materials for faster decomposition), the incinerating toilet (which burns the excrement), and the tree bog (a simple system for converting excrement to direct fertiliser for trees). The pig toilet from the Indian state of Goa which consists of an outhouse linked to a pig enclosure by a chute is still in use to a limited extent but the subsequent use of the pigs for food carries a significant risk for human health.

The unsanitary 'flying toilet' used in African slums where plastic shopping bags are first used as a container for excrement and are then thrown as far away as possible." This practice has led to the banning of the manufacture and import of such bags in Uganda, Kenya, and Tanzania.

A toilet that pays its users has been opened in Musiri, Tamil Nadu, India. It is the first of its kind. The feces it receives are composted, and the urine is used as fertilser for bananas and other food crops. Users are paid up to the equivalent of 12 US cents a month.

Before the introduction of modern flush toilets it was common for people to use a chamber pot at night and then to dispose of the 'nightsoil' in the morning; this practice (known as slopping out) continued in prisons in the United Kingdom until recently and is still in use in the Republic of Ireland. The garderobe was used in medieval times, and replaced by the privy midden and pail closet in early industrial Europe.

UD toilet, UDD toilet, and UDDT system

These toilets have two compartments. One for urine diversion and one for the feces. A urine diversion toilet, *UD toilet* or *UDT*, flushes one or both compartments with water. A urine diversion dry toilet, *UDD toilet*, or *UDDT* is more similar to a dry toilet. The term UDDT can also refer to a system incorporating a UD or UDD toilet to recover water or utilise wastes as a fertiliser or biofuel. Astronauts use a UDDT to recover potable water in the space station.

Chemical toilets

Chemical toilets which do not require a connection to a water supply are used in a variety of situations. Examples include passenger train toilets and airplane toilets and also complicated space toilets for use in zero-gravity spacecraft.

Public toilets

Public urinal (Limbourg, Belgium)

A public toilet, frequently called a restroom, is accessible to the general public. It may be within a building that, while privately owned, allows public access. Access to a public toilet may require a fee, (pay toilet), or may be limited to business's customers.

Depending on culture, there may be varying degrees of separation between men and women and different levels of privacy. Typically, the entire room, or a stall or cubicle containing a toilet is lockable. Urinals, if present in a men's toilet, are typically mounted on wall with or without a divider between them. In the most basic form, a public toilet may be not much more than an open latrine. Another form is a street urinal known as a *pissoir* after the French term (see Urinal).

In more luxurious variations there may be an attendant, towels, showers, etc. A fairly common feature in more modern toilets is an area to change baby diapers.

A charge levied in the UK during the mid-20th century was one British penny, hence the generally adopted term "spend a penny" meaning to use the toilet.

Portable toilets

A bucket toilet

A line of portable toilets

The portable toilet is used on construction sites and at large outdoor gatherings where there are no other facilities. They are typically self-contained units that are made to be easily moved to different locations as needed. Most portable toilets are unisex single units with privacy ensured by a simple lock on the door. The units are usually light weight and easily transported by a flatbed truck and loaded and unloaded by a small forklift. Many portable toilets are small molded plastic or fiberglass portable rooms with a lockable door and a receptacle to catch waste in a chemically treated container. If used for an extended period of time they have to be cleaned out and new chemicals put in the waste receptacle. For servicing multiple portable toilets tanker trucks, often called "Honey Trucks", are equipped with lage vacuums to evacuate the waste and replace the chemicals.

High-tech toilets

"High-tech" toilets include features such as: automatic-flushing mechanisms that flush a toilet or urinal when finished; water jets, or "bottom washers" like a bidet; blow dryers; artificial flush sounds to mask noises; and urine and stool analysis for medical monitoring. Matsushita's "Smart Toilet" checks blood pressure, temperature, and blood sugar. Some feature automatic lid operation, heated seats, deodorising fans or automated paper toilet-seat-cover replacers. Interactive urinals have been developed in several countries, allowing users to play video games as with the "Toylet", produced by Sega, that uses pressure sensors to detect the flow of urine and translates it into on-screen action.

Floating toilets

A *floating toilet* is essentially an outhouse built on a platform built above or floating on the water. Instead of wastes going into the ground they are collected in a tank or barrel. To reduce the amount of waste that needs to hauled to shore, many use urine diversion. It was developed for residents without quick access to land or connection to a sewer systems. It is also used in areas subjected to prolonged flooding. The need for this type of toilet is high in areas like Cambodia where the World Bank cited in 2008 that nearly 10,000 people died as a result of poor sanitation.

Chamber pots

A chamber pot is a receptacle in which one would excrete waste in a ceramic or metal pot. Among Romans and Greeks, chamber pots were brought to meals and drinking sessions. Johan J. Mattelaer said, "Plinius has described how there were large receptacles in the streets of cities such as Rome and Pompeii into which chamber pots of urine were emptied. The urine was then collected by fullers." This method was used for hundreds of years; shapes, sizes, and decorative variations changed throughout the centuries. This method is no longer used in developed countries, with the exception of hospital bedpans.

Garderobes

Garderobes were toilets used in the Middle Ages, most commonly found in upper-class dwellings. Essentially, they were flat pieces of wood or stone spanning from one wall to the other, with one or more holes to sit on. These would go into pipes that would lead outside the castle or manor. Garderobes would be placed in areas away from bedrooms to shun the smell and also near kitchens or fireplaces to keep the enclosure warm.

Garderobe seat openings

View looking down into garderobe seat opening

Exterior view of garderobe at Campen castle

Urinals

Although it is possible for urinals to be used by females, they were originally designed for males. They are intended for the disposal of liquid waste, not solid waste. Urinals are meant to be used for the convenience of male users in a standing position. They typically have no door or stall enclosure, and thus take up less space. These fixtures are most commonly found in public places, but can occasionally be found in a private home

Victorian public urinals

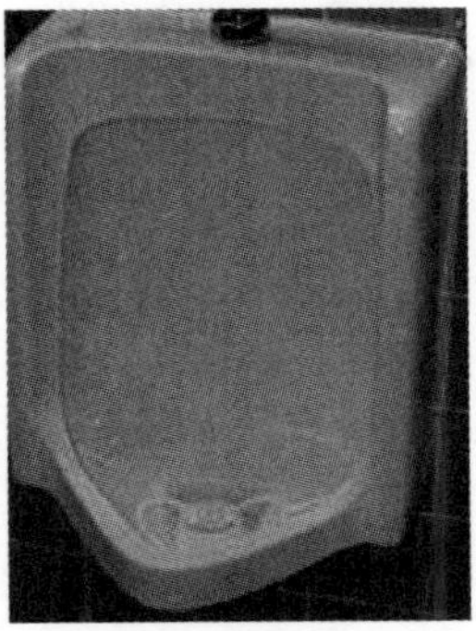

A single urinal, with a bright pink urinal cake

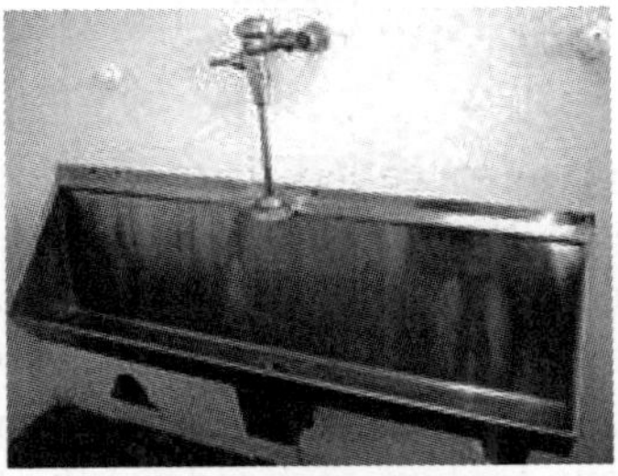

A stainless steel trough-style urinal

Dutch retractable street urinal, in The Hague

Urinals in men's room at OsloOpera house

Men's room with a view, on the 38th floor in the JR Tower (Japan)

Squat toilets

The squat toilet (also called "squatter" or "squatty-potty") consists of a hole in the ground. However, common modern versions flush like a modern seated toilet, and are not to be compared to a contemporary portable toilet with no plumbing. To use this toilet, one is in a squatting position rather than sitting, by placing one foot on each side of the toilet and squatting over it. Modern versions are in separate stalls when they are in public lavatories, and include toilet tissue rolls for the user's convenience. The squatting method is accompanied by advantages as well health benefits that connect to easiness of procedures such as child birth. The squat toilet is most commonly found in Asia, Africa, and the Middle East but can also occasionally be found in some European (Romania), Mediterranean, and South American countries.

Squat toilet as seen in some parts of Europe and Asia

Squat toilet (Rome, Italy)

Squat toilet in Topkapi palace (Istanbul, Turkey)

Squat toilet in Topkapi palace

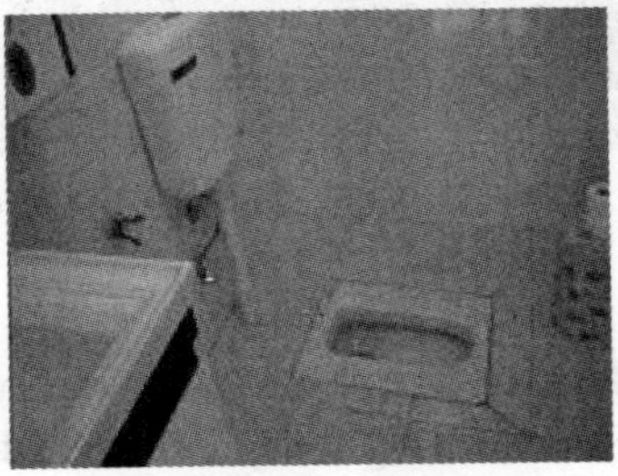

Porcelain squat toilet, with water tank for flushing (Wuhan, China)

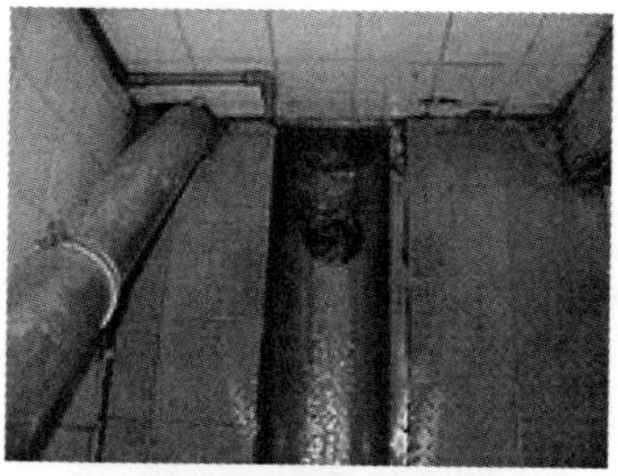

Old-style squat toilet (Hong Kong)

Etymology

In *La Toilette* from Hogarth's *Marriage à la Mode* series (1743), a young countess receives her lover, tradesmen, hangers-on, and an Italian tenor as she finishes her toilette

Portable potty on top of a mountain in China

Toilet

The word **toilet** came to be used in English along with other French fashions. It originally referred to the *toile,* French for "cloth", draped over a lady or gentleman's shoulders while their hair was being dressed, and then (in both French and English) by extension to the various elements, and also the whole complex of operations of hairdressing and body care that centered at a dressing table, also covered by a cloth, on which stood a mirror and various brushes and containers for powder and make-up: this ensemble was also a *toilette,* as also was the period spent at the table, during which close friends or tradesmen were often received. The English poet Alexander Pope in *The Rape of the Lock* (1717) described the intricacies of a lady's preparation.

The word *toilet* may also be used, especially in British English to describe the room containing the fixture, for which euphemisms such as *restroom* or *bathroom* are used in American English. Prior to the introduction of modern flush toilets, most human waste disposal was done through the use of household chamber pots, or took place outdoors in outhouses or latrines. Pail closets were introduced in England and France in an attempt to reduce sewage problems in rapidly expanding cities.

And now, unveil'd, the toilet stands display'd

Each silver vase in mystic order laid.

These various senses are first recorded by the *OED* in rapid sequence in the later 17th century: the set of "articles required or used in dressing" 1662, the "action or process of dressing" 1681, the cloth on the table 1682, the cloth round the shoulders 1684, the table itself 1695, and the "reception of visitors by a lady during the concluding stages of her toilet" 1703 (also known as a "toilet-call"), but in the sense of a special room the earliest use is 1819, and this does not seem to include a lavatory.

Through the 18th century, everywhere in the English-speaking world, these various uses centredaround a lady's draped dressing-table remained dominant. In the 19th century, apparently first in the United States, the word was adapted as a genteel euphemism for the room and the object as we know them now, perhaps following the French usage *cabinet de toilette,* much as *powder-room* may be coyly used today, and this has been linked to the introduction of public toilets, for example on railway trains, which required a plaque on the door. The original usages have become obsolete, and the table has become a *dressing-table.*

Vestiges of the original meaning continue to be reflected in terms such as *toiletries, eau de toilette* and *toiletry bag* (to carry flannels, soaps, etc.). This seemingly contradictory terminology has served as the basis for various parodies e.g. *Cosmopolitan* magazine ("If it doesn't say 'eau de toilette' on the label, it most likely doesn't come from the famed region of Eau de Toilette in France and might not even come from toilets at all.")

The word *toilet* itself may be considered an impolite word in Anglophone North America, while elsewhere the word is used without any embarrassment. The choice of the word used instead of *toilet* is highly variable, not just by regional dialect but also, at least in Britain, by class connotations. Nancy Mitford wrote an essay out of the choice of wording; see U and non-U English. Some manufacturers show this uneasiness with the word and its class attributes: American Standard, the largest manufacturer, sells them as "toilets", yet the higher priced products of the Kohler Company, often installed in more expensive housing, are sold as *commodes* or *closets*, words which also carry other meanings. Confusingly, products imported from Japan such as TOTO are referred to as "toilets", even though they carry the cachet of higher cost and quality. When referring to the room or the actual piece of equipment, the word *toilet* is often substituted with other euphemisms and dysphemisms (See *toilet humor*).

As old euphemisms have become accepted, they have been progressively replaced by newer ones, an example of the euphemism treadmill at work. The choice of word used to describe the room or the piece of plumbing relies as much on regional variation (dialect) as on social situation and level of formality (register).

Lavatory

The term lavatory, abbreviated in slang to lav, derives from the Latin: *lavâtôrium,* which in turn comes from Latin *lavô* ("I wash"). The word was originally used to refer to a vessel for washing, such as a sink/wash basin, but eventually came to mean a room with such washing vessels, as for example in medieval monasteries, where the lavatorium was the monks' communal washing area. The toilets in monasteries however were not in the *lavatorium* but in the reredorter. Nevertheless the word was later associated with toilets and the meaning evolved into its current one, namely a polite and formal euphemism for a toilet and the room containing it. Lavatory is the common signage for toilets on commercial airlines around the world, see Aircraft lavatory.

Loo

The origin of the (chiefly British) term **loo** is unknown. According to the OED, the etymology is obscure, but it might derive from the word Waterloo. The first recorded entry is in fact from James Joyce's *Ulysses* (1922): *"O yes, monloup. How much cost? Waterloo. Watercloset".*

Other theories are:

- That it derives from the term "gardyloo" (a corruption of the French phrase *gardezl'eau!* (or maybe *gardel'eau!*) loosely translated as "watch out for the water!") which was used in medieval times when chamber pots were emptied from a window onto the street. However the first recorded usage of "loo" comes long after this term became obsolete.
- That the word comes from nautical terminology, loo being an old-fashioned word for lee. The standard nautical pronunciation (in British English) of *leeward* is *looward*. Early ships were not fitted with toilets but the crew would urinate over the side of the vessel. However it was important to use the leeward side. Using the windward side would result in the urine blown back on board: hence the phrases 'pissing into the wind' and 'spitting into the wind'. Even now most yachtsmen refer to *the loo* rather than *the heads*.
- That the word derives from the 17th century preacher Louis Bourdaloue. Bourdaloue's sermons at the Saint Paul-Saint Louis Church in Paris lasted at least three hours and myth has it that wealthier ladies took along "travelling" chamber pots that could be hidden under their dresses whenever the need arose to avoid the need to leave. Due to the popularity of the myth the bowls became known as Bourdaloues after the preacher and the name became corrupted to portaloos and sometimes just plain loos due to the habit of shortening words in slang.

- That the word comes from the French word *lieu* (place), as in *lieu d'aisance* (literally: "place of ease", a common euphemism for lavatory) or *lieu à l'anglaise* (literally: "English place"). From around 1770 the term *lieu à l'anglaise* began to appear in France, referring to this English invention which was sometimes installed for the benefit of English visitors. (Ashenburg p. 138)

WC

The **WC** refers to the initial letters of Water Closet, which, despite being an English language abbreviation, is not in common use in English-speaking countries – but is widely used internationally: in France (pronounced "le vay-say" or "le vater"), in Italy (pronounced "vi-ci" or "vater"), Romania (pronounced "veh-cheu"), the Netherlands (pronounced "waysay"), Germany, Switzerland and Hungary (pronounced "ve-tse"), Denmark (pronounced "ve-se"), Norway (pronounced "vay-say"), Poland (pronounced "vu-tse"), Spain (pronounced "uve-cé" or "váter"), China, and others.

Other

LexicographerEric Partridge derives khazi, also spelt karzy, kharsie or carzey, from a low Cockney word *carsey* originating in the late 19th century and meaning a privy. Carsey also referred to a den or brothel. It is presumably derived from the Italian *casa* for house, with the spelling influenced by its similar sound to khaki. Khazi is now most commonly used in the city of Liverpool in the UK, away from its cockney slang roots. An alternative derivation is from Christopher Chippindale, who states that khazi derives from Army slang used by expatriate officers of the British Empire who took a dislike to the habits of, and steaming rain forest inhabited by, the Khasi people of the Khasia hills on the northern frontier of India.

The Dunny is an Australian expression for an outside toilet or outhouse. The person who appeared weekly to empty the pan beneath the seat was known as the "dunnyman". The word derives from the British dialect word *dunnekin*, meaning "dung-house". It is now an informal word used for any lavatory and is most often used referring to drop or pit lavatories in the Australian bush, which are also called *thunderboxes*.

The Privy is an old fashioned term used more in the North of England and in Scotland; "privy" is an old alternative for "private", as in Privy council. It is used interchangeably in North America for various terms for the outhouse.

The netty is the most common word used in North East England. Many outsiders are often bemused when a Geordie or a Mackem states they are "ganninte the netty" (going to the bathroom). The etymology of the word is uncertain, but it is believed to be either derived from a corruption of "necessity" or from graffiti scrawled on Hadrian's Wall. It is linked to the Italian word *gabinetti* meaning "toilets" (singular *gabinetto*).

Latrine is a term common in the military, specifically for the Army and Air Force for any point of entry facility where human waste is disposed of, which a civilian might call a bathroom or toilet, regardless of how modern or primitive it is. Traditionally the Royal Navy along with the United States Navy and Marine Corps use the nautical term "Head" to describe the same type of facility, regardless of whether it is located on a ship or on the land.

The Jacks is Irish slang for toilet. It perhaps derives from "jakes", an old English term.

The standalone toilet enclosure has been variously known as a "back house", "house of ease", "house of office", "little house", or "outhouse". The house of office was a common name for a toilet in seventeenth century England, used by, among others, Samuel Pepys on numerous occasions: *October 23, 1660: going down into my cellar..., I put my foot into a great heap of turds, by which I find Mr Turner's house of office is full and comes into my cellar.*

In the Philippines the abbreviation CR (*Comfort Room*) is commonly used.

Culture

There are many different ways to clean oneself after using the toilet, depending on national mores and local resources. An important part of early childhood education is toilet training.

In the Western world, the most common method of cleaning after using a toilet is by toilet paper or by using a bidet, which has been increasing in popularity. In the Middle East and some countries in Asia, and South Asian countries such as India and Pakistan, the custom is to use water, either with or without toilet paper. Traditionally, the left hand is used for this, for which reason that hand is considered impolite or polluted in many Eastern countries. The Islamic faith has a particular code, *Qadâ al-Hâjah* describing Islamic toilet etiquette.

Toilet humour is a name given to a type of off-colourhumour dealing with defecation, urination, and flatulence.

Men's toilet designed by artist and architect Hundertwasser

Toilet in Delftware style

Toilet Bus in Samsun

APPENDIX-3

Glimpses of Sulabh

Breaking centuries-old tradition, widows of Vrindavan celebrated Holi at MeeraSahabhaginiSadan on March 14, 2014

The 'NGO Leadership and Excellence Award', instituted by the World CSR Congress, was given to Pathak on the occasion of the World CSR Day at Taj Lands Hotel, Mumbai on February 18, 2014

Justice Samaresh Banerjee confers prestigious Michael Madhusudan International Bongo Moni award to Dr Bindeshwar Pathak for his work among the widows of Vrindavan

Santa Claus brings joy and happiness in the lives of "Widows of Vrindavan"

Dr Pathak and members of the Sulabh family attending to widow trainees of the first computer class, during the opening of the Sulabh Vocational Training Centre at Deoli Village in Uttarakhand.

Hon'ble Supreme Court's intervention changed the lives and destiny of the widows of Vrindavan. They came to have a glimpse and pay respect to the great institution.

Index